SURVIVING

THE

FLIER

HOW MUCH IS "TRUE" AND HOW MUCH IS "STORY?"

This tale is classified as historical fiction because I had to invent all conversations. I kept names, descriptions, and events as close to the facts as possible, relying on various sources to provide details. I also tried to seek out and utilize first person or period sources whenever I could.

Still, for the purposes of storytelling, I had to invent certain scenes to explore backstory or provide exposition. While the conversations as I wrote them may not have happened word for word, the stories or information they convey were drawn from Flier's deck logs, war patrol reports, transcripts, letters to and from the front, and interviews with various people involved. When possible, I tried to cross check these stories with other information in order to present the most complete story possible. But as anyone who studies history knows, our perception of what may have happened can differ from what actually happened as new or different information comes to light.

In the end, I tried to tell this story as accurately as possible, seeking to honor the lives and memories of these men, their boat, and the Submarine Service of WWII.

For further reading, my list of sources can be found at the end of the book.

R.J.H.

SURVIVING
THE
FLIER

BASED ON THE TRUE STORY

Based on the memories and unpublished memoirs of the last survivor, Alvin Jacobson, the gripping story of the only WWII submariners to escape their sunken sub, elude the enemy, and return home.

R. J. Hughes

PHOENIX FLAIR PRESS

Surviving the Flier
By R.J. Hughes

http://www.survivingtheflier.com
http://www.ussflierproject.com

Edited by Jennifer Harshman of Harshman Services

Printed in the United States of America
Second Edition

ISBN: 978-0-9846124-1-3

Published by Phoenix Flair Press
Muncie, IN

Cover design by R.J. Hughes
Maps created by R.J. Hughes

DEDICATED TO ALL THOSE
"ON ETERNAL PATROL"

PARTICULARLY THOSE WHO
REST WITH
USS FLIER BENEATH THE
BALABAC STRAIT.

ACKNOWLEDGEMENTS

When this project started more than six years ago, I had no idea how large and complex this would be and how many people would become a part of this. I need to thank so many people, especially:

God, who has been the Author of my life, and He is the one I need to thank first and foremost. He has given me more than I ever would ask, even when it wasn't what I was asking for!

My wonderful husband, Justin, who is nearly as much an author of this piece as I am! Yes dear, this is the point at which a writer says, "I couldn't have done this without you," but guess what? That doesn't mean it's not true! You're my best friend and my support. Thank you for helping interview, work the website, edit the manuscript, and put up with me during this whole project.

My mom and dad, siblings, and in-laws, who all stayed interested in this project, helping me talk through points, critiquing the manuscript and making this a better story. We've always been there for each other, and I hope always will be. I'm so blessed to have you.

Alvin Jacobson Jr. and his family. They opened their lives to me so I could see and write this story with as much accuracy as possible. They put up with a lot of interviews, e-mails, phone calls and questions, as well as provided tons of information about their father and the men with whom he served. My one regret is Al isn't here to see this project for himself.

The family of Lt. James Liddell, USNR, who opened their home and library to me in my search for *Flier* information and sources. It was a great insight into another point of view of this story, and a visit I won't forget.

James Alls, who, through a twist of fate, became the last man standing from the *Flier*. Without him, we would never have known some of the particulars of *Flier*, and without him, so much of this book's new life would not have been possible. He brought stories about these men to light and allowed me to see so much that I forgot to ask until it was (almost) too late. Thank you Jackie Alls, for all your help and hospitality.

The crew of *USS Redfin SS-272*, particularly Jack March, Larry Coleman and Charles "Red" Schwertfeger, for sharing the history of their boat and their stories, and for supporting this project sharing their time, expertise, photos, and documents.

Charles Hinman of *USS Bowfin* Museum, who helped me with details about the *Flier* and her men through his websites, "On Eternal Patrol" and "*USS Flier*," numerous e-mails and phone calls.

To Timothy Loughman, son of *USS Macaw's* Executive Officer, Lt. Gerald Loughman, who helped me get a greater understanding of *Flier's* Midway incident and supplied new photos of *Flier's* life.

Michael Sturma, author of the USS Flier: Death and Survival on a WWII Submarine, which was invaluable to my research.

Jo Ann Cosgrove of Taylor University, who located and acquired a large number of obscure books for my research through the Interlibrary Loan Program. I often wondered if she cringed when she saw my bizarre requests, or if she considered it a challenge.

To my editor Jeni Harshman, who helped me make changes and caught my errors and have me feedback for this second edition. It made this book so much better for your attentions, Jeni. Thank you, Heather Kittleman, Wendy Skorupa, and Elizabeth Dean, who read this at various times and gave me feedback.

Lt. Aerik LaFavre, Associate Professor of Naval Science at the University of Michigan's NROTC for doing research for me about U of M's NROTC program during WWII.

Heather Panozzo and Liz Butler for all your assistance in the past year

The staff of the National Archives and Records Administration, and Mary and Dick Bentz, for locating and mailing various records of this story to my home.

The families of the lost crew, who shared letters, photos and stories with me, helping to tell the story of the lost men of Flier.

To all those whom I didn't mention by name and those who requested anonymity, thank you

Last, but certainly not least, I want to thank the men of *USS Flier*. In a way, I'm sorry this book is written, because they paid the ultimate price and gave their lives so my family and I can live in freedom decades later. Thank you for being willing to do so. May you never, ever be forgotten.

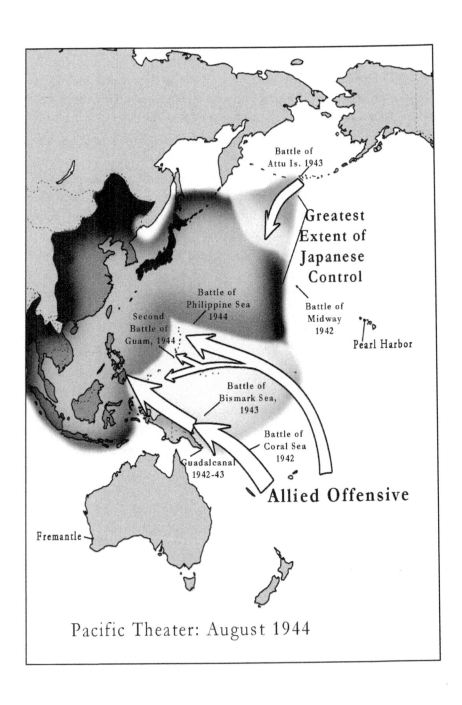

Battle of
Attu Is. 1943

Greatest
Extent of
Japanese
Control

Battle of
Philippine Sea
1944

Battle of
Midway
1942

Pearl Harbor

Second
Battle of
Guam, 1944

Battle of
Bismark Sea,
1943

Battle of
Coral Sea
1942

Guadalcanal
1942-43

Allied Offensive

Fremantle

Pacific Theater: August 1944

TABLE OF CONTENTS

USS Flier Motor Machinist Mate James Alls, at work aboard submarines at the Submarine Base, Pearl Harbor, HSawaii. Courtesy of USS Flier crewman, James Alls.

-PROLOGUE-

FREMANTLE, AUSTRALIA, JULY 1944

"This is taking too long." The two shore patrolmen walked down the street in Perth, a crowd of disgruntled sailors behind them walking to the parked busses nearby.

"Look Jim, I know it's against regs, but what if we divide and conquer? If we're careful, this shouldn't be a problem, and no one has taken a swing at us yet."

"Telling guys that liberty is cancelled for the rest of the night is not popular."

"I know, so let's just get this done as fast as possible. We're shore patrol, it's more trouble than it's worth for these guys to take a swing at us. Just be careful."

The next pub Jim Alls entered featured a few American sailors who all groaned and argued for a moment before reluctantly trooping out to the waiting busses. All except one.

An Army Ranger Sergeant, more than a little drunk, was standing at the end of the bar arguing with some newly-arrived New Zealand soldiers.

"Okay, Sarge, that's enough," the seventeen-year old Alls gripped the man by his arm. "Liberty's been cancelled for the night, everyone has to report to their bus in the park across the street."

The Ranger saw the SP badge on Alls's arm, and gave a curt nod and grunt. "Fine, you fellas are lucky," the Ranger roared at the laughing Kiwis, as Alls lead him away.

It happened so fast. One last insult spat, the empty beer stein grabbed by a Kiwi, and Alls's world went black.

Searing pain woke him up hours later. It was dark, the street deserted and quiet. Alls struggled to his feet in the alley behind the bar he last remembered, his face on fire and sagging strangely.

Stumbling to the street, he saw the glaring headlights of some kind of vehicle heading for him, and flagged it down with one hand, holding his jaw with the other.

"Holy cow, mate, what happened to you?" the Australian driver said when he pulled up next to Alls.

"Came out worse in a bar fight, no big deal," Alls said, trying not to gasp in pain, as he jumped in the passenger seat. "Give me a ride back to my hotel, the Wentworth? That's where my crewmates are staying."

"Be happy to give you a ride mate, but I'm taking you straight to the hospital. That's not just a swollen jaw you've got there, something is seriously wrong." Alls didn't argue.

The jaw wasn't just broken, it was shattered. Since Alls, an American sailor, had been dropped off at an Australian hospital, the doctors at the hospital and the American military medical team debated who had the better set up and methods to help him. After two days of agonized waiting, Alls was transferred to the American base.

The next morning, still in blinding pain, Alls met the dentist, who entered the examination room flanked by two huge sailors.

"Your jaw is shattered, sailor, as you know. I have to reset it this morning, and I'm sorry, but I can't put you under or give you any anesthetic, since I'll need you to open and close your mouth several times so everything lines up when I'm done. These gentlemen-" pointing at the two sailors with him "-are going to help me."

"Oh no," Alls moaned, shrinking back into his chair, "they're here to hold me down, aren't they?"

"I am sorry," the dentist said, picking up his first tool.

By the time the jaw was set and wired, Alls was shaking in pain and shock, the dentist and his assistants were nearly deaf from the screaming, and a rather large crowd had gathered at the exam room's window. They apparently found it quite entertaining.

To Alls, worse than confinement to the hospital ward and the enforced liquid diet, was the knowledge that he wouldn't be allowed to rejoin the crew of his submarine, the *Flier,* when she left port for her second patrol in just days. He had been with them since before *Flier's* commissioning, and in many ways, those guys had become family to him. With dozens of submarines pulling in and out of port every month, the chance that he'd be reassigned to the old *Flier* once his jaw healed was too slim to hope for.

"Hey, Jim, I hear you've got a new nickname."

"Lt. Liddell," Alls' eyes lit up, and he saluted *Flier's* Executive Officer, struggling to get the words out past his wired teeth.

"Calling you 'Mush Mouth', or some such nonsense?"

"Just a scratch, sir, I'm ready to go." He said, trying to sound as normal as possible.

"No, you're not Jim, and we both know it. That jaw of yours would play havoc every time *Flier* dove and the pressure jumped around. We can't have you flat on your bunk in pain, not even for a day, if we can avoid it."

"Sir, I-I don't want to leave the *Flier* sir," Alls started, not sure how to explain himself without sounding like he was crying or whining.

"Which is why I came to tell you," the young officer continued smoothly, "that you're not weaseling away from us that easily. Captain Crowley put a retainer on you. When you're cleared, and *Flier* is next in port, you'll be reassigned to our crew, simple as that. We're not going to lose one of our best Motor Macs over something this minor."

Alls grinned, showing a mouth of steel wire. "Thank you, sir, I won't let you down."

"You'd better not. Just because you've managed to extend your R&R by six weeks or so, doesn't mean we don't expect you to be in top form and ready to baby those V-16s when we get back."

"I will, sir." Alls saluted from his bed.

"All right, now that that is settled, I have to get back. Captain is at headquarters, getting orders for this new patrol, and we're expecting your replacement any day now."

"Sir? Can I ask a question about a friend?"

"Sure, if I know the answer."

"Is Red Snyder still a Chief?"

Liddell looked confused. "Yes, Snyder is still a Chief. Did he expect otherwise?"

"Well, he wasn't sure if he should spend the money on the chief's uniform until after R&R," Jim admitted, grinning.

"Huh?"

"Well, sir, since Chief Hudson promoted Red to Chief while we were at sea, Red had no Chief's uniform. So when Red and I were on the bus to the Wentworth after we got to port, he was still wearing his old Motor Mac's blues. I told him, 'Let's go get your new chief's uniform before we go out, I want to see you in it.' Red opened the bag on his lap and showed me a Chief Motor Mac's uniform and said, 'I borrowed this from Billy Brooks so I wouldn't have to get one.' I asked him, 'Why would do that when you can just purchase one of your own?' He said, 'Because I know I'm going to get busted back down to Motor Mac before we go to sea again and I don't want to waste my money!' "

Liddell burst out laughing. "No, despite whatever gilly[1] and girls he may have gotten into, he's still Chief. He wasn't even one of the bigger problems this R&R."

"Oh?"

"I'm sure you'll find out in a few weeks, Jim."

"I'll miss you guys."

"Eh, we'll be back before you know it, and you know your Engine Room crew will give you hell for missing out on the fun."

"I sure hope so, sir."

"All right then, Alls, we'll see you in a few weeks."

"Yes, sir. Good luck, sir." They shook hands, and Lt. Liddell disappeared down the hall.

Days later, the *Flier* left on patrol, leaving Alls, stir crazy, in the hospital.

He knew there would be no public word from the *Flier* for weeks, possibly even more than two months. When she finally returned, whether here or Brisbane or Pearl Harbor, Alls was determined to be the third thing on the boat when she finally moored, right after the long-awaited mail and the fresh, cold milk that was always delivered. If he jumped that line, the guys would jump him.

He could only wonder where she was: near the Marianas where the most recent battle was fought? Or was she near Siam where some of the biggest Japanese bases were rumored to be? Fremantle boats often patrolled the Philippines. Some even went as far away as the Sea of Japan.

---

[1] "Gilly" a.k.a "Bug Juice" a.k.a "Torpedo alcohol": the 180-proof grain alcohol that powered a torpedo. Sailors would distill it to remove the poisons added to discourage consumption, then mix it with fruit juice.

After a few weeks of confinement, and shortly after his jaw was freed, Alls went to his doctor. "Doc, my jaw's almost healed. Would it be possible for me to go walking around town this afternoon? It's a beautiful day, I'm sure stretching my legs would do me a world of good."

"Oh no, Mush Mouth," the doctor said. "I'm not letting you out there where you can drink alcohol and eat all sorts of who-knows-what. Your body has been on a liquid diet for a long time, we have to reintroduce food to it gently, and certainly not in some questionable pub."

"What if I promise I'll just walk around, not eat anything at all and not drink anything more interesting than plain old water?"

"You promise?"

"If that's what it takes to get me out of here for a few hours today…or everyday…"

"All right, all right, anything to get you out from underfoot for a while."

It felt great to get outside, feel the sun on his face, smell the salt in the air. This late in August, it was still technically winter here, and some Aussies were bundled against the brisk wind. It made Alls laugh. A native of Washington D.C., it felt like high spring, maybe sixty degrees, perfect walking weather.

The weeks confined in the hospital, however, had taken their toll. Alls had lost a lot of weight and found he had to take it easy. After several blocks, he decided to go inside one of his favorite dives for a bit of a rest before heading back to the hospital.

Once inside, he spotted an old friend from the States eating lunch at the counter.

"Hey! What are you doing here?"

"Oh hey, Alls, I got transferred to the Communication division here in Freo a few weeks back. How about you? What are you doing out here?"

"Just waiting for my boat to get back so I can go out on patrol."

"Really? Which boat?"

"The *Flier.*"

The man's face went white and he looked quickly away. Then, so low Alls almost didn't hear him, he said, "Sailor, that boat ain't comin' back."

Captain Herber "Tex" McLean, Commander of Submarine Squadron Sixteen, awards Flier's CO, Lt. Cmdr. John D. Crowley a Navy Cross for his successes during the first patrol. Flier's crew also earned a number of commendations. Taken aboard USS Flier while she was docked beside Submarine Tender USS Orion in Fremantle, Australia between July 5 and August 1, 1944. Official US Navy Photo.

1

FREMANTLE, AUGUST 2, 1944

"Sign here," the Petty Officer said, handing me the clipboard and receipt.

"Are we all set, sir?" Thomas "Doggy" Donovan called up from down below.

I glanced down the main hatch and said, "Get me James."

Two seconds later, the face of our head cook, James Westmoreland, appeared at the end of the tube. "Sir?"

"Did we get everything? The last load of coffee? The right stuff?"

"Last load of Hills Bros. arrived two hours ago; we're all set for stores. I stuck the *Redfin* with that mistaken load of Navy coffee."

I glanced at our sister sub moored to our starboard-side. "Poor bastards," I grinned.

"No kidding, sir," he shouted back. "Once we fill the showers with those potatoes, we're done. I'm still asking for volunteers to take miscellaneous boxes and cans, but we've received everything we ordered."

"I have an open compartment in my cabin if you need a place to stash some of the smaller stuff."

"I don't know that you do, sir. A new ensign reported aboard in the last hour and he will have to hot bunk somewhere in Officer's Country."

"Oh well, worse can happen. Keep the deck clear for a few minutes."
I turned to the impatient Petty Officer. "All set," I said, signing the receipt. The Petty Officer signaled his men, and they quickly dropped bag after dusty burlap bag of potatoes down the hatch to the Crew's Quarters below. When done, I slammed the heavy steel hatch down, and cranked the wheel until it locked. Moments later, I heard the sounds of the inch-thick steel plate being bolted to the bottom of the hatch, permanently sealing it until we returned to port. We'd been given enough food money for a standard six to eight week patrol, but one never knew.

The Petty Officer and his crew quickly left our deck and headed across the submarine nest to their ship, the submarine tender *USS Orion*.

"Ensign Jacobson!" someone yelled at me. I looked up to see a young enlisted man waving from the lookout platform. "I was supposed to bring the battle flag in, sir. I found those four small Jap flags, but the steward, Mr. Turner, said I missed *Flier's* battle flags. But sir, where-?" He pointed at the bare periscope shears above his head, then to the periscopes of the other two submarines in our nest, both flying colorful fabric records of their patrols. "Turner insisted we have a flag, but I've never seen it."

"Yeah, we do things a little differently around here, kid. What's your name, anyway?"

"Wesley Miller, sir, Motor Mac third class," he said proudly. He looked only a little younger than I was. The fact he was a Motor Mac meant he might have come from the surface fleet, or has been on the tender fleet for a while. I'd heard this was his first sub.

"Well, Miller, you'll find our flags, such as they are, hanging on the rail of the forward cigarette deck."

Miller leaned out over the lookout rail and then looked back at me. "Do you mean those life rings, sir?"

"You got it."

"I thought those were trophies." He jumped down to the bridge deck, ducked through the forward hatch and hauled one over the rail. "Sir? Is it true that these are life rings from Jap ships you sank last patrol, or are the guys telling me a sea story?"

"Yup, came from *Flier's* first victim." We'd painted our battle flag on some canvas and attached it to the back of the life ring before hanging it on the rail. It certainly caught a lot of attention when we'd pulled in. The sight of all those gold-braided Captains and Admirals standing on the dock, open-mouthed, pointing at our unconventional flag, with Captain Crowley standing boldly on the bridge, was not one I'd soon forget.

"What was her name?" Miller asked.

"No idea. If you can read Japanese, be sure to tell us, right before we turn you over to the Marines," I joked. "There's another one on the other side, don't forget."

"Thanks for the help, sir."

"No problem."

A couple of minutes later, I heard, "Uh-sir? Aren't these things supposed to fit through the hatch?"

Based on extensive interviews with Flier crewman James Alls, Flier's unconventional flag may have looked similar to this.

I burst out laughing. "Sorry Miller, I forgot. We couldn't fit them down the hatch when we retrieved them in the first place, so we had to saw them in half. Find the tape, we painted over it, then break them in half there."

"Thank you, sir!" A moment later I heard a ripping sound, and then he was gone.

Without those life rings, *Flier* was now black and nameless. Only Old Glory flapping at the aft end of the bridge, and the Starry Jack[2] at the bow

---

[2] "Old Glory" and "Starry Jack": Old Glory is a common nickname for the 48-star flag of the United States which was in use in 1944. A "Jack" is a flag, generally different from a nation's flag, which is flown from a military ship to distinguish it

remained to identify us as an American submarine, and we would stow those the moment we cast off. Once out in the open sea, we'd be in as much danger from our own planes and surface ships as the Japanese, especially if they shot first and asked for identity later.

Mooring lines splashed in the water and thudded onto the deck of the *Redfin* as crewmen started to cast off. Restrained now by just two lines rather than her usual six or seven, *Flier* pulled heavily against those, as if eager to get underway.

I climbed up to the Bridge to take the first watch as we navigated out of the harbor. It was incredible to think that, less than a year ago, I had been a struggling engineering student at the University of Michigan, listening to Cmdr. Scott tell us about the Submarine Force and his adventures on his submarine, *S-43*, during my ROTC[3] classes. He was the one who inspired me to request the Submarine Force, along with a dozen other guys. Now I was a commissioned Ensign, starting out on my second patrol, and my first as a fully-qualified submariner.

"Morning, Ed," I called to my mentor and friend, Lieutenant John "Ed" Casey, as he climbed to the Bridge from the Conning Tower below, his ever-present cup of coffee in his hand.

"Morning, Jake," he yawned, lifting the mug in greeting. "Thanks for the coffee."

"You know, personally, I don't taste a difference, but whatever makes the crew happy."

"Good boy. You'd taste the difference after a couple of months out at sea, I guarantee it. I think Navy coffee can chew a hole through the mugs *and* the intestines."

"Yeesh. I've had coffee in my day, but James seems to try to make it so strong it can stand up on its own. What does he do? Double the recommended amount?"

"I know he does something, because I can tell when one of the other

---

from a civilian ship of the same nation. In 1944, the US Military Jack was 48 stars on a blue field, hence the name, "Starry Jack".

[3] ROTC: Reserve Officer Training Corp: A program for college students where they train for the military while in college. The military often pays a significant portion or the entirety of the tuition and board, and in return the graduated student becomes an officer in the military for at least four years upon graduation.

hands makes the stuff. Gotta have something to keep me awake during my shift, especially after runs like the one last night." He took a loud slurp and sighed contentedly. "This is the good stuff."

"I take it the sound test went well?"

"Sure did. That new starboard prop is purring quieter than a kitten now, so no need to go back into drydock."

"I don't know, a part of me feels a little uneasy about going out with a spare prop. It's like starting on a cross-country trip with a spare tire."

Ed laughed. "Our 'spare' is still a solid brass prop, Jake. I don't think we'll have a flat somewhere out in the Pacific."

"If you say so, Ed. Hey, how's the family? Heard much from your wife?"

"Letter upon letter, almost as many as I wrote to her during our last patrol. Want to see the latest photo?" He was already digging his wallet out of his back pocket. "There we are. That's my Betty Ann and little Ricky. She said he's growing by leaps and bounds, and giggling all the time." He handed me the photo of a young, pretty girl, proudly standing behind a baby boy, who was hanging on to her fingers as he walked across the lawn. Both smiled at the camera. Despite the fact that the photo had to be new, the corners were already bent and frayed, showing how often he must have looked at it since mail call nearly four weeks ago.

"Gee, you're not a proud father, at any rate, are you?" I said.

"No, not at all," he smiled, taking back the picture and touching the surface tenderly, as though he could touch his family. "He's grown so much since I saw him last. I was there the day he was born, you know. I still remember the nurse coming into the waiting room and telling me I had a boy. That was the same month *Flier* was commissioned, but we didn't leave for the front for another six weeks, so I got to spend some time with them. Last spring, when I went home, he was giggling and already starting to scoot across the floor. And now he's walking," Ed sighed. "When we get back to port, I'll have to find him something for his first birthday and ship it home. With luck, it might even get there in time."

"If we come back here, you'll find some great stuff. I sent a lamb's wool rug and three boomerangs to my parents. I didn't realize I'd need to get them all inspected and authorized in duplicate to send home, though!"

"Be glad that's all you had to do. Maybe I'll find him a stuffed koala or a boomerang."

"Send him a kangaroo."

"Somehow, I doubt the Navy would authorize that," he laughed. "I would also like my wife to still be speaking to me when I get home."

"Spoilsport."

He tucked the photo back into his wallet, and said, "How about you? How's that large family of yours?"

"Pretty well. Mom said my brother Charles is still okay on the *Boise*. I think they're in that mess in the Marianas right now, but you know how censored the mail is these days, it's only a guess. David graduated from high school this past May, and has enlisted in the Army Air Force. I think he might be leaving soon for Europe, or maybe the Pacific, she didn't say."

"You two scare him off of the Navy?" Ed joked.

"Believe it or not, David gets severely seasick. He loves to sail, but if he's in Lake Michigan or anything larger, he's feeding the fish over the side. I guess he decided to head as far from the ocean as possible, I just didn't realize he was thinking vertically.

"My sisters are getting ready for school. Edna Mary and Marilyn are at U of M, and Muriel gets to have our folks to herself while she finishes up High School. Mom did say that she thinks Edna Mary is likely going to be engaged soon, so she's all excited."

"Congratulations. Soon, I'll have you married off to a beautiful girl."

"Oh no, you had your chance. I even wrote Muriel about your little plan, and despite everything, I still managed to escape Fremantle without a wedding ring on my finger."

"What about that dark-haired beauty I saw you with several times over R&R? What was wrong with her?"

"Not a thing, believe me. But she's also one of Admiral Christie's drivers, so I didn't want to get too involved! She just needed to talk, and I liked to listen."

"Well, there are worse ways to pass the time. Speaking of which, I missed your crew barbecue this time around."

"No you didn't. I never threw one. I was able find things in Hawaii. I didn't even know where to begin here."

The Flier crew enjoying a barbecue and baseball game on Hawaii prior to her first patrol. Photo courtesy of the family of Walter "Bud" Klock, Chief Radioman, USS Flier.

"You just need the help of an experienced hand at these things. I could throw a better party in my sleep than the ones at those hotels."

"Is that an offer?"

"Good morning, gentlemen," our XO[4], Lieutenant James Liddell, said, as he climbed up through the Bridge Hatch. We quickly stood at attention, and just as quickly Liddell said, "At ease. Are your units ready for departure?"

"Yes, sir," we chorused.

"Good." He turned to look over the Bridge Wall, and I could almost hear him mentally checking off the various duties that should be done by now on deck: torpedo skids closed and latched, all storage containers closed and latched, bow light folded to deck and secured, the starry Jack still flying at the bow, with crewman waiting to stow her as soon as we cast off…

Yeoman[5] Walter Dorricott climbed out of the Bridge Hatch at Liddell

---

[4] XO: Executive Officer, second in command.

[5] Yeoman: A Ship's secretary and recorder who takes care of all paperwork. *Flier* carried two Yeomen, Dorricott and James Elder.

and Ed's feet, holding *Flier's* immense Sailing List,[6] as well as his ever-present clipboard.

"Good morning, sirs!" Yeoman Dorricott saluted when he scrambled to his feet.

"Everyone accounted for?" Liddell asked, as we saluted back.

"Yes, sir," Dorricott was grinning widely, smiling at some private joke. Lord knew what it was, and it would likely be dangerous to ask. "I just received the paperwork officially transferring Donald See aboard in place of Alls, and transferred Alls' paperwork onshore along with all of his personal effects."

"What happened to Alls, anyway?" I asked.

"He wound up on the wrong side of a Kiwi's fist while on shore patrol duty. Shattered jaw," Liddell said.

"Too bad, he was a good kid. Now he'll be assigned elsewhere," Ed said.

"Nope, Captain put a retainer on him. As soon as he's cleared and we're back in port, they'll reassign him here, even if they have to fly him to Pearl to meet us," Liddell said calmly, looking over the list.

"We also had two last-minute additions to the crew," Dorricott continued. "A new Ensign under instruction, Phil Mayer, and a Torpedoman named Lucius Wall. That brings our total of new hands to thirteen. " I'd heard that some sailors, hearing the ridiculous rumors that Flier was 'jinxed' had tried to get their orders changed. Having thirteen new hands aboard wasn't going to help the matter.

"I understand Mayer is fresh out of Sub School, so he'll be studying for his quals then," Liddell said.

"Yes, sir, along with twenty of the enlisted men this tour."

"All right, then. All those who went back to the States accounted for?"

"Yes, sir. George Laderbush was the last one back and is stowed and ready to go."

"How is his mother doing, back in…Maine, wasn't it?"

---

[6] The Sailing List is a list of the name, rank, and serial number of every person on board a submarine any time it leaves the dock for any reason. In addition to those names were the names and contact information of next of kin for every person, as well as last wills and testaments.

"Yes, sir. George says she's just fine, still kicking…oh, which reminds me," Dorricott glanced around, leaned in closer to us and lowered his voice as we leaned towards him. "Kit Pourciau just received news of his mother's passing in the last incoming mail call. I gave him time to write a letter home before last outgoing mail call. I told the Chief of the Boat about it and he said he'd keep an eye on Kit, but if you notice that he's not his usual self…"

"Thank you, Dorricott," Liddell sighed, raking his hands through his hair as we stood straight again. "Now, this issue with the chief…" Liddell raised an eyebrow in our direction.

"I saw him with my own eyes a moment ago," Dorricott said, his smile returning.

"Everything's taken care of, sir," I jumped in. I had bailed our Chief Gunner's Mate, Charles Pope, out of Fremantle jail because he confused a bathroom with the middle of a busy street after what had to have been a thoroughly enjoyable evening. "There will be no civilian charges for the uh…incident…this time."

"Good." Liddell muttered. He looked at the list of names quickly, almost muttering to himself. "I notice Baumgart has decided to stay for the patrol, despite everything." Sometime over R&R, Baumgart had gotten busted from Motor Mac to Fireman. For what, I never heard, and no one was talking. His reduction in rate meant not only a cut in pay, but some of his watches would now be outside on lookout duty rather than his favorite engine room.

"Yes, sir," Ed said, "though scuttlebutt is he's planning to ask for a transfer and fight the charges when we return from patrol. He feels a few beers shouldn't have busted him down in rating, especially when other guys were just as drunk during R&R but not demoted."

"He can try to take it up with the Captain, and good luck, he'll need it." Liddell eyed Dorricott again, sighed, and said, "All right, what is it? Grin any wider and your face will split in half."

"Sorry, sir, I just got a telegram this morning, it had some good news."

"Oh?"

"My Barbara had a baby boy, sir, I have a son!"

"Well congratulations, Dorricott!" We all clapped him on the back and shook his hand while he grinned even more widely.

"I can't wait to see the photos in her next letter when we return," he said, "I wish I could go home to see him, but…"

"I know, we all want to go home. I know several men who have children they've only met through letters and photos. Congratulations, all the same," Liddell said, swinging down to the deck beneath us, Dorricott at his heels.

Almost on cue, an Admiral from COMSUBSOWESPAC[7], followed by two Marines, and our CO[8], Lieutenant Commander John D. Crowley, strode out of one of the immense doors in *Orion's* hull. They quickly stepped down the steep iron stairs to the deck of the *Hake,* then crossed to the *Redfin*. Sailors from both subs and the *Orion* snapped to attention as they passed.

Crowley stepped smartly across the gangplank to where Liddell and Dorricott stood at attention. Dorricott handed Captain Crowley the Sailing List. Captain turned around, stepped back across to the *Redfin,* saluted, and handed it to the Admiral. The Admiral accepted the list, said something to Crowley briefly, and then saluted back, the Marines mirroring the action. They looked familiar to me, though I couldn't quite put my finger on it.

Captain crossed back to *Flier,* and the *Redfin* sailors hauled the gangway back almost as soon as his foot cleared it. Captain Crowley gave the order to fire up the engines, and a minute later, after the order relayed inside, *Flier's* engines coughed, then roared to life, spewing black, greasy clouds of diesel smoke across her stern. As Captain Crowley, Liddell, and Dorricott climbed up to the Bridge, Captain gave the order to cast off. Liddell plunged into the Conning Tower as the final two lines were hurled to *Redfin's* deck and *Flier's* great brass props churned the brackish water to foam. The close gap between the subs began to widen as she delicately maneuvered away from our tender's nest while the few of us on the deck waved our farewells.

"Hey, Ed," I asked him as we picked up speed, "did those Marines at the dock look familiar to you? You think they were the same ones—"

"I think they were," he said. "They came and got our little friend when

---

[7] COMSUBSOWESPAC: Short for <u>Com</u>mander of <u>Sub</u>marines in the <u>So</u>uth <u>We</u>st <u>Pac</u>ific

[8] CO: Commanding Officer. Frequently called "Captain" regardless of actual rank.

USS Flier, 20 April 1944. Official US Navy Photo.

we pulled into port." We had run across a fishing vessel just before leaving enemy territory on the last patrol. One of the fishermen indicated that he wanted to go with us, so we gave some food and supplies to the other four, and took the fifth aboard. He didn't speak English, we didn't speak his language, but we quickly figured out some sign language, and eventually, some of the crew started to teach him basic English.

"Still think they're holding a grudge?" I resumed.

"Well, you have to admit," Captain broke in, "if the boys in the Torpedo Room wanted to teach our guest some English, they could have started with 'Hello' rather than 'All Marines are-' "

A ship whistled as we passed.

"Though, in retrospect, teaching him to bow first was an interesting touch." Captain finished.

At the mouth of the harbor, we passed *USS Harder,* the current and, if we had anything to do about it, soon to be defeated leader of the Submarine Force. She appeared to be returning from a training run, her flag and fourteen brag rags flying boldly from her periscope and most of her crew out on the deck, enjoying the sun. Captain waved to her captain, Sam Dealey, who waved right back.

"I see scuttlebutt is right, as usual, sir," I said to Captain.

"Yup. Dealey gets to take her out for one last patrol before stepping down," he replied.

"Chances of scuttling her record?"

"If *Flier* performs as well as her last patrol, *Harder* will soon be eating our wake on the scoreboards."

"I like the sound of that, sir."

When we were finally free of the harbor and all of the protective mine fields and anti-sub nets, *Flier's* props bit deep and she flew through the waves, forcing a fierce wind and fine salt spray against my face, which made me shiver despite my coat. A full complement of officers and lookouts were on deck standing watch. Though we were more than four days from enemy territory, it was still not safe to be complacent in these waters.

My morning shift passed quickly and uneventfully. Allied planes circled overhead, watching for anyone outside the Bombing Restriction Lane. I slipped comfortably back into my watch routine: with the binoculars, sweep the horizon from starboard to port, then the sky from port to starboard, then the sea from starboard to port, then look around with my eyes for a whole picture, all while subtly adjusting my balance for the drifts and drafts of a boat gliding on top of the waves.

We pulled into Exmouth Gulf the evening of our second day at sea for a standard refueling, and stayed the night.

The following morning, I took my first cup of coffee out onto the Bridge for some fresh air and sunlight, two things which would become scarce in the coming weeks. Though early, the city and harbor hummed with workers intent on their duties, doing everything they could to ship us back and forth as quickly as possible. There were few Australian accents, since most of the Aussies who had joined the military were in the European and African Theaters. Instead, I heard a lot of American, British, and Dutch accents from various quarters.

I enjoyed these few quiet moments, and wondered where we were being sent this time. On our first real patrol, *Flier* left Pearl Harbor, patrolled near Formosa, through the Philippines, and ended in Fremantle.

Now, there was apparently a lot of activity in the Marianas, and of course lots of rumors about the Philippines and the South China Sea. It would be later today before we found out where we'd been assigned.

Captain climbed out into the cool morning air and moments later, the engines thrummed under the decks. "Morning Jacobson," he greeted me.

"Morning, sir," I stood at attention, while still holding my mug.

"As you were," he told me with a half-smile. I resumed my station looking over the chest-high wall that shielded the bridge.

"Permission to hold target practice this morning, sir?" I asked, before I

Lieutenant Commander John Daniel Crowley standing on the lookout deck of Flier during her construction in 1943. The structure next to him is the support tubes for the SD Radar and Aft Periscope. Courtesy of family of Cmdr. John D. Crowley

lost his attention.

"That target Ed told me about last week?" he said, sipping the coffee.

"Yes, sir, we passed it on our way in, I believe."

"Very well, I'll sail her there for you. We should be there by 1100 hours."

"Thank you, sir."

I dropped through the Bridge Hatch and the cool, salt smell of the harbor vanished instantly under the combined stench of diesel oil, sweat, and cigarette smoke. The new scents of fresh paint and floor wax would fade too soon under the body odor and old cooking smells yet to develop and ripen into a healthy "sub air" mix.

From the Conning Tower, already full of men checking systems and coming on duty, I dropped down again to the Control Room, packed with pipes and instruments, a maze of highly polished bronze, brass, steel, and copper. Stepping through the aft hatch, I found Pope finishing his morning chow. I caught his eye, and pointed forward to Officer's Country. He nodded and tossed his tin tray into the already full sink, then followed me to the Wardroom, where I found Ed, who happened to be our Chief Gunnery Officer, finishing his own breakfast.

The three of us went down the two-foot wide passage to the "privacy" of Ed's cramped three-man cabin for a quick consultation about the morning's exercise.

"Captain said he'll sail us up to that target for gunnery practice," I said without preamble, jerking the curtain "door" closed behind us.

"ETA?" Ed asked, sipping his coffee.

"1100 hours."

"Good. I think I'm favoring a surprise practice this morning, how about you two?" Ed said.

"I like the idea, sir," Pope said. "It's the only time we'll have a safe environment to have a surprise practice. Keep the men on their toes."

"It's sort of expected, though," I replied.

"Expected is different from 'definitely going to' sir," Pope pointed out, "and no one on the gunnery crews knows *when* we'll get there, so they'll be able to practice dropping everything, grabbing their gear, and getting on deck."

"Sounds good to me," Ed said. "Aren't you due to be on watch when we get there, Jacobson?" He asked me.

"Yes, sir," I said. I always called him sir in front of the enlisted men.

"That'll help. I'm supposed to be in the Conning Tower, so it'll be easy to announce the gunnery practice when you sight the target. Pope?"

"Technically off duty, sir, but I'll be all right."

"Sounds like a plan then. Dismissed."

Pope ducked out of the room, while Ed marked something in a book on his desk. Many more photos of his wife, son, in-laws and extended family were taped to the desk and the wall next to it.

"Do you have enough photos yet, Ed?" I teased.

"Not nearly, Jake." He grinned. "You'd better get to work."

"Yes, sir," I said. "First order of business: *Breakfast!*"

Our steward, John Turner, smiled when I entered the Wardroom. "There you are, sir, I knew I was missing someone."

"Hope that doesn't mean I've missed breakfast."

"Never let that happen. Been keeping it warm for you. Here you go: eggs, sausage, toast, biscuits and gravy, fresh doughnuts, and coffee."

"Wonderful. Finding everything back there, then?"

"Never better, James even took the morning off, left it to Alvin, Clyde and me. Melvin, of course, made the bread and the biscuits."

"Fantastic, I love his biscuits. Thanks, Turner."

"No problem, sir."

After breakfast, with another cup of coffee to ward off the morning wind, I scrambled back up the ladders to the Bridge just as *Flier* was pulling out of Exmouth's harbor.

A few hours later, the call came from the lookout rings, "Target in sight, sir."

I trained my binoculars on the landscape and saw it: the long, low silhouette in the water.

"Attention all hands! Target Approaching! Man the guns!" Ed's voice crackled over the ship's radio as the General Quarters Alarm sounded. In moments, Ed and Pope leapt out of the Bridge Hatch, and about ten seconds later, the gunnery crews, some still pulling on their flak jackets and holding their helmets to their heads, flooded out and ran to their various stations.

One team, under Pope and Fire Controlman Donald Tremaine, leapt to the deck below, ran forward and released the muzzle of the large four-inch .50 caliber gun from its support frame.

My team rushed to the 40-mm Aft Bridge gun. Two men, the pointer and trainer, leapt to the seats on either side of the gun and cranked her hard to port, while one loader jumped to the deck below and cranked open the ammo locker and began handing the rounds to the other loader on the bridge deck.

Tunk–tunk–tunk–tunk. Ed's team on the 20 mm machine gun on the Fore Bridge started their assault on the target. *Flier* jumped with each shot, causing most rounds to veer wildly off-target. "Move it, men!" I called, ramming cotton wads in my ears.

The fourth round slammed into place in the feed, and *Flier* lurched under the *"Boom!"* of the 40–mm. I clutched the wire rails surrounding the gun deck to keep my balance.

"BOOM!" Flier pitched as the 4-inch gun roared beneath me. Soon the water around the target surged and foamed under the assault, as *Flier* danced and the men adjusted their aim to account for her pitches and rolls.

We flew past the old thing, then heeled around hard starboard and shot from the other side. It was nearly impossible to see the target now between the blue-grey fog of gunpowder smoke swirling around us and the water frothing and spraying high for yards around the target. The smell of gunpowder probably wasn't going to come out of my hair for days now. I just hoped I couldn't still smell it by dinnertime.

"Cease fire!" Ed boomed, and the frantic energy ground to a halt. We couldn't waste all our ammo on an exercise. "Excellent work!" He shouted over the wind, "Restore the equipment and reload the lockers. That'll be all."

In minutes the spent drums and shells were hurled into the sea and the exterior ammo lockers restocked from the main ammo locker deep in *Flier's* belly. Then the crew vanished through the Bridge Hatch into the sub, and the sea was quiet with only the six of us on the deck maintaining the watch once more. I focused my binoculars on the silhouette, now easier to see despite the glittering waves. According to the gunnery officers in Perth, that old wreck had the dubious distinction of being the most shot-at ship in the world. Every passing battle ship, submarine or airplane would target it. It was hardly more than a rusted-out tube now, full of holes. [9]

Flier's engines roared again and she turned her nose north and west. Australia faded from a crisp red-brown rocky shore to a bluish shadow then vanished in the afternoon haze. She had been a great and gracious hostess, and already, the crew was vociferously wishing to return to Fremantle after patrol.

I knew in my gut that I would see Fremantle again. I just didn't know that when I did, I would be scarred, severely sunburned, and under a top-secret gag order.

Based on photographs, this is the wrecked freighter Mildura as she would have appeared in 1901 and as she appears currently. Most of what remains are her ribs, keel, and boilers. The majority of her wood and fittings were scavenged for local homesteads.

---

[9] This "target ship" was likely the SS MILDURA and what's left of her is still visible near Exmouth. She was grounded on Ningaloo Reef by a typhoon March 12, 1907 and was used as a target by warships and planes during WWI, WWII and decades afterward.

2

GATEWAY TO WAR

Hours after Australia vanished beyond our stern, Captain ordered an officer's meeting in the wardroom, leaving the Chief[10] in charge. Breakfast had long since been cleared away, though the coffee pot was full, and fresh doughnuts beckoned from the sideboard. We helped ourselves and took our seats, waiting for Captain.

He entered carrying the new, tightly rolled charts under his arm, which he placed at his seat. He drew the green curtain doors of the room closed, and Ed did the same with the other doorway. Then Captain grabbed the ship's com. "Attention All Hands! Our Patrol Area is the South China Sea."

Through the curtains, I heard the excited conversation of the men, as they digested this small bit of information. Captain turned to us, his face all business. Though he spoke low to limit people hearing the meeting as they passed by, we all knew everything he said would be common knowledge among the entire crew shortly, and probably before we adjourned. On a submarine, secrets didn't stay that way for long.

"Our orders are straightforward. We're to proceed through Lombok Strait, to Makassar Strait and Sibutu Passage, then, unless told differently, we're to take Balabac Strait via the Natsubata Channel. For the next five weeks, we're assigned Patrol areas 201 and 202 in the South China Sea, beginning with 201. We'll switch patrol areas every Sunday.

"If all goes well, after sundown on September 11, we'll head back, via Mindoro Strait, Sibutu Passage, Makassar, Lombok, and yes, home to Fremantle and Perth by the end of September." That brought a quiet cheer from us, and moments later, a much louder one from the Forward Torpedo Room. Captain smiled, shook his head, and continued. "As usual, we're

---

[10] "Chief of the Boat" sometimes called "COB" is a senior enlisted man aboard. He advises the CO and XO about the crew and disciplinary matters in addition to being in charge of day-to-day operations. While not strictly in the chain of command, the COB and his opinions carry a lot of weight with both enlisted men and officers. According to Al Jacobson, *Flier's* COB was CMoMM Edgar W. Hudson. According to Jim Alls, the COB was CTM Kenneth Gwinn. There is no official military paperwork that formally identifies the COB of *Flier*.

Philippine
Sea

Mindoro
Strait

Sulu
Sea

Axis controlled

Allied-controlled

Patrol
Area

Saigon

Balabac
Strait

Celebes
Sea

Makassar
Strait

J a v a S e a

Lombok
Strait

Indian
Ocean

FLIER'S PLANNED
SECOND PATROL:
2 August 1944-
approx. 22 Sept.
1944

Exmouth
Gulf

——— *Flier's* **Planned
Route to
Patrol Area**

········· *Flier's* **Planned
Route Back to
Fremantle**

Fremantle

engaging in unrestricted submarine warfare with the enemy, so keep your eyes open for any and all convoys as well as any fools traveling alone.

"This time, HQ has given us a wide hunting ground free from friendly submarines because we are to watch for and sink four Japanese supply submarines that are likely operating out of Saigon. Once we get there, any periscope is not friendly. Keep your eyes peeled."

For three days, *Flier* plowed northward without seeing a soul. Captain Crowley tested us with emergency dives and surfaces, forcing *Flier* to go from surfaced to submerged in less than forty-five seconds. This tested the nerves of those of us on watch outside, because the first dive warning we usually received was the loud "hiss" of air escaping the ballast tanks as she began her dive, while we scrambled for the Bridge Hatch.

Between duty shifts there was always the great food and entertainment to be found on board. During the daytime hours and between training runs, Captain allowed those crewmembers who wouldn't be allowed on deck after crossing Lombok to come outside for tanning, fresh air, and exercise. After dark, we indulged in our Navy-supplied library, radio, record player, and even our own movie theater complete with projector, screen and reels. Most of us also brought our own books, stationery, and decks of cards for the inevitable poker games. Some had managed to bring special things aboard. Last time he was home, Leon Courtright had talked his sister out of her hand-cranked phonograph and collection of records.

Several men on the crew had been on the battleships and destroyers during Pearl Harbor. I knew Don Tremaine had been on *USS Maryland* and Jarrold Taylor on the *Pennsylvania* that day. Some were regular Navy, but others, like I, were Reservists that had been activated. Some had been Skimmers[11] before entering Sub Service while others tried to join as soon as they were free to volunteer out of boot camp. Almost a fifth of us were under twenty years old, and only a few were over thirty.

At forty years old, the old man among us was Ken Gwinn, the Torpedo Chief. He'd been born in Indiana, and grew up working in his parent's diner, but apparently had military plans from early on. I overheard him once telling Captain that he joined the Army at thirteen, trying to get into

---

[11] Skimmers: a term for surface sailors.

World War I. His father had to track him down and prove his age before they let him go. Gwinn had been terribly disappointed, and joined the Navy after he was eligible. Now he'd served on dozens of boats, from S-Boats to *Flier*.

If Gwinn was the oldest, the youngest must have taken after him. Dick Lambert, who had been on *Flier* since she commissioned last year, was due to celebrate his seventeenth birthday this month. He must have been barely fifteen when he joined the Navy, well below the age to enlist even with his parent's permission, though no one noticed anymore. He was one of many military wide. Not to mention, he was a good torpedoman.

Of the officers, we ran the gamut from the experienced Navy men like Captain to the new guy Mayer. Liddell had been in ROTC too, and activated as soon as he graduated, before the war began. Herb Miner and Herb "Teddy" Baehr were "mustangs", enlisted guys who had worked their way to the officer ranks. Though we shared the same rank of ensign, they were much older than I, and could run any system on *Flier* blindfolded, if need be. Everyone respected their opinions, from the enlisted to Captain.

We came from all over the country: I heard southern drawls, the unique accent of New England, the familiar cadence of the Midwest. Several men came from New York City, another group from Chicago, and at least four guys had been born abroad. Despite our differences, we were like brothers, teasing each other mercilessly, but heaven help the person who picked on any one of us.

One night before we entered Lombok, I entered the galley bleary-eyed to get a cup of coffee and a bite before my night shift began. The Mess Hall had been taken over by the men and the stainless-steel walls were now blanketed with posters, photos, news articles, anything and everything that took our minds off of the danger into which we were heading. The carefully prepared and posted menu was now all but covered by a Betty Grable poster, though no one minded, least of all the galley staff. Rita Hayworth's smile gleamed from over the water fountain, while postcards from Hawaii, Panama, New York, San Francisco, San Diego, Perth, and other exotic locales were pasted in between photos of cars, girls from home, and other "lucky" items.

In a place of pride hung the original framed *Flier* insignia, painted by a

Disney artist.

Boxes of food were crammed between the various pipes running overhead, and mesh bags full of fresh fruit, carrots, turnips and other root vegetables hung from the ceiling. The fresh stuff would be used first, saving the canned food, some of which was currently jammed under the racks and inside the men's personal lockers, until the end of patrol. That is, if it hadn't already been eaten by someone. Thank goodness for the actual storage room, that kept the bulk of the food safe.

The Andrews Sisters finished up their rendition of "Boogie Woogie Bugle Boy" before the record hissed softly on the last groove. Melvin, and Skow, were taking freshly-baked bread out of the oven. I closed my eyes and breathed deeply, suddenly remembering my home in Grand Haven, and my mom and sisters baking bread and rolls for dinner.

"Whoa! You'd better open your eyes when you go waltzing through here, sir!" Clyde Banks's voice called. The trapdoor to the Cool Room was open at my feet, and our Second Cook, along with another new hand, Tommy Bohn, looked up at me from the chilly bottom.

"Whoops! Sorry about that, Clyde."

"No problem, sir, I just didn't want you joining us. It's rather tight quarters as is."

"You sure? I think I see a spare inch just to your left there," I said with a grin.

"Very funny, sir."

Clyde and Tommy were trying to stand on the same square foot of space, which was already on top of a bunch of packages of frozen something-or-other. The rest of the room, I knew, was packed solid. "Actually, sir," Clyde said, "I was about to send the non-qual[12] to find you," he said, jerking his thumb back to Tommy. "Those pork shoulders seem a bit older than we thought they were when we got them."

"Making a change in tomorrow's menu then, I take it?"

"Yes, sir. The T-Bones seem to be holding their own, so I think I'll swap the scheduled steak dinner for some pulled pork. James already agreed

---

[12] Non-Qual: A submariner who is not yet qualified. After Submarine School, a submariner is not qualified until he completes his exams on the job. Each non-qual has a year to finish his qualifications, though many do so much sooner.

On the left, a detail from a Flier *menu drawn on June 25, 1944, showing the* Flier *insignia as it appeared in 1944. Based on the initials, three crewmen, Vernon McLane, Vernon Moench, or Victor Murawski, could be the artist. On the right, the insignia as James Alls remembers it. Image on the left courtesy of the family of Lt. James Liddell.*

with me, so if it's all right with you, I'll make it official."

"You'd better hold those T-Bones, I put in an order for steak on my birthday in two weeks." Skow said with a grin.

"For you? We'll serve gruel." Clyde laughed. "So how 'bout it, sir?"

"Whatever you want; as Commissary Officer[13], I know better than to mess with you guys, because you have the power to serve us all gruel for breakfast, lunch and dinner if you want!" I said.

"And don't you forget it, sir!" Clyde playfully wagged his finger at me from his position waist-deep in the deck.

"You know, the crew would probably hang *me* by my toes for upsetting you!" I continued, "I can hear Lt. Casey now, 'We don't have the best cooks in the Navy just to let some wet-behind-the-ears Commissary Officer offend them three days out!'"

"You learn quickly, sir," he said, hoisting himself up onto the deck. "I'll keep that toe-hanging in mind though, it might come in useful."

---

[13] Commissary Officer: One of the junior officer positions; he requisitions, receives, stores, and accounts for all ship's stores. In addition, he is involved in the meal planning and oversight of the galley staff, including coordinating with the sub's Pharmacist's Mate so he can provide proper nutritional supplements.

"All right, all right, I'd better stop now before I give you any more ideas. Menu change is fine by me, need me to inform Doc?"

"If you would, sir," he bent down to grab Tommy's forearm to haul him up.

I searched out Doc[14] and quickly informed him. At this point in the patrol, changes in the menu were not a problem, but later, we had to keep track of nutrients and the vitamin supplements that might be needed to keep the crew healthy. The lack of sunlight for two months caused a number of surprising health issues.

Returning through the sparsely populated Mess Hall, fully intending to fill my coffee mug this time, I caught an interesting conversation between Pope and Earl Baumgart.

"Come off it, Earl," Pope said with a laugh, relaxing against the wall.

"All I'm saying," Baumgart was quietly insisting, "is something doesn't feel right. I've been on lots of different ships and this one feels off. Like she's jinxed."

"You keep that talk up, and the Japs really will get you," Oliver Kisamore joked, looking up from his book and glass of Coke.

"Besides," Pope grinned, lighting a cigarette, "*Flier's* not jinxed, I am, don't you know?"

"What?" Tommy looked confused.

"I don't think he's heard that story, Gunner," Oly said, grinning.

"Well then, I'll tell you why we had so much hard luck for a while, and this ain't no bull. Before I came on submarines, I worked in battleships. One day, I just finished swabbing the deck, when this albatross swoops in, lands, and shits all over the deck! He wasn't looking at me, so I snuck up behind him, crouched behind the capstan, and rapped him smartly on the head with my swab. Feathers went everywhere. I didn't mean to kill the stupid bugger, but there it was, dead as a doornail. So there you have it,

---

[14] Pharmacist's Mate or "Doc": the only medical person on a submarine. Even today, sub work is too risky to allow a highly-trained person like a doctor or nurse to patrol, so a Pharmacist's Mate is assigned. While his job technically was to oversee the crew's health, provide first aid, and inform the Captain if someone's condition warranted a transfer to a larger vessel, some Pharmacist's Mates during WWII also performed surgeries including minor amputations and appendectomies. *Flier's* "Doc" was Peter Gaideczka.

that's why we had bad luck, because no sailor ever kills an albatross, it's bad luck."

The few guys in the room laughed appreciatively. It was a silly and oft-told tale, and Pope was the best storyteller on the boat.

"You don't take things seriously, Chief," Baumgart told him.

"Not when it's smoke and mirrors and superstition, no. What happened at Midway was because of a storm, the lack of a pilot, lots of things, but not some crazy jinx."

"What happened at Midway?" Tommy said, sweat-faced, slamming and latching the cool room trapdoor.

"Tell you what kid," Pope said, "put on some Glenn Miller and I'll tell you."

Tommy jumped on one of the Mess Room benches and shuffled through the shelf full of records. Clyde, finished with his inventory paperwork, winked at me as he passed, pulling his well-worn deck of cards from his pants pocket saying, "I have the last bit of my salary burning a hole in my pocket. Who's up for a game of poker?" He slid onto a bench at another table.

"I'm in." Baumgart slid into place across from Clyde.

"Me, too," Pope strolled over, "especially if Lady Luck will not desert me." He affectionately patted Betty Grable's bottom on her poster. "Sir? Are you in?" He asked me.

"No thanks," I said, waving my cup, enjoying the scene. "I'm more of a cribbage man."

Trumpets blaring erupted from the record player. "Hey, can I play?" Tommy grinned, turning around.

"Sorry kid. You know the rules. No playtime until you're fully qualified. Hey, Skow, you in?" Pope said.

"Sure am." He grinned. "And I have some dishes the kid can do, unless you still need him." He looked at Clyde.

"He's all yours."

Tommy rolled his eyes. "Dishes?" he asked in disbelief.

"I know of a few oil filters that need to be cleaned, if you'd prefer…" Baumgart offered with a grin.

"No, no, dishes will be fine. At least then I can hear the story."

"Sure thing, kid," Pope turned to Clyde, "Deal 'em." I still had a few minutes and tucked myself in to the table next door. I'd heard bits and pieces during the last patrol when I was a rookie, but this was the first I'd heard the whole tale.

Clyde flicked the cards around the table with a practiced grace as Pope lit another cigarette and took a long draw on it. "Now where was I?" he mused. "Ah, yes, Midway."

"Well, first of all, Midway is a tricky base to get into even on a calm day. It's this ring of reefs surrounding two spits of sand, and the harbor and channel have to be dredged regularly to keep them deep enough for ships and subs. Whenever you come to Midway, they send a pilot who's familiar with the waters out to the sub to help guide you in.

"Of course, the day *Flier* attempted it[15] was in the midst of one of the worst winter storms that season. It was one of those storms that howled for days on end. The moment we hit the shallower waters around Midway, the waves started to break over the deck. Half the time, the waves and rain were so bad you couldn't see the islands at all."

Pope glanced down at his hand, told Clyde, "Eh, I'll take three," and tucked these in his hand with barely a glace before resuming. "Midway radioed us to stand by for the pilot, but by the time he came out on the tug, it was far too dangerous to transfer the man aboard, so the tug signaled us to follow her wake into the channel. Captain slowed down a bit to let the tug get well ahead of us, then followed her wake.

"Now what we didn't know is there is a tricky cross-current that jets right across the mouth of the channel. If you don't go fast enough, you get pushed east. And just to make things more interesting, one of the two eastern buoys was missing, so we had no idea where the east side of the channel really was.

"Anyway, just after we passed the entrance buoys, this massive swell comes out of nowhere, picks up *Flier* and shoves her to port. Captain ordered us hard to starboard to correct Mother Nature, then then another massive swell coupled with that current grabbed us, shoved us out of the channel starboard-side. Captain ordered *Flier* to port when a final wave

---

[15] January 16, 1944.

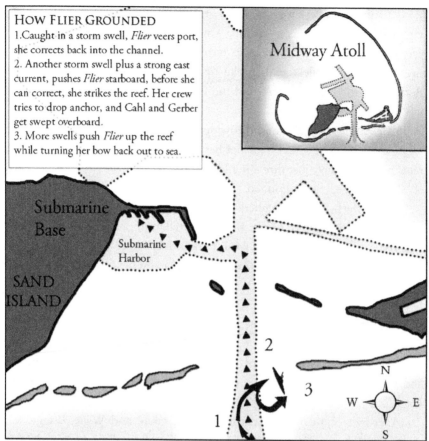

HOW FLIER GROUNDED

1. Caught in a storm swell, *Flier* veers port, she corrects back into the channel.
2. Another storm swell plus a strong east current, pushes *Flier* starboard, before she can correct, she strikes the reef. Her crew tries to drop anchor, and Cahl and Gerber get swept overboard.
3. More swells push *Flier* up the reef while turning her bow back out to sea.

Taken from the records of Flier's *investigation into her grounding at Midway, this shows the approximate final grounding position.*

picks her up and bounces her on a reef, neat as you please. Came down so hard, she bounced Baumgart here out of bed, didn't she?"

"I wasn't the only one." he grunted looking at his cards, and throwing a few quarters in the pot.

"Oh man," Clyde added, "I had just finished the lunch clean up and was prepping dinner. *Flier* had been rolling a bit in the waves, but when she suddenly hit, then hit again, the clean dishes went flying across the Mess and I found myself on the floor wearing dinner. Had no idea what happened, but then the alarms were screaming and everyone was running everywhere."

"To make matters worse," Pope grinned, warming to his story and the rapidly-growing audience drifting in from Crew's Quarters, "some screwdriver got thrown into main terminal, and the short-circuit started a fire that spewed thick, oily smoke up and down the sub. Seawater was flooding in the engine rooms and the Forward Torpedo Room, everything was chaos.

"Meantime, Captain was throwing *Flier's* rudder back and forth and trying desperately to either back her back off the reef, or throw her over the reef. But every wave just threw her higher and higher."

"Full house," Skow grinned.

"What the—!" Pope laughed.

"Apparently, you'd better be a storyteller or a card player." Skow smirked, "'Cause you sure as hell can't do both at once!"

"Nah, you were just lucky that time. I'll get you next round," Pope said gathering and shuffling the cards. "I'm watching you."

"You're also just jabbering without finishing the story."

"Yeah, yeah. So, in the meantime, the anchor detail had gone to the foredeck to try to drop anchor to prevent *Flier* from climbing higher up the reef, and this huge wave swept two guys, Jimmy and Gerber, overboard, and Dag got slammed into Conning Tower, laying open his side, didn't it, Dag?"

A crowd of men now surrounded the table, and Waite Daggy was standing in the back. "Sure did," he said, proudly pulling up his shirt to reveal the jagged, red line that trailed down his side. "Don't forget this one," he said, pointing at the scar running from his lower lip to his chin, "and my winning SMILE!" He grinned, revealing a mouthful of missing teeth. "Couldn't shut my mouth and damn near broke my jaw. Took the dentist at Pearl forever to fix me up."

"Dentist at Pearl?" Doc snorted. "I like that! Do you even remember who it was who sewed you up and removed that giant shaft of wood out of your face?"

"Should I?"

"True, when they dropped you down the hatch, you were covered in blood and nearly unconscious. I made sure you stayed that way too, between alcohol and morphine."

Macaw *and* Flier *caught on Midway's reef. Top photo dated January 16, 1944. Bottom photo dated January 17, 1944. The land in the background is Eastern Island. Both photos courtesy of the family of USS Macaw's Executive Officer, Lt. Gerald Loughman.*

"That would explain my headache the next day."

"Your head was the only thing that ached? I did pretty well, then."

"What happened?" Tommy asked them.

"Dag here, decided to take on the Conning Tower and deck using his face as a battering ram," Doc said. "Chief Gwinn hauled him single handedly up to the bridge, then down to the Conning Tower, the Control Room, and back to me in my Alley. Had a spar of wood about yea big"-he held his thumb and forefinger about four inches apart-"thrust through his lips. The electricity was off more often than it was on, and wouldn't stop flickering even when it did decide to cooperate, so about five or six guys sat all around Dag on the other racks, holding battle lanterns just so I could see him properly.

"*Flier* would get hit by a swell and lean so far over we had to hang on to the rack frames to keep our footing, then she'd slowly right herself and pause for just one moment before keeling over the other way. Those moments were the only time I had to try to fix his face, that gash down his back, and those broken teeth and jaw."

"Are you sure you fixed his face?" Pope said, squinting at Dag.

"I'm a Pharmacist's Mate, not God, Pope. Some things he has to take up with the Man Upstairs." He clapped his hand on Dag's shoulder, as we all roared. "All I could do was keep him from walking around with half the deck sticking out of his lips."

"Yeah, yeah, go on about yourself, why don't cha?" Pope grinned. 'Like Doc said, *Flier* kept getting battered. She would scream as she rolled and pivoted every time a big wave hit her. She actually managed to turn herself back out to sea rather quickly, but was still stuck fast. Cap ordered the ballast tanks and two fuel tanks dumped, hoping that would lighten us enough that the next big wave combined with our churning props would push us off, but the storm wouldn't cooperate. The shafts got banged to hell and began leaking water. We were running all trim and bilge pumps and a bucket brigade besides, to keep ahead of the flooding in the stern.

"Up on deck, Banchero spotted Gerber in the water, threw him a life ring, then the crazy fool threw himself in the drink when the ring didn't fly far enough. Both of them were swept out of sight into the lagoon, and we hoped they would be okay.

"Suddenly, there was this beam of light shining through the rain, and the silhouette of a massive ship. It was one of the newest sub rescue ships, *Macaw*. Word passed down to us that she was coming, and we set up a cheer. We were saved! Since we were already pointed out to sea, *Macaw* decided to anchor outside the entrance buoys and get a lightweight messenger line to us, which was connected to her tow cable. Once that was hooked up, it'd be a simple matter to haul *Flier* off her perch and out to deep water. *Macaw* tried to float the messenger to us, sent a small launch, even a tug boat our way, but the sea and currents would not cooperate and it was too dangerous to bring two vessels that close anyway. Their gunnery officer even tried to shoot it to us, but the winds forced it down several feet short every time.

"So they had a new idea: since there was a current streaming out of Midway and another strong one heading east, *Macaw* decided to head back into Midway and turn around, then attach the messenger line to a flotilla of life jackets and whatnot and feed it out as *Macaw* passed by us again on her way back out to sea, using the currents to our advantage."

Baumgart won that hand, dealt another, but the story continued with hardly an interruption, and the Mess was now packed with avid listeners. "The sea was so fierce that *Macaw's* starboard anchor chain snapped when they tried to haul it in, and she was pitching and rolling in the waves. Minutes later, they sent a three word message: '*We are aground.*'" The room groaned. "Sure enough," Pope resumed, "there she was, just next to us, with all of her men scrambling all over the deck trying to pry her free, too."

"For days the storm continued, sometimes calmer, sometimes furious, but never quite enough to pull either *Flier* or *Macaw* free.

"Six days later, on a Saturday, the storm finally cleared and we could see the *Macaw's* sister ship, *Florikan,* standing by outside the reef—"

"WITH the *Jack* AND the *Gudgeon*, who were trying to get into Midway, but we were blocking the channel," Baumgart interrupted.

"Well, more the *Macaw* than us, her stern was the one hanging in the channel."

"Still humiliating," Baumgart grunted, with several of the old hands agreeing. "Especially when the *Kingfish* managed to get into Midway during that storm by maneuvering around *Macaw* and us."

"Okay, granted, it wasn't our finest hour. By this time, there was only a skeleton crew on both vessels. During the few lulls, nearly a third of our crew had been evacuated to the *Macaw* via the most rickety looking boatswain's seat you've ever seen."

Baumgart shuddered, and Pope, noticing, laughed. "Yeah, you wouldn't have fond memories of that, would you?"

"Well, you weren't dropped by that thing, were you?"

"Dropped?" Tommy asked.

"You see," Pope continued in grand form, as Baumgart glared at his cards, "when you hear, 'grounded boat' you sort of think of one that isn't moving, but that wasn't true at all. Both girls were stuck hard on one point of their hulls, but floated and pivoted with the waves everywhere else. *Flier's* stern was stuck pretty solid, but her nose heaved and rolled like a roller coaster. *Macaw* did too. So, if you can imagine this pair of pants, suspended from a cable tied between the two ships, that's how we were getting guys back and forth. Baumgart gets in, and halfway across, these waves hit the *Flier* and *Macaw*, rolling them toward each other, and dropped Baum in the drink, neat as you please. Wasn't a thing he could do about it, but the girls quickly rolled back over and lifted him out again.

"Anyway, Baum got the *Macaw* in one soggy piece and went with the rest of the guys to Sand Island, where they found Gerber and Banchero already in the hospital, Gerber nursing a broken arm."

He paused for a moment to consider his cards, and Wes Miller piped up, "What happened to the other one, Kohl?"

"Cahl, James Francis Peder Cahl," Baumgart replied solemnly. "A guy who got off at Freo, Joe Lia, tried to go in after him, but Cahl was too far out to sea. He drowned. Jim Alls told me that he talked to some of the Midway pilots who told him a strange tale. When they were coming in to land, they saw some dolphins pushing something to shore. When the guard went down to the beach, they found Cahl's body, still guarded by the dolphins. Once they pulled him ashore and onto a stretcher, the dolphins left. Those of us who were evacuated to Sand Island buried him at sea with full honors." Baumgart concluded.

"Jimmy's belongings that were in his locker and bunk were sent to the *Macaw* via the boatswain's seat, along with the letter Captain had to write to

Another aerial view of Flier *and* Macaw *grounded on January 17, 1944. The white caps at the top of the photo are breaking over the western coral wall, while the light water near Flier's stern is the eastern coral wall. Macaw's stern is in the eastern portion of the channel. Photo courtesy of the family of* USS Macaw's *Executive Officer, Lt. Gerald Loughman.*

Cahl's new wife, giving her the news. Everything was shipped stateside from Midway," Pope said quietly, tossing his hand back at Baumgart.

We all sat in respectful silence once again for a few moments until Pope resumed. "*Flier* was banged to hell. Steering was shot, our rudder bent beyond use. The prop shafts leaked everywhere. The engines were clogged with crushed coral sand, the port prop wouldn't work at all, and the starboard prop was real sluggish. Every wave that hit brought a shriek of protest from *Flier*. We didn't know if she would float once we pulled her off.

"Those of us left aboard had been wearing our lifebelts for six days, and Captain and the Exec were at each other's throats—"

"Lt. Liddell?" Tommy asked, incredulously.

"No, no, Lt. Liddell was our Engineering Officer at that time. No, our Exec for that patrol was a guy named Adams. He and the Captain couldn't see eye to eye on anything. We weren't the first ship, or submarine, to ground at Midway[16], but it still wasn't good for a CO's career. Captain was already under the gun, trying to do what was right for the remainder of what he probably thought was his last command, and Adams was feeling the pressure too. Something blew between them, and by the time *Flier* made it to Cali, they refused to speak to each other. I heard that Adams even threatened to leave the Sub Force altogether rather than patrol with Captain again. Few days later, he got orders to transfer as the XO of *Albacore*.

"As soon as Captain realized he would need a new XO, he marched up to HQ, looked them square in the eye and said, 'I'd like to promote my Engineering Officer than take on some unknown from your pool of 'XOs-In-Waiting'. You want results; I want to work with the best, and that's Liddell'." They took him at his word, which is how we got Liddell as the youngest XO in the war, not that you'll ever find *that* in the official record."

Jimmy Elder, our other Yeoman, burst out laughing. "Yeah, that sounds like the sort of thing that wouldn't make the official records. The best stuff is always left out."

"Really? How much of the 'best stuff'?" Pope asked.

"Well, not you Pope, you're in a lot of the records. Makes for better reading!"

"Eh, I always knew I'd make my mark on history. May my future descendants enjoy it!

"Anyway, in the end, it took the tug that tried to guide us into Midway, plus the *Florikan,* AND a floating crane to pry us free of the reef, and then we checked her bow to stern. Surprisingly, despite the fact that she couldn't steer, couldn't dive, and couldn't run her engines for long, and only the starboard prop had a hope of working for short sprints, the one thing she could do perfectly well was float. So, we hooked her up via a towing bridle,

---

[16] *USS Trigger* (SS-237) grounded on Midway's northeastern reef on June 6, 1942, *USS Tarpon* (SS-175) grounded at the same spot as *Flier* on 10 December 1942 and *USS Scorpion* (SS-278) grounded on the western side of the channel on 13 August 1943.

loaded everyone up and headed out for Pearl. Got there a few days later." [17]

"Without incident?" I grinned. "Not the way I heard it, Pope."

"No, no," chorused a bunch of the old hands. I had not been on the Midway patrol, but I had heard this part of the story again and again, usually from someone trying to explain the phenomenon that was Pope to a new hand.

"Way I heard it, *Florikan* and *Flier* ran into another winter storm a few days later, and the tow cable snapped. And *someone* volunteered to reattach it himself," I said slyly.

"Fished the crazy idiot out of the water," Dag grinned. "He tried to ride *Flier* like a bucking bronco in the waves, clinging to the deck as she threw him under water then high in the air, then over the side! It's a good thing you had that lifeline around your waist!"

"I got her reattached though, didn't I?"

"With *a lot* of help!"

"Jinxed," Baumgart muttered under his breath.

[17] The *Macaw* wasn't so lucky. Despite numerous attempts, she could not be pried off the reef. Salvage crews boarded, assigned to take every item of value and then blow her free of the reef, but during another winter storm on 12-13 February 1944, the sea pushed *Macaw* into deep water and she sank, taking five hands with her, including her commanding officer Lt. Cdr. Paul W. Burton. She partially blocked the channel, and was finally demolished using explosives. Her wreck has been surveyed and can be dived today at Midway.
Photo on the left, taken February 13, 1944, shortly after Macaw sank, courtesy of the family of USS Macaw's Executive Officer, Lt. Gerald Loughman. Photo of Macaw wreck on right taken in 2005 during a survey for the National Oceanic and Atmospheric Association (NOAA). Credit: NOAA; Schwemmer

"Oh get off it," Pope rolled his eyes, "She got through that just fine, and went on to have a spectacular first patrol. Moreover, we got rid of Adams and promoted Liddell, kept the Captain, had the latest technology installed, and to top it all off, we never would have been in the position to stalk those three convoys if we had gone on our original patrol." Several of the men nodded their heads and chorused, "That's right.'"

"You know what they say about serving three patrols on the same sub though," Jarrold Taylor broke in, "It's not good luck!"

"Please! This is her second—"Pope said.

"Third! Midway was still a patrol, even if it ended early," Taylor cut in.

"Trouble stalks her wherever she goes," Baumgart growled, several other men nodding in agreement.

"Good!" Pope snorted, throwing down his cards. "A submarine who can't find trouble can't earn any record or any glory. Look at the *Harder!* Rumor has it, Jap destroyers made a special target of her and she turned right around and made dinner of four of them, a fleet record!" The argument was growing, expanding into several of the listeners, who were echoing, "That's right!" "She'll be a top scorer yet!"

"Hey, are we playing poker or not?" Clyde broke in. "I signed up for a poker game, not insanity!"

As the only officer in the room, I decided to head this off before it got any worse, "All right, gentlemen, that's enough, just—"

"I don't care what anyone says." Baumgart stood up at the table, towering over Pope. "I've been around submarines for years and on this boat ever since she touched water, and I'm telling you, she's ji—"

"You had better not finish that sentence Mr. Baumgart," Captain's voice rang out. He stepped through the bulkhead, coffee in hand, eyes blazing, with Liddell right behind him. The men and I flattened ourselves against the walls, opening a direct path from the Captain to Baumgart. Captain continued in a softer, but authoritative voice, "unless you were *not* going to say something against my boat."

Baumgart backed down. "She...she's a joy to work on, sir."

"Glad to hear it. From this point forward," he announced to the crew in general, "I will not tolerate any more talk about *Flier*'s luck, at least so-called bad luck, from anyone. She's as lucky as any other boat in the fleet

This photo, declassified in 2011, shows Flier's damaged propellers and broken rudder after Midway. The propeller on this side could work for short periods, and Flier used it when she was adrift from Florikan during the second storm. The other prop and bent shaft are visible beneath the body of Flier. Taken at Pearl Harbor, 1 Feb. 1944. Inset: the intact stern, rudder and props of USS Bonefish, a sister submarine. Official US Navy Photos. Thanks to Timothy Loughman.

and she takes the same chances. Is that understood by all?" We were silent, and all nodded our heads. "All right Mister Liddell," he turned to his XO, "what's the movie feature this evening?"

Liddell held up the film canister he was carrying in his hand and there was a collective groan. "Don't worry, it's not "Saratoga" again," he announced. "We've got a new one boys: Destination Tokyo, starring Cary Grant. Supposedly, it's about submarines, we're starting a pool to see who spots the most mistakes."

The poker game was cleared away, the sheet hung, and the projector quickly assembled. Baumgart slipped out, probably back to an engine room. My shift started, I went to the Navigation Table in the Control Room, then up to the Bridge for lookout duty. I left to the smell of popping popcorn and sounds lively commentary, not all of if about the movie.

I woke shortly before dawn of August 7th for my morning shift and splashed my face and hands with water and washed myself down with a washcloth. It had been over a week since my last shower, and I was allowed to take one tomorrow. I just wasn't sure if it was worth moving all those potatoes yet. I leaned in to the mirror to shave when *Flier* suddenly bucked and exploded, smashing my face into the stainless steel mirror and dropping me on my bunk.

Cursing under my breath, I rushed down the passage in my stocking feet and shorts, some firemen and Motor Macs hard on my heels.

"What happened?" I asked no one in particular when I reached the Control Room, as another Motor Mac pushed past me with a muttered, "Excuse me, sir," and continued on his way toward the stern.

"Not sure, sir," one of the Helmsmen said, keeping a tight grip on his wheel. "Something's gone wrong in the engine room."

Captain Crowley, still in his pajamas, ducked through the bulkhead into the room. "What happened?"

Before the helmsman could repeat himself, Lt. Miner slid down the ladder from the Conning Tower. "Don't know exactly yet, sir. One of the engines may have overheated or malfunctioned or something. Baehr and Liddell ran back there, so we'll probably hear something soon."

On cue, Baehr stomped back into the Control Room. "Damn V-16s. They pick the worst times!"

"What happened, Baehr?" Captain said.

"Number One cracked a cylinder liner and hydro-locked beautifully. Liner, piston, connecting rod, maybe part of the crankshaft, all shot to hell."

"Can you fix it?" Captain said. I could see him figuring whether or not this repair would cost us our time slot to cross into enemy territory, or even force us to turn around. He might have ordered the jinx talk deep-sixed, but if we limped back to Fremantle already needing more spare parts, or an engine overhaul, the talk would be impossible to stop or ignore.

"My team and I can handle it, we've got all the spares on board, but it will require us to almost completely disassemble the engine. Pain in the-"

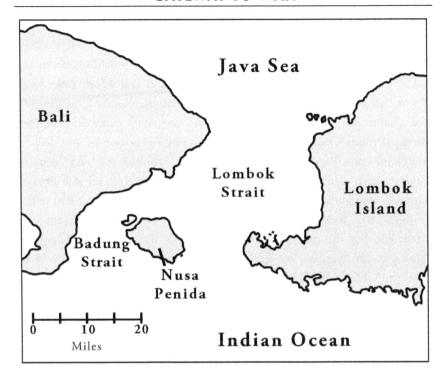

"How long?" Captain interrupted.

"Up to a day, sir, depending on how extensive the damage is, or whether the crankshaft sustained any damage we can't handle. I'll know more in a couple of hours."

We were only twelve hours from Lombok.

Crowley's eyes were bloodshot and tired and he sighed as he raked his hands though his hair and glanced at his watch. "I think I'm going to change and come on duty. Keep me posted of any developments until then." He turned and went back to Officer's Country.

Flier soldiered northward. On her three remaining engines, she could still make close to full speed, but the loss of one quarter of her power this early was serious, if Baehr couldn't fix it.

I tried to ignore the possibility that we would have a second scuttled patrol while I plotted our passage through Lombok Strait on the charts. In addition to Commissary Officer, I was Assistant Gunnery Officer, Assistant Torpedo Officer, and Assistant Navigator. Essentially, I was Assistant We-need-someone-to-do-this Officer. At least I was never bored, and the new ensign, Phil Mayer, would soon be able to shoulder his share.

Lombok was one of the main passages from the Indian Ocean to the South Pacific. Ten miles wide at the narrowest, and nearly forty miles long, it was flanked by the island of Bali on the west and Lombok on the east. For a submarine, it was a difficult strait to cross. With every tide, the fast, strong currents changed direction, and despite being one of the deepest routes into the Pacific, those currents made Lombok too dangerous to traverse safely while submerged. The slopes of Lombok and Bali bristled with anti-ship guns, and the strait itself was patrolled by at least two patrol vessels. They were usually rickety wooden vessels with little arms or armament, but the real danger was their radio, which could light up the shore guns in minutes. The best bet was to cross at night, when we'd be nearly invisible to the shore guns, and try to elude the patrol vessels.

This time of year brought another problem. Phosphorescent algae were blooming, and if we moved too fast in the water, they could light up our bow and stern wakes like landing lights. Unable to submerge, unable to run, parading through Lombok was a bit like casually strolling out of prison through the front gate, at night, while carrying a small flashlight, and hoping that the guards won't notice.

We had already planned to arrive at Lombok at dusk, when we would be difficult to see, and then cross during slack tide of oh-dark-thirty. The wait time would allow us to watch and count the patrol boats and track their movements.

When I reported back on duty at the map table that evening, I saw that Liddell had given some details and alterations to the chart and also some notes about charting the rest of the upcoming journey. '*Of course*,' I thought to myself as I picked up my tools, '*all this work will depend on…*'

Number One roared triumphantly from the stern. Teddy, riding a wave of backslapping, greasy Motor Macs, was striding through the Crew's Quarters on his way to the Control Room. "We're all set, Captain," he announced. "You have the final say, of course, but turns out it was more bang than busted."

"How many more spares do we have?"

"Enough that I don't think we need to return for more, but I wish this hadn't happened this early. I'll be glad when we get home safe and sound."

"Well, let's see what you did." Captain followed Teddy back to the Engine Rooms.

The problem now was our margin of safety. Crowley's quiet nickname among some of the crew was "Cautious Crowley," and even though the engine was repaired, I wondered if we'd turn back for more spares just in case.

"Ensign Jacobson," Captain said as he stepped back into the Control Room. "What's our ETA for Lombok?"

"About two hours, sir, we'll arrive just before sunset."

"Very good," He nodded and climbed up to the Conning Tower.

To allow Teddy to rest after his nearly triple shift, I took the midnight duty as the Junior Officer of the Deck or JOOD. The cool night wind struck me like a blow as I stepped onto the Bridge, and lifted the ever-present sheen of sweat off my skin. Soon I was shivering beneath my coat.

The moon, a large waning gibbous, hung low over the eastern horizon, illuminating the eastern shores of Bali, though the strait itself was still shrouded in shadow. If we were quick enough, we would be through the strait before the moon lit the water.

Captain climbed to the Bridge shortly after. "Status?"

"Radar has spotted one patrol boat," Paul Knapp, the Officer of the Deck, said, "about 6500 yards ahead of us in the mouth of the strait. We can't see the other one yet. The current has slowed, but slack tide[18] is still a half-hour away according to our calculations. There are no sightings of the algae yet."

"Very good," Captain said, "The gunnery crew is standing by. All ahead, standard speed." A gun battle in Lombok was suicidal, and we all knew it, but the possibility was very real. I took my position on the Aft Bridge, watching our wake for signs of a following enemy.

Flier slid through the waves, entering the main channel. With sixteen feet of draft beneath us, we had to maneuver delicately through the shallow places near the shore. The plan was to stick as closely as possible to

---

[18] Slack Tide: In places where the tides impact the currents, slack tide is the time at the height of high or low tides when the current rushing one direction slows, stops, and then reverses as the other tide takes effect.

Lombok's shadowed side and hide in that for the entire transit.

"Three thousand yards..." I heard Radar in the Conning Tower report on the distance to the patrol boat. The shores and water around were eerily quiet.

"Two thousand yards..."

Still quiet, with no sign of either patrol boat.

"One thousand yards..."

The sea around us suddenly flared brilliant green. "Reduce speed to one-third!" Crowley ordered, and *Flier's* props slowed, causing her nose to dip and create another splash of glowing algae. The new speed still caused some algae glow, but it was much dimmer, and hopefully, difficult to see from the island.

"Status of the chaser?" Captain asked Radar.

"She's eight hundred yards and closing, but shows no signs of having seen us. She should pass about five hundred yards in front of us, and turn," I heard from below.

All we could do was sit dark and silent in the shadow, hiding in plain sight hoping the chaser wouldn't see us. I combed the shores of Lombok with my binoculars, but saw no sign of alarm from the jungle save the occasional scream of some animal or bird.

The low humming I had become gradually aware of evolved into the thrumming of a ship's motor ahead on our portside.

"I see her, sir," I heard one forward lookout quietly call.

"All stop," Captain said in a softer tone speaking directly into the Conning Tower hatch, and soon *Flier* drifted slowly to a crawl.

I turned briefly to look over the port bow and saw not the chaser, but the brightly glowing green lines of her bow and stern wakes. She approached at a good clip, in a straight line, never deviating, or showing that she had seen anything.

As she reached the shores of Lombok, I could make out her details. Sure enough, she was a small wooden fishing vessel. If it wasn't for her radio, and the noise made destroying her, it would be easier to sink her than tiptoe around her.

She sped past us and a couple hundred yards ahead and thankfully turned away from us, re-crossing our bow even further away than before as she started her patrol back across the strait. As the sounds of her engines died away, and we breathed a collective sigh of relief.

When Radar reported that the chaser was two miles away, *Flier* pushed forward again. With the algae scattered in patches throughout the strait, we had to move carefully, and more slowly than we would have liked. At times, she seemed to crawl along. Hours ticked by. The moon was cresting Lombok's mountain when Radar reported another hit.

"Second target acquired, five thousand yards ahead at three–two–seven relative and heading west." She was ahead of us and slightly to our portside then.

"ETA to crossing her path?" Captain quietly asked down the hatch.

"Approximately thirty-four minutes."

"Projected course of chaser at that point?"

After a slight pause Liddell's voice said, "She should be approximately a half-mile from Bali's shore, and turning."

"Wonderful," I heard the smile in Captain's voice. "Maintain course and speed."

Flier nosed through the waves, the algae a faint line at her bow and stern. Because the chaser was far enough away, we slowly maneuvered into deeper water farther from shore, hoping the algae's dim glow would be harder to see from farther away. Radar watched the chaser as she charged for Bali, but she never deviated from course, nor saw us as we crept across her path.

Well ahead of both chasers now, all we had to do was keep hidden long enough to get out of range of the guns.

The mountains of Lombok and Bali flanked the exit of the strait. The famous volcanic mountains of Bali gleamed silver and black in the moonlight, rippling down to the water's edge. Some of the guys said that the women of Bali are as beautiful as their island. If that was the case, I thought, they must be breathtaking indeed.

Soon, the sea opened up before us. 'A *clean getaway*,' I thought with relief.

By 3 A.M., with Lombok and Bali rapidly fading against the horizon, *Flier* finally roared ahead, lifting her nose gracefully out of the water. The gunnery crew stood down, and life resumed its familiar pattern.

-3-

CHANGE OF PLANS

The next six days were largely uneventful. We crossed the Java Sea, passed through Makassar Strait to the Celebes Sea, then Sibutu Passage to the Sulu Sea. We sighted Bancoran Island and rounded its north side, lining up to the entrance for Natsubata Channel. We always traveled above water at night, and dove as soon as we spotted the first aerial patrol of the morning. The only ships of any kind we saw were native fishing vessels which we left alone. Sonar heard nothing except the sea life swimming and eating around us.

"I thought we'd see more action," I heard a few of the younger hands complain to Chief Gwinn, during an afternoon when he was showing them the finer points of torpedo maintenance.

"Be grateful," he replied. "Trust me, we'll see action before you know it, and maybe then you might not be so eager."

The qualifying boards began for the unqualified hands. Despite the intensive training at submarine school, there was no substitute for working on an active submarine, and the new guys were constantly underfoot. I would be working my station in the Control Room and turn around to find a non-qual intently inspecting the air bank gauges, sketching electrical systems, or hovering over my shoulder watching me plot our course on a chart. It was a little nerve wracking, but I had been in that position last patrol, and cut them a break.

I did, however, enjoy watching the quals from this side. Ed loved to ask the strangest questions, to see how well we'd really learned a system. The first time he asked a potential qual, "How would you pump five gallons of lube oil from the tank through the whistle?" I think I got a good idea of the bewildered look I must have had on my face when he asked me that! It was possible to do, once you thought about it, but not something that would occur to anyone off-hand. Another potential qual looked confused and slightly panicked when Captain Crowley told him that yes, making a full multi-gallon pot of coffee *was* part of Crowley's version of the quals, and he wouldn't qualify anyone who couldn't make a decent pot.

Not only did these guys have to learn how to work on a submarine,

"All Hands Below" by Georges Shrieber Watercolor, 1943. Talking, sleeping, card games, and letter writing were all normal ways of passing the time between duty shifts. Due to space constraints, the men took their ease anywhere they could, like this torpedo room, working relaxation around those still on duty. From Department of the Navy: Navy Historical Center. Gift of Abbott Laboratories.

they had to learn the peculiarities of *our* submarine. *Flier* had her own little quirks in her systems and her crew. Billy Brooks' tattoos almost needed their own bunk, they were so large. The inked snake that wrapped itself around his arms seemed to twitch to life when he expertly shuffled and dealt cards in the Mess Hall. And if he wasn't eating, working, or sleeping, he always seemed to be playing poker. Chief Hudson often walked around with his shoes untied and had a habit of popping in a room to announce something and pop just as quickly out, often leaving some rather startled people in his wake. Chief Gwinn was tough. The first time a sleepy-eyed newbie tried to sit down for breakfast without his shirt on, Chief Gwinn promptly stood him up, turned him around, and told him that a decent man didn't appear at the table without his shirt on. It never happened again. He was a tough old bird, but a near father-figure for many. Firm, generous with guidance, and the last person you wanted to see when you were goofing around.

The poker pool quickly settled into a regular schedule, and whenever

Captain judged it safe, the crew ran the radio, listening to music, or news, or whatever sporting event was being broadcast from the States.

Early Saturday morning, I stepped into the Crew's Mess to see if Skow had left his usual midnight plate of sandwiches out, when I found a much larger crowd of people than I expected before breakfast.

"I can't believe it, Braves lost?! After that brilliant shut out yesterday by Red Barnett?"

"You can't expect any man to throw a perfect game two days in a row, even against the same team. Why do you think I bet on the Reds this time?"

"No matter, I'll get it back in the poker tournament. You can't bluff to save your life."

So that was it. The radio was signing off on a baseball broadcast over in the States, because, strangely enough, it was Friday night there. A lot of our sporting events took place over bacon and eggs, rather than burgers and fries.

The men were moving out now, some sliding very slim billfolds into their back pockets and some clutching a small bunch of battered Hawaii dollars[19] in their fists.

They'd also eaten all the sandwiches and drunk all the coffee.

I filled the massive multi-gallon coffee maker with water and grounds and eyed the pile of freshly baked biscuits waiting for breakfast, when I noticed that there was still someone there.

In the back of the room sat Don See, Alls's replacement, with his qualification notebook open in front of him, though he wasn't looking at it very studiously.

"Hey kid, how's the quals coming?" I called to him.

"Ensign Jacobson," he jumped, "Uh, sir, I was studying, sir, I really was."

"Well, I see the notebook out, so I can believe you were just sitting here, studying quietly, minding your own business when the guys came in to

---

[19] During WWII, residents of Hawaii, as well as all Pacific and North African troops, were paid with, and used, American dollars with the word "Hawaii" stamped on the front and back. In the case of invasion of Hawaii or capture of these troops, the Hawaii bills would not be honored, preventing a financial windfall to the enemy.

listen to the baseball game. It's not like you were running the pool."

He laughed, "That's actually pretty close to what happened, sir, to be honest. And I wouldn't bet on a baseball game. Football's more my style. My whole family is obsessed with it."

"Really?"

"Yes, sir. My full name is Donald Nesser See. Ever hear of the Nesser brothers?"

"Uh-"

"Well, see, my grandfather was Pete Nesser, and while *he* wasn't interested in football, nearly every one of his brothers was. Seven of them became the backbone of the Columbus Panhandle football team. They invented football plays, traveled the country, even got the Panhandles into the National Football League. They were just crazy about it. Most of them still are, come to think of it. They were devastated when the Panhandles finally disbanded when I was a kid. Thankfully, Columbus still has the Buckeyes, or I think they'd go crazy." He laughed.

"Uh-oh, you almost had me."

"Sir?"

"You're talking to a True Blue Wolverine, kid. You almost had me there with your talk of your family's pro team and football nostalgia. Then you just had to go and bring up the Buckeyes."

He saw I was (partially) joking with him, and grinned. "Well, they are the best team in college football, sir, with all due respect, of course."

I snorted. "U of M is going to mop up the Buckeyes again this year."

"With all due respect again, sir, last year was a complete fluke, and if memory serves, we took out the Wolverines in '42"

"We have one of the strongest lineups in school history. I knew a lot of the guys on the team. They were with me in NROTC. You don't stand a chance."

"Most of those guys were activated after last season from what I'm hearing. They're probably no closer to a football field than we are, sir. The Wolverines practically have a rookie lineup this year. Our team is still intact and better than ever, they've had longer to work together."

"Not so fast there, See. We still have Don Lund, and Bob Wiese, and Coach Cristler. Ohio's toast. I'd put money on it, but you don't bet."

"I said I don't bet on *baseball*, sir. With all due respect, are you offering to put a wager on the outcome of The Game this year?"

"Have a burning need to part with your money, sailor?"

"Not at all, sir. A seaman could always use an extra dollar or five in his pocket though."

"Just a fiver?"

"*I am* just a seaman, sir."

Liddell and Ed entered the room, heading for the now-full coffee maker. Standing next to See, I looked over his charts, as though I was checking his work. "I think you're mistaken, See." I said, continuing our conversation.

"I have to say sir, given the evidence, I can't agree with you."

Ed looked at us oddly, then slurped his coffee as Liddell poured his cup. Ed frowned as he swallowed, looked in his mug, then at me and the pewter water pitcher in my hand.

"Ah, I told you, Jacobson, I can always tell when James doesn't make the coffee."

"Oh?" Liddell took a sip. "A little weak, but hardly undrinkable."

"I doubled the recommended amount," I said in weak protest.

"You sure Cap'n passed him on the coffee maker quals?" joked.

"Tastes like Navy coffee to me." Liddell said, as he ducked back through the bulkhead.

"That's the problem." Ed mock-groaned, as he followed.

I quickly poured a mug and tried it myself. "I still don't get it, I can't taste a difference." I said. "

See got up and grabbed a mug for himself. "Tastes fine to me sir. Course, I only started drinking this stuff."

"I don't know what James does that makes it 'Official Flier Coffee'."

See looked down the corridor, and apparently saw no one else nearby. "So sir, what do you say?" he said eagerly.

"All right then, five dollars, so long as I can find you come November." I'd been aboard *Flier* for two patrols already; I might be rotated out next cycle or two. He might be as well.

"Don't worry, sir. I'll be right here."

Flier approached Natsubata Channel, the safest route through Balabac

Straits, on Sunday, August 13. I was plotting our course on the Control Room map table when our chief radio man, Bud Klock, dashed out of the Radio Room and flew up the ladder to the Conning Tower. Moments later, he jumped down to the Control Room again, Captain hard on his heels. Captain pushed past Klock to the radio room where Klock's assistant, Bernard Fite, was standing at attention in the hallway. Captain bolted into the Radio Room, and bolted the door shut behind him. That could only mean one thing: an Ultra.[20] Several minutes later, Captain emerged from the room, and went up to Officer's Country. Ten minutes later, I was called into the meeting along with Teddy Baehr, because we were going to be sharing navigational duties with Liddell that night. Liddell was poring over a chart of Balabac Strait when I arrived, along with a set of bearings, and was marking a path through the strait.

"The *Puffer's* on the west coast of Palawan and attacked a large southbound convoy this morning," Captain stated once all four of us were in the room. "GHQ wants us to try to hit it, and estimates it'll be here," Captain pointed to a position outside the strait, "twenty-five miles off the west coast of Balabac, by 0230 hours tomorrow morning. In order to do that, we're going to have to run full speed on the surface through Balabac tonight, instead of picking our way through slowly.

"Balabac is believed to be mined, so they sent us the track the *Crevalle* took when she went through here a few weeks back. That's what Liddell's marking out now. Due to the limitations of enemy mines, we want to keep *Flier* in the deep water of Natsubata Channel, more than one hundred fathoms[21] if possible. Anything less than fifty might be dangerous."

Liddell, finished marking the *Crevalle's* track, said, "Are we being ordered to follow *Crevalle's* track?"

"No, it was specifically noted to be informative, nothing else."

"This looks similar to what I already planned. I'm seeing a couple of things here: one, the *Crevalle* must have been coming from the north. If we

---

[20] Ultra: The most top-secret classification of message transmission in the US Navy during WWII. Only the commanding officer of each vessel was permitted to receive, decrypt, and destroy the message. It was jokingly called the "burn before you read" code level. WWII Ultras led to wild goose chases more often than not, but did help track down and destroy significant numbers of ships.
[21] Fathom: A fathom is 2 yards or 6 feet of depth.

were to deviate to follow her track precisely, it would take us too long to reach our rendezvous in time. They also tracked very close to Natsubata and Roughton Reefs, far too close for my comfort.

"They didn't tell us *when* the *Crevalle* went through here, did they?"

"No," Captain replied.

"So we don't know when or what time of day it was when she did this. If she went through at a slack spring high tide, that might have bought her a few more feet of clearance or weaker currents." He was talking more to himself at the moment, but Teddy and I listened closely. "We're just past the last quarter moon, so we'll have weaker neap tides rather than a spring tide. And at the rate we're going, we'll get there..." he did some rapid calculations, "between the low and high tide, such as they will be, and that will be when the currents will be the strongest. Moonrise isn't until three tomorrow morning, either."

He looked up at the three of us. "Captain, the dangerous point is here: the bottleneck between the Roughton and Natsubata Reefs to the north and Comiran Danger Bank to the south. Natsubata Channel, which is deep enough to avoid mines, lies closer to the reefs than the island, and, as you can see, it's steep, and quickly rises to shallow, minable waters on the reef side, more slowly on the island side. *Crevalle* stayed in the deepest point of the channel, but unless we know what day and time she went through here, there's no way to tell how she took her bearings to stay that close to the reefs without running aground or into minable water. If it was daylight, or a spring tide, or a full moon, it would much easier than tonight."

"What do you suggest, then?" Captain asked him.

"This path," Liddell pointed to a line drawn slightly south of *Crevalle's* track. "With the lack of moonlight and the strong currents we'll be facing, I think we need to stay a little farther away from those reefs. They'll be almost impossible to see with lookouts or Radar, they're so close to the water's surface. If we take radar bearings on Balabac, Comiran, and Palawan, and take continuous soundings, we should be able to keep to this track fairly easily. Additionally, if we happen across any patrol or local vessels, we'll have more room to maneuver, we won't be blocked in on our starboard side. It looks like we can intersect *Crevalle's* track here, just past that bottleneck, without too much loss of time or safety."

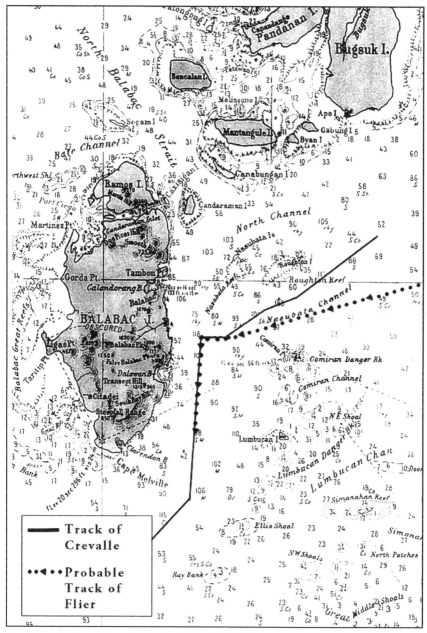

Based on testimony at the investigation into the loss of USS Flier, this is the track Crevalle took on 8 May, 1944, heading east through Balabac Strait. The track of the Flier is conjectured based on testimony from the Flier's navigator, Lt. Liddell.

"What's the weather like this evening?" Captain asked us.

"Cloudy, sir, possible storms coming in from the west," I said.

"Very well, that will help hide us from the known Japanese bases on the eastern coast of Balabac. We'll have to pass within five miles of those."

"There a light or lighthouse on Comiran, sir," Teddy interjected.

"We'll have to keep an eye out and see if that's true then. All right, we'll be running dark tonight. This close to the enemy, I don't want so much as a cigarette on deck. I'm also going to post the full complement of lookouts on deck and the Bridge, and battle stations in the Conning Tower. As we get closer, I may put more lookouts on deck."

He continued, "As soon as we sight Comiran Island by radar or lookout, we'll begin continuous soundings, and we'll take bearings by radar every five minutes."

"Yes, sir," We chorused.

"Does anyone have anything else to contribute for passage tonight?" Captain asked. No one did. "Very well. Hopefully, the fates are smiling on us all. Dismissed."

The afternoon wore on as *Flier* flew south-west. The lookouts on deck were rotated every four hours to keep them alert. No one else was in the area, not even fishing boats. That was a good thing, because some of the fishing boats carried radios and reported ship locations to one side or the other, but the complete lack of seagoing population as we got closer to the archipelago made me nervous for some reason.

Dinner came, Turner serving us some of James and Alvin's fabulous stew with Clyde's and Melvin's fresh bread and biscuits. News of the convoy we were ordered to destroy had already filtered among the crew, and the growing anticipation became almost palpable.

That night, Teddy and I were assigned to rotate every four hours between the Map Table in the Control Room and Junior Officer of the Deck on the Bridge outside. Teddy, sopping up the last bits of stew with a biscuit, "volunteered" to take the first shift on deck. "I need to see the sun for a bit, I think," he grinned and stretched.

"Sure, leaving me with the freezing temps of midnight, I see."

"It'll help keep you awake, don't you know. Besides, you young'uns need to let your elders have what little perks there are, that's the right way of the world."

"I suppose you're right. I mean, you're what? Forty?"

"Thirty-three!"

"Yup, getting up there."

"You know, as a Michigander, you should know better than to mess with a Flint boy."

"Ooo, shaking in my shoes."

"Do I have to pull this sub over and separate you two?" Ed said, smiling.

"No, sir!" We chorused.

Everyone erupted in laughter. Then, before I could move, Teddy stood up, grabbed a set of binoculars, called "Topside!" and dashed out of the room.

Plotting is tedious work at best, and when constant readings are being called from the Sonar and Radar Stations, along with more bearings from the deck, it quickly gets exhausting. The time just seemed to crawl by until 2030 hours, when I would relieve Teddy topside and get a chance at some fresh air myself. Half an hour before, I put on my red goggles to dilate my eyes and prepare them for night lookout duty. They leached all the color from the Control Room, turning the brass and copper pipes, the dark green linoleum floor, and the steel wheels various shades of blood red and black.

Chief Hudson, Chief of the Watch tonight, stood in the Control Room, watching over his crew. Two of our seamen were manning the Planeswheel Stations in case Captain ordered a crash dive. Electricians continuously checked the circuits on the starboard wall, while others checked the pneumatic systems for the ballast tanks. Men strode through the room in a semi-constant stream of traffic, often in their stocking feet, or their depth charge sandals. This supposedly cut down the chance that a heavy, booted footstep could be picked up by a sharp-eared enemy sonar operator during the forthcoming attack. Despite that, sound reverberated all around me. I heard the hum of the ice cream machine, the slap of cards in the Mess Hall. Turner, his hands full of our dinner dishes, stepped past me with an "Excuse me, sir," on his way to the Galley. A moment later, he stepped through the bulkhead and chatted with the galley crew while they finished the dinner clean-up and setting up the night round of sandwiches.

Jimmy Elder dropped from the Conning Tower with the Deck Log tucked under his arm and walked forward to the tiny closet that the Navy called the Yeoman's Office. Soon, he and Dorricott were talking, while typing and filing the immense amount of paperwork and records the Navy required on each patrol.

Someone had moved one of the record players and was blasting Duke Ellington from Crew's Quarters. Excited chatter seemed to bubble all around me, and underpinning it all was the growling vibrations of *Flier's* engines and the swish of the water sliding past her hull.

My time up, I packed up, stowed my navigation tools and stretched.

"Lookout duty?" Asked Hudson.

"What? The red goggles didn't give it away?" I grinned.

"Lucky dog," he said, as I mounted the ladder to the packed Conning Tower.

The sounds from below were now overlaid with the sounds of a submarine's business: the rustle of charts, the whine of the radar, the sea sounds picked up by the sonar. As I climbed up to the Conning Tower, my crewmates crowded around me. Knapp stood at the Torpedo Data Computer, adjusting trajectories for any moves *Flier* made in case we had to fire a torpedo quickly. Howell and Tremaine had their backs to me, their faces buried in the radar screens at the back of the room. Next to them, Pope was listening at the Sonar Station. Crowded on either side of the ladder to the Bridge were Russo at the Helm and Liddell at the plotting table, where they could quickly relay messages and respond to orders to and from the Bridge. I squeezed between them and scrambled up the steel rungs. A moment later, all sounds of sub life vanished completely under the roar of the evening wind.

Captain stood next to Ed, who was the Officer of the Deck, on the Bridge outside, straining their eyes and binoculars over *Flier's* bow. The island of Balabac loomed ahead, guarding the channel. High overhead the lookouts leaned over their guardrails: Gerry Madeo and Baumgart were the aft lookouts watching the stern of the boat with Teddy, while Wes Miller and Gene Heller covered the bow with Ed. Teddy stood alone on the Aft Cigarette deck, next to the 40 mm gun, scanning our wake for any sign of danger.

"Eighty Feet Below" Geroges Shrieber, Watercolor, 1943. The men at work in the Control Room. Planesmen hold their planeswheels, which control the submarine's dives, another checks the Christmas Tree, the bank of lights that records which valves are open or closed. The map table like that Jake worked at appears in the corner, as someone goes up the ladder to the Conning Tower overhead. From the Department of the Navy, Navy Historical Center. Gift of Abbott Laboratories.

He was so intent on what he was doing, he didn't hear me walk up behind him, and jumped slightly when I tapped him on the shoulder. "I am ready to relieve you, sir," I said quietly.

He recovered quickly, however, and continued the ancient ceremony, "I am ready to be relieved." He looked at me and said in a quieter voice, "I'm sure you know our position. Balabac is straight ahead, but no lights or enemy have been sighted yet, neither has Comiran Island."

"Radar hasn't reported it yet either, though it should be off our port bow soon, according to the charts," I told him.

"I guessed as much. Everything is quiet. No planes, not so much as a fishing boat."

"Thank you," and in a slightly louder voice I said, "I relieve you, sir."

"I stand relieved," Teddy intoned. "Attention Bridge, Ensign Jacobson has the Conn."

"I am Ensign Jacobson and I have the Conn."

"Thanks, Jake," Teddy said, in a lower voice, the formalities finished. "I'll see you in four hours."

"Thanks, Teddy."

I handed him the red goggles and clapped him on the back. He crossed the deck and dropped below. I never saw him again.

Sunset had just passed, and the last dying rays coloring the high clouds overhead a blood red, while dark storms built themselves over Balabac's mountain.

I quickly fell into my pattern, watching the skies and sea for a plane, a wake, anything that said we weren't alone, but it remained quiet.

Flier cut through the sea with ease, her engines humming happily, vibrating the deck beneath my feet. The scent of baking bread vented up to me from the nearby kitchen exhaust. The smell made me hungry.

"We should be coming up on Comiran in a few moments, sir," I heard Liddell's voice, a half hour after I had come out on deck.

"Begin taking continuous soundings," Captain told him.

The clouds, which had been building and thickening to the west, now started to push overhead, obscuring the few stars that were appearing.

An hour after I replaced Teddy, a lookout called out, "Captain, there's a light off the port bow, sir."

I turned and saw a tiny point of light barely visible in the darkness.

"Ensign Jacobson, pass me the Conn," Captain called back to me.

"This is Ensign Jacobson, Commander Crowley has the Conn."

"I am Commander Crowley and I have the Conn."

That was odd. Normally, as Junior Officer of the Deck, I would have command of the engine speed and direction, or Conn. In such a delicate and close space, Captain must want that control until we were past Comiran Island.

Moments later, he called out, "Battle Stations."

Ensign Phil Mayer and Lt. Bill Reynolds climbed out on deck, Reynolds taking position watching over the starboard side, Mayer the port.

"Ninety-five fathoms," Liddell's voice boomed out from the Bridge hatch.

No one spoke. We just all kept straining to see any threat to our boat.

"Sixty fathoms, with radar reporting Comiran Island seven thousand,

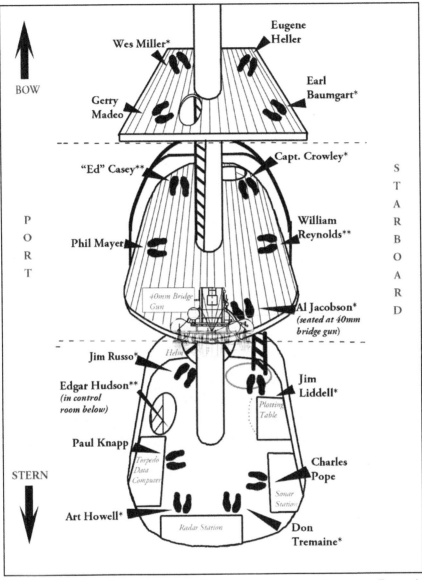

Eugene Heller

Wes Miller*

Earl Baumgart*

BOW

Gerry Madeo

"Ed" Casey**

Capt. Crowley*

PORT

William Reynolds**

Phil Mayer

40mm Bridge Gun

Al Jacobson*
(seated at 40mm bridge gun)

STARBOARD

Jim Russo*

Helm

Edgar Hudson**
(in control room below)

Jim Liddell*

Plotting Table

Paul Knapp

Torpedo Data Computer

Charles Pope

STERN

Sonar Station

Art Howell*

Radar Station

Don Tremaine*

This chart shows the probable positions of the Flier crew at the moment of her sinking. During the investigation into Flier's loss, Capt. Crowley testified who had been on the Lookout Deck, Bridge and in the Conning Tower as well as which stations were manned. Those marked with a single asterisk testified to their own position. Those names marked with a double asterisk had their position stated during the same investigation. Those without were recorded as being on duty on the deck on which they are shown, though their exact location may never be known for certain. The layout of the Conning Tower is based on USS Cod, a sister submarine built at Groton only a few weeks before Flier. Those not shown were deep inside Flier.

eight hundred yards ahead off the port bow, bearing two–one–one true."

I suddenly realized that the rushing of the water was now competing with the rushing of my blood in my ears. I took a deep breath, rubbed my eyes quickly and dropped into the starboard seat of the 40 mm deck gun to steady my binoculars.

"Comiran Island six thousand seven hundred yards ahead, bearing one-nine-zero true," I heard Liddell say. "Sounding, seventy-one fathoms."

Minutes ticked by, as I continued to take deep breaths to steady myself. I turned to look around for a moment's rest. Balabac loomed ahead still, illuminated by the flickers of lightning that shot through the storm clouds. There was a faint shadow of the mountains of the main island, Palawan, to the north, and Comiran easily seen off the bow. The darkening sky was turning a deep shade while the sea glowed as it always did moments before night truly fell. Whenever my family and I had sailed Lake Michigan, this had always been one of my favorite times of day. Despite the danger, it was the most beautiful scene I'd ever witnessed, and for a moment, I just took it all in.

"Forty-one fathoms." Liddell's voice sounded urgent.

"Forty-one?" Captain questioned, crouching down to the Bridge hatch. "Are we drifting away from course?"

"Not according to the charts, sir. A finger of a reef might extend here, could be all. We could be in deeper water in moments."

"Can we turn south a bit to adjust and find deeper water while maintaining sea room in case of a surface ship?"

"I believe so, if we adjust head—"

It happened so fast.

Flier suddenly bucked and thrashed violently to port, throwing me against the gun. Reynolds crashed into me, and we tumbled together in a tangle of arms and legs. Air was roaring from somewhere. *Flier* groaned.

"Aaah! My side!" Reynolds shouted.

"Lie still!" I shouted back, extricating myself. "Hang on a second, I'll see what happened."

Mayer pounded past us in two strides and threw himself over the guardrail.

I could hear screaming erupting from behind me, accelerating in terror and volume, and the roar of the ocean was now too close. A moment later, *Flier* drove herself under the sea, dragging me twenty feet down in the space of a hastily gulped breath.

'*The props!*' I thought, panicking. I could imagine the propellers shredding my body in moments, a bloody mess for the sharks.

I tore for the surface, pushing myself as hard as possible from *Flier's* deck even as she fell away beneath me. Her props, still drumming at full speed, agitated the water and threw me like a rag doll, spinning me around until finally, with lungs bursting, I broke the surface of the water.

I gasped, heart hammering, and thrashed about in the sludge for a moment before I could face the horrifying truth.

I was shipwrecked, and it had taken only seconds.

-4-

DEATH BELOW, AND ABOVE

I floated easily in the warm sea. The oily sludge that had been *Flier's* lifeblood now weighed down the waves and coated my head and face. I ducked my head again and again to try to clear my eyes, but couldn't rid myself of it. It clung to every part of me. The sea glowed an iridescent blue wherever the stands of oil separated. We were in another area of algae again.

As the ringing in my ears slowly faded, I became aware of the sounds of splashing and yelling. At least I wasn't alone. I scraped my eyes clear as best I could, and saw heads bobbing in the water. Voices I should recognize sounded strange and muffled. Suddenly, Captain's voice roared, "Men! To me!"

In the distance, one shadow, lit from below by the algae, appeared to be waving.

I tried to swim, but my clothes and shoes weighed me down. *'If you're ever stranded in the ocean, kick off your shoes and remove your clothing, it will make it easier to swim for extended periods,'* my drill instructor's advice from boot camp rushed back to me.

I kicked off my shoes, and shed my shirt. I tried to grab my knife out of my pocket, but it slipped out of my grasp when I fumbled with my belt. Fortunately, my binoculars had apparently survived the sinking, and floated next to me, attached to the strap around my neck.

"Men! To me!" Crowley kept calling. I kicked over to him, and heard a babble of voices in front of me.

"Roll call!" Crowley ordered, when most everyone had gathered around him.

"Liddell!"

"Baumgart!"

"Casey!"

"Mayer!"

"Pope!"

"Knapp!"

"Tremaine!"

"Miller!"

"Madeo!"

"Russo!"

"Howell!"

"Reynolds!"

"Jacobson!"

The names tumbled over each other. With Captain we were just fourteen men...no, fifteen.

A brilliant bolt of lightning streaked overhead, and for a split second, I could see, wheezing in the water, so bloodied and bruised I could barely recognize him, Edgar Hudson. He gasped and groaned, one arm floating dead beside him, obviously broken. His hair was matted with streaks of oil and blood and his face was already swelling to grotesque proportions. Miller and Baumgart supported him as best they could. "Sucked...from...Control Room ... beneath... the ladder," He gasped.

'Blasted through two hatches,' I thought in horror. Other stories began spilling over each other.

"I pulled on the periscopes to get to the hatch where the air was rushing out," Pope said.

"Blast tore off my shirt before I landed in the water," Liddell said.

"I was thrown to the Aft Deck and she sank under me," Crowley muttered.

"There was no one on the Bridge when I got up. I called 'Abandon Ship,'" Tremaine said.

"I dove overboard..."

"...saw men tangled in the guardrails..."

"...where's Gene?! He was right next to me!"

"...didn't know where I was..."

"...happened so fast..."

"ENOUGH!" Captain yelled over the accelerating din.

Just fifteen remained out of the eighty-four men who had been eating, working, and sleeping, just moments before. Fifteen...and now fourteen. Hudson gave a long sigh, and relaxed in the waves. "God go with you, son," Captain murmured as we released him.

"What now?" someone muttered.

"Jim, what's our chance of finding land?" Crowley asked Liddell.

"There's land on three sides of us. There's nothing east. Comiran Island is the closest land to the south, only a couple of miles away, but it's tiny and if we miss it in the dark, it's fifty miles to Borneo, the next island to the south."

"Anywhere else?"

"Balabac is west, ten miles away, but the Japs are there. Our last option is Palawan Island and the little cluster of small islands to the north. Depending on which one we find, those are anywhere from…" he thought for a moment, "maybe nine to thirty miles away."

"Where *is* north?" Pope asked.

We said nothing, but looked around. High on *Flier's* deck, even without the lightning, Balabac was easily visible, as well as other islands. But now, I only saw water from horizon to horizon.

In the last few minutes, the clouds had finished blanketing the sky, covering any stars we could have used for bearings. We were hopelessly lost.

Lightning streaked overhead in a huge fan, and for a moment again, I could see everyone briefly, covered in oil and blood, floating in the fouled sea with fragments of cork and debris around us, but no land anywhere.

"There!" Liddell pointed. "If that storm is still mostly west of us, that way," he gestured, to the right, "should be north."

Lightning flashed again to the "north," then the "west," and then all sense of direction was gone.

"We can get lost this way," someone behind me muttered.

"We can't stay here," someone else said. "What if what hit us was a Japanese sub? They could be on their way here now to check for survivors."

"Moon rise is at three." Captain broke in. "That's four hours from now, and we can take a definite bearing then. Comiran is too risky, if we miss it, we're done. Balabac is nearby and large enough to easily find, but is also a known Japanese stronghold. I put the question to you men: do we risk the longer swim for the unknown islands to the north, or the shorter swim where we know we will have to deal with the enemy and their networks of garrisons?" Captain asked us.

"I'd rather die swimming north than risk being captured by them," Russo said.

We all agreed. The rumors that circulated in the pubs and halls about Japanese prison camps were enough to give anyone nightmares. Better to drown in the ocean or starve on a distant island than that.

"If we swim north," Jim Liddell said, his voice projecting away from us, probably still facing the "north" he had figured out earlier, "the current seems to be forcing the waves to slap us west to east. If we can swim, keeping the waves hitting us on our left side, we will be going north to…whatever there is."

"Agreed," Captain said. He paused, then took a deep breath. "One more thing, we have no idea how far we will have to swim, or how long. Some of us are stronger than others, some might be injured, but to insure as many people as possible reach our goal, and home…" he took another deep breath "…our swim needs to be 'every man for himself.'" He paused, allowing us to take this in. "Are we agreed?"

Captain was now the oldest Flier, around thirty-five, and a notoriously poor swimmer. He was acknowledging that he may not make it to "safety" by morning, just as much as any other man, and he was barring us from helping him. If letting him drown helped the rest of us get home, that was what was important.

One man, who was clutching his side, pushed himself away from another man who had been supporting him and muttered quietly, "Agreed." It sounded like Phil Mayer, who had run past Reynolds and me and over the guardrail. He must have hit something on the way down. We quickly agreed to the rule. I was not injured, but still wondered just how long we would have to swim, and if it would be long enough to find land.

"Let's go, then. Try to stay together if at all possible," Captain said.

As the men began to splash away, I noticed one veering off slightly. "Hey," I called out, "north is this way."

"Jake?" The swimmer stopped and turned…passed me, then thrashed back and forth in the water. "Jake, is that you?"

It was Ed, who was swimming with no direction, no sense of…sight?

"Ed, it-it's Jake, follow my voice." I came up behind him. "What happened to you?"

"I was blinded in the blast," he grunted, turning to face me. "Hot oil in my face. I think I hit something on the way down, too. I can't lie on my stomach."

"You're still fully dressed, let me help you."

"Wait, my knife. Grab my knife." His knife came out of the pocket easily, but without a way to strap it to myself or hold it, I soon lost it, too.

"No matter, I'm sure someone else has theirs," I said, hoping it was true. I steered Ed around until we faced the crew, swimming away. "Here, just follow me, and I'll keep you going straight." Because Ed couldn't swim on his stomach, he had to rely on his strong back and side stroke. We soon caught up to the others.

We all swam in silence, conserving our strength. Opening our eyes and mouths for a time was horrible as the diesel oil coated the surface of the water. I was still wearing my watch, but in the darkness I had no idea whether or not it still worked. The recent events, in some ways, seemed a distant memory rather than minutes or hours ago. I didn't even notice the thinning oil slick until it disappeared.

I switched between the breast, side, and back stroke as needed, all the while keeping an eye on Ed, who occasionally had to be called back to the group as he swam.

'*The Lord is my Shepherd…Yea, though I walk through the valley of the shadow of death, I will fear no evil: for thou art with me…*' Strange, I hadn't read that psalm in ages. Still, repeating over and over in my head was Psalm 23, a glimmer of hope in the dark.

Sometimes lightning flashed and struck what I hoped was the mountains of Balabac Island. If it was, we were still going north. If it wasn't…I thought that only once and refused to think it again.

'*He leadeth me beside the still waters…*'

My hand struck something hard in the water, and I recoiled. What was that? Something else brushed against my side, and I grasped at it even though I shuddered. I missed it in the dark. Then, the sea around me was thickly coated with a layer of thick, scorched oil.

"Ugh! Are we going in circles?" someone yelled.

"I don't think so," Liddell's voice was surprisingly close. "The lightning has stayed left of us, this could be moving with the current, and caught up with us."

I struck something again, and grasped it quickly, seizing it as well as I could in the slippery muck. It was a thin layer of cork, and with a sickening lurch, I realized that this was the insulation that had covered *Flier's* interior. They were useless; not even large enough to help with floating, even if my skivvies had pockets to put them in.

I tried not to imagine them down there, but I couldn't help myself. Just a while ago, we had been working, watching movies, playing poker, waiting for the morning, when the "action" was supposed to take place. Had Doc been checking his medical supplies, or writing home to his wife? Had Chief Gwinn been tinkering obsessively with his "Tin Fish" in the Forward Torpedo Room when it happened? Did he even know what happened? Walter Dorricott would never see even a photo of his new son. How long before his young wife was told he was never going to come home? We were not due back for six more weeks, and no sub was considered "overdue and presumed lost" for about six weeks after that. It was August now...dear God, it could be past Thanksgiving before any of our families found out we weren't coming home.

No. I shook my head. I was going to go home. I was going to hug my mother and father, and sisters, and tell them what happened. I wasn't going to be the one that didn't return, not now that I had a second chance.

"How much farther?" Pope's voice rasped. He sounded like he might be in pain. We were back in clean water, the oil slick mercifully behind us.

"Not far," Liddell's voice called from ahead now, and tried to sound encouraging, "Nine miles maybe."

"To hell with this," Pope muttered. He stopped swimming. Lightning flashed, and for a moment, I saw the exhaustion and hopelessness on his haggard face. He had already trailed far behind the group, and now watched us swim on. Moments later, when I glanced back again, he was gone. I turned away and kept swimming northward. There would be time later.

'I will fear no evil, for Thou art with me.'

We stuck to the rule, 'Every man for himself' with one exception: me. Ed kept swimming to one side or the other, lost in his blindness. I kept calling him back to the group, checking on him. He was my mentor and my best friend in the Submarine Force. I refused to fail him.

My first days on *Flier* had been difficult. I had been assigned to Mare Island fresh out of Sub School and hoped to get a submarine, not a tender or shore crew duty. Sure enough, there was room on a boat called *Flier*, out of drydock and in the final stages of her Midway repairs and sea trials.

"Ensign Alvin E. Jacobson, reporting for duty," I announced myself from the dock to the Officer of the Deck, Lt. Ed Casey. "Permission to come aboard?"

"Permission granted. Welcome aboard, Ensign Jacobson," Ed said, looking over my paperwork to make sure I was who I claimed. The Submarine Force was Top Secret, after all.

"Everything's in order, welcome to the *USS Flier*, one of the newest boats of the fleet."

"Thank you, sir, she's a beautiful sh—BOAT!" I realized my mistake almost instantly, and Ed laughed.

"Rule number one, kid, this is a boat, *not* a ship. To a submariner, a ship and a target are the same thing!"

Though *Flier* was beautiful and practically new, the crew was deeply divided. I heard some of the rumors about the Midway incident, and how Captain had nearly lost his boat there and then at the resulting investigation. Many of the original, experienced hands had also been reassigned to other boats during *Flier's* repairs, and most of us who filled the spaces were inexperienced and unqualified. Some of the remaining crew started to believe the *Flier* was jinxed…had she been? That idea quickly spread through the new hands and made the crew as a whole nervous and anxious.

I stepped into all of this, twenty-one years old, expected to be responsible for men older and more experienced than I, all while studying for my qualifications. It was a lot to manage, especially when I hadn't been the most studious person so far in my life.

Ed was a graduate of the Naval Academy, with all its rules and regulations, and at home in this environment. He quickly took me under his wing and became my mentor; helped me study, learn how to be an officer and take responsibility for others while not losing my own mind or sense of humor. It was like having my older brother back with me.

He did this for many men on the *Flier*, and was the favorite officer of the crew. In a way, he was the heart of the boat.

He also was swimming the wrong way again.

"Ed!" I called out as I swam over to him, "Ed! You're swimming the wrong way." I didn't say "again."

He stopped swimming but didn't turn toward me this time.

"Ed," I gripped his shoulder which bowed wearily in the water, "come on, let's rest a moment, then I'll push you back to the group."

"No," he breathed and slipped out of my grasp. "Every man for himself. We all agreed on that."

"Let me help you back to the group. Just put your feet on my shoulders, I'll push you."

"I don't need pushing, Jake. If I can't find my way, then I can't find my way."

"Ed, please. Just follow my voice back to the group."

He hesitated for a moment. "You're *not* going to leave, *are* you?"

"Not a chance, I'm not going to let Betty Ann and Ricky down. You still have to get Ricky his birthday gift. If we're lucky, it'll be you." If he really was blind, they'd send him home for good, but now wasn't the time to say that.

I heard him take a deep breath, and saw his shadowy figure nod. "Just don't...don't push me, I'll keep up, if you guide me."

We began to swim back, and I cast around in my head for an idea, any idea at all, to keep him from giving up. "You know, you still owe me a party in Fremantle. You promised me you could throw a better party in your sleep than the ones at the hotels I was going to."

"I did, didn't I? Guess I'll have to raid the Emu Brewery too, if you're going to hold me to my word. I also promised to marry you off to a pretty girl? If Christie's driver is out, did any other girl catch your eye?"

"No one in particular. All of Perth and Fremantle may be populated with beautiful women, but no one has yet managed to catch me."

"I'll find you the second most beautiful woman in the world, Jake, and she'll catch you."

"Second?"

"You can't have Betty Ann." I could hear the smile in that voice, weak though it was.

We kept talking, his voice low and hoarse with exhaustion, though sounding much more optimistic, as we swam back to the group. A few shadowy figures turned at our approach and nodded a greeting, too tired to talk. Ed's breathing was labored, and I was exhausted, though I would not admit it to anyone.

"Thanks, Jake. You can stop talking now. It's not fair for you to weaken yourself on my account. Every—"

"Man for himself. I know Ed, but it's not a big deal."

"I can hear you kicking the water when your feet or hands break the surface. If you keep ahead and to the side of me, I can follow you. Just don't splash me in my face, got it?"

I swam slightly ahead and to the side then rolled on my back and kicked the surface gently. "Can you follow that?"

"Sure can. Thanks Jake. I'll make sure to find you a gorgeous girl when this is all over."

I heard Ed swimming quietly just behind me for a while.

The storm eventually died away, and the clouds overhead pulled apart into wispy threads that showed the stars in small clusters. I saw the cluster Liddell once taught me was the "False Cross," and from my own days sailing in Michigan, I spied Capricorn and Sagittarius, but the clouds to the north stubbornly refused to reveal the Dippers or North Star. We were still only guessing at the direction.

It was breathtaking, and brought back the 23rd Psalm in full force.

> *The Lord is my Shepherd; I shall not want.*
> *He makes me to lie down in green pastures:*
> *He leadeth me beside the still waters. He restoreth my soul:*
> *He leadeth me in the paths of righteousness for His name's sake.*
> *Yea, though I walk through the valley of the shadow of death*
> *I will fear no evil: for Thou art with me.*
> *Thy rod and thy staff, they comfort me.*
> *Thou preparest a table before me in the presence of mine enemies:*
> *Thou anointest my head with oil; my cup runneth over.*
> *Surely goodness and mercy shall follow me all the days of my life:*
> *And I will dwell in the house of the Lord forever.*

It must have been about an hour later when I realized I didn't hear Ed's breathing or splashing anymore. "Ed?" No answer. "Ed!" I rolled over and looked around me. "ED!" The ocean behind me was empty.

I turned and kept swimming after the guys. The war forced a strange familiarity with death. You had to harden yourself to it, before you went crazy. It was worse on the submarines. They just went missing with no reason, no known grave. Friends just vanished into the ocean and you had to force yourself to keep going while promising yourself you would think of them later. Anything else and you'd go mad.

I suddenly remembered the expression on Oly Kisamore's face one night when I saw him in a pub in Freo.

"Hey Oly, what's with the look?"

He seemed to shake himself and smiled at me. "I'm sure it's nothing, sir."

"You looked like you'd seen a ghost."

"Just a rumor, sir, someone said the *Herring* is overdue, and no one's heard from her."

"Okay."

"My best friend is aboard, sir."

"Ah," Now I understood. "Look Oly, I'm sure he's fine, they likely ran into some radio problems or something, which is why no one's heard from them." It was no good dwelling on what could be until there was actually news. Lots of submarines came into port too late. Still, it was a desperate excuse, I almost felt ridiculous offering it.

"I'm sure you're right, sir. Thanks for the talk." He gave a half-hearted smile, excused himself, and wove through the crowds and out of the pub.

The few times I saw him afterwards, he seemed fine, talking and laughing, despite no more news about *Herring*[22]. That was the way we all had to cope, just promise that there will be a later someday.

I flipped over again onto my side. My muscles burned dully. I found I had to switch positions more and more often, trying to rest different muscle

---

[22] The *Herring* was sunk on June 1, 1944 by shore gun fire after destroying two Japanese ships anchored in the harbor of of Matsuwa Island (modern Matua Island). She went down with all hands, including Oliver Kisamore's best friend Andry Saarm of Michigan. Her resting place has not been found

groups in turn.

I looked around and realized that in my concern for Ed, I hadn't noticed that we seemed to be two more men short. It was impossible to see who it was in the night.

I changed position again and just thought to myself, '*Keep going, just keep swimming.*' Paul Knapp swam beside me for a while, but we drew farther and farther apart. I barely noticed the distance until I realized he too was gone. He must have felt his time was up and quietly left us for the few moments of privacy I desperately tried to delay or deny Ed. It was courage as I had never seen: to die alone and quietly, without distressing the rest of us, giving us the chance and hope to reach some sort of safety, and get back home.

The water's surface grew slippery with *Flier's* oil again. I was growing tired of the grisly reminder. It was like she was chasing us, or we had been wasting hours of effort swimming in circles. I didn't like either option.

The moon finally rose, slightly to our front and right sides. We'd been swimming northeast, but now we had a concrete bearing. The rainbow threads of the oil faded as I turned north, and, quickly thinking a prayer for my shipmates, I also prayed that I never saw that oil again.

No one talked; the energy and concentration couldn't be spared. My arms and legs felt like lead, but after so many hours, the swim strokes were automatic. I refused to think of the miles between me and some island, or I'd give up, I knew. I pushed myself to think of nothing but the next stroke taking us to safety, even freedom. Thoughts of family, friends, the *Flier*, the missing men, I violently shoved aside. Just think about the next stroke, the next, the next.

The moon was still low in the stars when the sky began to lighten at the horizon, telling me that it was at least six hours that we'd been swimming together . I had hoped to be practically on an island's beach, but in the pre-dawn light, I couldn't see any indication of land.

I kept going, trusting God would see me through one way or another again. '*Be prepared,*' I remembered my Eagle Scoutmaster telling me. This was about as unprepared as I had ever been, but I decided I would continue swimming until my heart gave out, and no sooner. If it were up to me, *Flier's* fate and those of her crew would be told.

'*Keep going, just keep going.*'

"We swam the wrong way!" Madeo suddenly shrieked.

"Madeo, wait, we may see more with the sunrise," Captain called. His voice was hoarse, strained and exhausted. "We may be nearly there."

I heard Madeo thrashing around in the water, "There's no land!"

"Wait for the sunrise, Madeo," Captain called back.

When the sun finally blazed across the sea, Madeo was gone, as were a number of others. Bill Reynolds, who'd crashed into me after *Flier* thrashed, and Phil Mayer, who'd run past us and over the side, and Miller, who'd asked me about *Flier's* now-lost "flag", were gone. There were just seven of us left, dark spots in the water.

Captain had been right; land was on the horizon, a low black mass of safety, provided the enemy wasn't waiting there for us, too.

5

DESERT ISLAND

"Make for the island as best as you can, don't try to stay together if you can make better time," Captain called out from behind me.

In the morning light, I could see Russo, younger and an excellent swimmer, far ahead and quickly pulling away from the group. Baumgart and Howell were within yards of me, and someone was swimming far to my right.

My muscles were screaming with pain and weariness now. I had to change positions every few minutes and even pause to rest, but still the island seemed to perversely, stubbornly, stay on the horizon. As the light grew brighter, I could make out the dark green of trees, but little else.

Only the sun climbing higher in the sky told me that I had been swimming for hours on end. The warm water and warming air was so soothing, I started to fall asleep, sometimes mid-stroke. I shook my head, and dove deep into the cooler water beneath me to keep awake. The lapping of the waves only compounded the problem. I forced myself to think about the island, food, anything to combat the fatigue, but that too seemed to blend in tempo with the waves.

At one point, it sounded like a bee buzzing around my head softly. I shook my head, and waved it off with my hands, but the noise didn't come closer or farther away, like a bee would. Stopping in mid-stroke, I looked up. The sky was dotted here and there with small clouds that clustered near the southern horizon, but the buzzing, slowly growing louder, was coming from nearby. There were no boats, no animals, no distant ships, just the few of us and our island. What was it?

I thought I saw something dark flicker for a second out of the corner of my eye. I glanced up, and saw the dark flicker again on the horizon. I grasped my binoculars and pointed them to the sky, searching for what I hoped was just my imagination.

Then, "God help us...PLANE!!!!" I roared as loudly as I could. I saw the Red Disc on the wings: a Japanese Zero.

As the plane drew nearer, we tried to stay as still as possible, waiting until she was nearly on top of us. "NOW!" I yelled, taking a deep breath and diving under, kicking as deeply as I could.

The shadow flickered overhead, but I stayed under until my lungs were ready to burst. Heart pounding, and all sleep a distant memory, I finally shot to the surface, exploding through to the air, gasping painfully. The plane had already passed over the island and was a distant speck. Baumgart and Howell's heads blasted out of the sea, and they shook the water from their hair and eyes. For a second, we all panted, too tired to do anything else.

"Figures," I finally grinned at them, "see a plane and every submariner in the area dives in seconds, sub or no sub."

They chuckled wearily. If we could laugh at that lame joke, we might just make it.

At least the island finally appeared to be getting closer. My muscles trembled with the effort, my breath dragged raggedly in and out of my lungs. Only a little farther, I told myself. Just keep swimming....

A pristine white beach spread itself beneath the trees and I thought, for a moment, that I saw a house sitting on the beach. I blinked hard, forcing the sea water out of my eyes, and shook my head. My vision was strained and blurry from the hours of sunlight glaring off the water's surface, and now, all I could see was a green blur on top of a white streak.

"Hey, is that a boat?" Howell croaked excitedly.

There was a low, dark shape in the water, with what appeared to be some people sitting at one end. I couldn't see movement, but quickly lifted my arm and waved frantically. "Hey!" I rasped, "Hey! Do you see us?"

Howell and Baumgart started waving and hollering too, but no one moved, or even acknowledged our existence. They sat so still, it was unnatural.

"Do you think they're friendly?" Howell finally asked.

"They have to see us from this distance," Baumgart said, waving his arms over his head in wide gestures.

"If they won't help a guy in need, we'd better give them a wide berth," I said. "No telling who they are, or if they'll report us."

We swam away from it, and suddenly, my hand smacked the binoculars, still floating beside me! *How tired am I?* I thought, sheepishly bringing the glasses to my eyes. Seconds later, I burst out laughing. "It's a palm tree! It's just a stupid palm tree!"

Caught in the current, it came for us rapidly. Sure enough, when it got closer, we could clearly see our "native boat" was an old palm tree floating in the waves, and the "people" were the remains of its once broad fronds, now bent and broken at bizarre, twisted angles.

We laughed, slapping each other's hands and the waves in joy. It was the first bit of luck in the hours that we'd been in the water. We splashed over to it in excitement and clambered aboard, straddling our new ship proudly. Baumgart and Howell broke off some of the larger fronds for paddles, and, as the Commanding Officer, I straddled the trunk and scanned the water with my binoculars for the rest of our men.

Russo was too far ahead, and was already wading in the hip-deep water toward the beach; there was no point to trying to get to him. I scanned behind us, and saw Captain and Liddell struggling feebly, clinging to what might be a piece of driftwood. "Men!" I pointed, "To the Captain!"

The fronds made for lousy paddles, and soon we realized they would have to swim at least part of the way to us, or we'd be out here another whole day. We stretched our raw, hoarse voices to the limit, yelling, whistling, throwing sheets of water in the air to get their attention, while trying to steer our "ship" out to sea to get them. They glanced our way once or twice, then suddenly stopped and stared in amazement, before laughing and pushing hard for our tree as we kicked and paddled our way to them.

"I had almost given up," Crowley croaked out when he joined us. Despite the hot sun that was burning me, his face was nearly grey and dead-looking. He didn't even have the strength to haul himself aboard for a few minutes and simply hung on to the trunk weakly. "Almost given up hope," he panted again, "when this bizarre vision yelled at me. By God, I never thought I'd be grateful to see one of these again."

"At least this time, it really *was* a ship, sir!" Liddell laughed.

"You'd been at the periscope, what was it, five hours chasing that so-called ship last patrol? You thought it was a sailboat, then two sailboats?" I said.

"Yes, then it was a massive sail ship with men in the riggings," Liddell replied.

"…and about everything else under the sun, until we surfaced and there was a…"

"*Floating Palm Tree!*" All three officers chorused, and everyone laughed.

"Hey, I'm not the only one that's happened to. You should hear Sam Dealey go on and on about all the driftwood and deserted islands he's stalked!" Captain was laughing as hard as the rest of us.

We hauled Captain and Liddell aboard the "*USS Palm Tree,*" and turned her to shore. Russo was staggering up the last few feet of surf, but Tremaine was struggling in the water far to the east. We screamed and hollered at him until he turned and waved, but kept pushing on to the far end of the island. We watched him go, confused, but with no more Fliers in the water, we made for the beach, using all the fronds as paddles, as well as using our hands and feet.

Now, sitting above the water, and closing in on the island, I could see that there was no house or any man-made objects, just a smooth white beach spread beneath the tall jungle. It looked like the perfect tropical island, and also perfectly isolated.

The water beneath us was crystal clear and covered with colorful corals, with hundreds of fish darting about, a scant few feet below.

"It's looking like we're going to have to wade the last bit in," Liddell said.

My feet brushed a large chunk of coral as it passed under us, and a moment later, I grunted in pain.

"Jacobson, what happened?" Liddell asked.

"I'm not sure, sir," I said, reaching down to examine my sole. My skin, wrinkled and tender from the hours underwater, now sported a thin, deep cut, neat as though carved with a razor. A watery trail of blood trickled freely from it. "I think I might have cut my foot on a coral."

By the time the *Palm Tree* shoaled a couple of blocks from the beach, most of our feet and ankles and been neatly slit and scraped open. Finally forced off, I clenched my teeth and tried to step delicately onto the rocks and coral, but every step just found new places to slice open, the saltwater rushing in to carve even deeper. I just forced myself to keep moving forward.

It seemed like hours later when I finally dragged myself onto the powdery beach and collapsed, too tired to move farther. I heard the thuds of other bodies striking the beach around me, gasping and panting. I could feel the water streaming off of me, and the warmth of my blood welling and running down the soles of my feet.

Moments later, I became aware of the sound of ticking; a very rhythmic, precise ticking. By some miracle, I had forgotten completely about my watch, and despite it all, it still worked! I squinted at the face, wondering if it was merely moving, or if that really was the time of day.

"Fifteen thirty?"[23] Captain asked me, glancing at his own.

"That's what mine says," I replied.

"Same here," he dropped his arm and lay on the beach, shielding his eyes from the mid-afternoon sun.

We'd been in the water for seventeen hours.

Russo had been the only man on the beach when we got there, and was still lying flat out on the sand, breathing deeply. "'Bout time," he murmured, not moving, "though I like the improvised ship."

"How long you been here?" Liddell asked.

"Dunno, sir, maybe ten minutes?"

Liddell looked around, "Have you seen Tremaine?" None of us had noticed when he had vanished, only that he was no longer here.

"I couldn't see anyone except you guys after I landed," Russo said, sitting up and squinting around him. "I didn't see Tremaine at all after the sun rose."

"He was here only an hour or so ago, drifting east," Liddell muttered. He sighed, then struggled to his feet, and trudged eastward. I may have drifted off then, for it seemed like only a moment later, Liddell returned with Tremaine in his wake.

"You were on that native canoe?" He said when he got close enough to talk without straining his voice.

"It was a palm tree. You saw us; you waved at us when we hollered at you," Baumgart said.

"I couldn't hear anything. I thought you were native fishermen waving at me, but if you weren't friendly enough to come help a guy out, I wasn't

---

[23] 3:30 p.m. *Flier* sank around 10 p.m. the previous night.

The first island the men landed on, as seen from a ship a number of years later. The pale streak in the water is the submerged reef they crossed. Courtesy of the family of Ens. Alvin "Jake" Jacobson.

going to take my chances."

We laughed feebly, and together limped up the beach and threw ourselves onto the shaded sand. Every one of us was stripped to his skivvies, burnt red. The fine grains of sand clotted our bloody feet, but worked themselves in deeper with every step. I kept taking deep breaths when I put weight on my feet, to keep from showing signs of pain.

Tired, wounded, hungry and thirsty though we all were, we had to make some kind of shelter quickly, before the sun set. Getting soaked and battered by a storm would only weaken us further.

We scavenged everything we could: driftwood, palm fronds, the fibrous vines that covered the trees. Despite my hopes, we quickly discovered that somewhere on the bottom of the ocean lay all of our knives. With no alternatives and light running out, we hauled with all our strength to wrench those blasted vines from the trees and bushes. By the time the sun touched the horizon, we had a sorry excuse for a shelter. I suspected a stiff breeze would have no trouble dismantling it, but in the rain, it might be better than nothing.

"How about some dinner?" Howell suddenly said, holding up a coconut. "I managed to snag this on the way to shore. Now if only we can...well..."

"Open it?" Tremaine said.

We smashed it against tree trunks and rocks until it cracked open. The smell of sweet coconut milk flooded my nostrils, making me nearly dizzy with hunger. We passed that small coconut around, each taking a small swallow of the milk, then shattered the shell for the meat. I scraped it off the shell with my teeth, savoring every bit.

Minutes later, my stomach clenched painfully. I staggered from camp and pitched toward the sand, losing my meal and then some. My muscles trembled as I curled on my side, hearing the others also lose their dinners. We would get through this, I promised myself. No matter what, we would get through this.

The sun vanished over the horizon, and soon, the temperature dropped. Shaky and weak, we walked back to our shelter and huddled together for some warmth and sleep. I couldn't stop shivering, and despite the fact that my sunburn was already serious, I wished for sunrise if only for the warmth it would bring.

No one even suggested building a fire. We all knew the Japanese were still camped on Balabac Island, now in sight again, and it was more than possible that a random patrol may see a fire here on the beach.

None of us had slept well when the sun broke over the horizon the next morning. We trembled and stumbled into the early light, trying to warm as fast as possible, limping up and down the beach, swinging our arms to ease the stiffness and pain.

Howell gasped and groaned when he tried to stand. His knee was badly swollen, mottled with deep bruises.

"I think I banged it on the Bridge Hatch when..." he shivered.

"Up you get," Tremaine told him, seizing Howell's arm and ducking under his shoulder, lifting him bodily. Russo dashed forward and grabbed his other shoulder, and together they hobbled out into the sun. The unspoken submarine culture was unbroken: we were in this together.

Today was Tuesday, August 15. We'd been on our own for a day and a half.

"Men," Captain said when we all had stopped shivering badly. "We're as rested as we're going to get today, and we must take stock of the situation and explore the island. We need food and water, and to know if we're alone here. Howell, because you're unable to walk, you will be in charge of trying to reinforce the shelter. Do I have volunteers to stay with him?"

"We will, sir," Tremaine and Russo said, and Captain nodded his acknowledgement. "Okay, that leaves Jacobson, Baumgart, Liddell and me to explore. Liddell and I will head east and Jacobson and Baumgart will head west," he looked at us and we nodded our assent. "You three," he said to the camp crew, "watch the strait and search this area when you're done with the shelter. We need water and food. If we can't find it, we'll have to weigh our options from there. I have a watch and so does Jacobson, so try to return no later than 1800, agreed?"

"Yes, sir," I said.

"Don't strain yourselves." He warned. "We can't risk anyone overheating when we have no reliable source of food or water."

I left my binoculars with the shelter group, and Baumgart and I headed west. In the early morning light, before the humid haze rose, I easily could see the dark purple shadow that was Balabac Island. To the west, a couple of miles away, was another island. It looked larger than ours, and also heavily forested. Compared to these giants, we had landed on a spit of sand.

The fine, silky grains of the powdered beach quickly gave way to broken chunks of coral as we got closer to the western edge of the island, and my feet were soon raw and bloody again. I longed for my shoes. I could have tied them together and slung them around my neck, couldn't I? Maybe have tucked my knife inside them?

"Is it just me, sir?" Baumgart grunted as he, limped beside me, "or is this whole island intent on killing us slowly?"

"I'll side with you on this one," I replied. "Seems to be deserted, too. I hear birds and the occasional monkey, but there are no signs of people."

We limped and grunted down the beach, as the humidity slowly shimmered above the waves until Balabac was hidden. Another patrol plane buzzed overhead around nine in the morning, but we were already under the spreading fronds of several palm trees, so just watched it pass.

We rounded the end of the island, and what little of the beach that was left vanished into a pile of coral chunks that covered the short distance from the trees to the shore. Washed up on these weathered razors were hundreds of coconuts.

"You think they're any good?" Baumgart asked me, eyes alight.

"I sure hope so."

"Let's break one open and make sure, before we lug these things back to camp," Baumgart said.

We each grabbed a coconut and banged them against tree trunks and the shattered rocks until they finally cracked. The sickening sweet smell of rot assaulted me.

"Ack!" I hurled the rotten nut into the trees, and clutched my stomach, gagging for a moment. "Okay, okay, there's dozens of coconuts on this beach, there's got to be some good ones."

"You'd think so," Baumgart croaked out. "But I'm from Milwaukee, I'd never know a good coconut if it bit me."

"Well, I wouldn't eat the one that bit you," I joked, "Might be a bit too fresh." We laughed wearily. "I wouldn't know the good ones either, these trees don't exactly grow in my neck of the woods. Should we...knock on them like melons?"

He chuckled. "Your guess is as good as mine, sir. It's at least worth a shot," he said, nudging one with his toe and picking up another one.

We picked our way carefully along the shore, knocking on coconut after coconut until we found one that sounded whole and hollow, but it too was rotten inside. Some were already broken open, the inside eaten by tiny black ants that swarmed up our arms and legs. Despite all our efforts to choose only the most inviting sounding coconuts, they were all rotten and inedible.

Baumgart slumped beneath a palm tree. "We're never going to find anything to eat."

"Nonsense," I replied, keeping a laugh in my voice. It was the first rule of survival my pack leader taught me in Boy Scouts: don't panic. Panic or resignation kept one from seeing solutions, just problems. "One of these has got to be good. Come on."

Another patrol plane flew overhead at around three that afternoon. This place might have been deserted, but it certainly was patrolled regularly.

I was about to suggest to Baumgart that we turn back for camp, when I spotted a human figure emerge from the trees some distance ahead. I tried to haul Baumgart behind a bush at the same time he tried to shove me under cover, and we landed in a heap behind a screen of thick fronds.

"Did he see us?" I asked as we untangled ourselves.

"No idea. I don't think so." We peered out at the unknown person from behind our blind.

"If he has, he sure didn't show any signs of it," I said.

"What do you think, sir?" He asked me.

"Beats me. It's got to be a native or an enemy scout. Doesn't seem to be in much of a hurry, does he?"

The man was meandering all over the beach, occasionally prodding a coconut with his foot. He didn't seem to be armed.

"It can't be a scout. I heard that those bastards never go anywhere without being armed to the teeth," Baumgart said.

Who could he be? I wondered. I too, had heard no Japanese soldier ever went unarmed, but at the same time, I had heard that they sent small patrols to check islands that did not have garrisons on them. He wasn't walking like someone who had a purpose like hunting or fishing, or even looking for something. His gait was stiff, like he was old or had arthritis.

Regardless, if he kept coming, he would eventually find our camp. I started to root around for a large enough piece of coral, or a stout branch, or something.

"Are you thinking what I'm thinking, sir?" Baumgart whispered, as he quietly picked up and hefted some fallen branches.

"Well, whoever he is, we can't let him find the camp, and I don't know about you, but I don't think I can chase him down with my feet like this."

"Same here. Let him pass then get him?"

"Unless you've got a better idea. I don't want to attack an unarmed man, but we can't let an enemy, armed or unarmed, find the camp, and we won't know who he is until we take him."

We watched him continue his slow walk toward our hiding place. He appeared to be limping now, rather than walking stiffly.

I wished fervently for my binoculars, which would have helped me see him better. My eyes were still weak from the glare of the sun on the water the day before.

Baumgart and I crouched, rocks and branches in hand, breathing deeply and quietly, watching, waiting for our quarry to limp even closer.

"Wait a second…" Baumgart raised his head a little higher to get a better look at him from over the palm fronds. "Wes?" he breathed. The figured limped closer. "Oh my God, Wes!" He yelled, stepping out from behind the bush.

The man leapt a mile in the air and then staggered in our direction. "Earl! Thank God! Are you a sight for sore eyes! I thought I was the only one that made it!"

It was Wes Miller, who had vanished before dawn the day before.

"Where have you been?" Baumgart asked.

"I figured we kept swimming in circles after we crossed *Flier's* oil twice, so I struck out on my own. By dawn yesterday, I was nearly past here and swam to shore. I'm so relieved! I thought I was the only survivor left!" He laughed.

"You nearly swam *past* this island?"

"Sure did."

"Well, I think that beats Russo's record for fastest swimmer then." I said, "What do you think, Baumgart?"

"Without a doubt!"

"Russo's alive? Where is he? Are there more than you two-or three?"

"No, there're seven of us, eight with you," I told him.

"I'm so relieved," he repeated. "Last night it was so cold, I didn't know what to do, I couldn't believe I was the only one left. I was just looking for food or water, can't even find a coconut around here," he said in disgust.

"Well that answers that question," I told Baumgart. "But I think the others will like what we found on our half of the island better than coconuts anyway."

"Who all is left, sir?" Wes asked me.

"Of the officers, there's only myself, Captain, and Lt. Liddell. Besides you and Baumgart here, we also have Don Tremaine, Art Howell, and of course, Russo. Howell got banged up pretty badly when it happened, and he is back at base with Russo and Tremaine. We were sent by Crowley to scout this island for food, water or any supplies. I take it there's nothing farther down the beach."

"Not unless you want rotten coconuts," he grunted, kicking one away with his feet. "I spent most of yesterday cracking the damned things open to find nothing. No water on my end either. Or much of a beach to speak of."

He turned north and pointed to a small point some distance away. "I landed just around the corner from that point. The coral turns into a sharp cliff, a little higher than me, with a strip of rocks under that. Tore my feet up pretty badly..." he looked at our feet. "Apparently it's the same on your side too."

"Only if you count very small razor blades as sand," Baumgart said.

"Wherever you are has to be better than where I landed. Lousy place to try and sleep or survive. I spent the day hoping to see anyone from *Flier*. I couldn't tell if I had been swept east or west or farther forward or farther behind. I thought it was just possible that I was the only one who made it. But I couldn't find food or water, so I made up my mind this morning to explore, and if I had to, head for that island," he pointed to the large island next to us. "It didn't look that far away, but boy! Am I ever glad to see you fellas."

"I never got a chance to ask: why were you on lookout duty last night? I thought you were supposed to be in the engine room" Baumgart said.

Wes looked a little embarrassed, I thought—maybe sad. "Hazards of being the new guy and the non-qual, I guess. The guy scheduled for lookout duty...bugger, I'm still trying-was trying-to learn names...decided he'd rather sleep and informed me of his decision to swap shifts with me."

"Wow."

Chances of fate, I thought. Had Teddy not bagged the first shift on deck...

"I guess that's it then," I said, standing. "We have to head back."

The air was now heavy and saturated with humidity, and the breeze did little other than re-distribute the sweat on our bodies. In the distance, I saw rain squalls form and dump rain on the ocean. I licked my rough tongue over my cracked lips and wished one would sweep over us.

The rocky shore slowly gave way back to the sandy beach as we turned to the southern edge of the island. After hours of negotiating the razor rock, it felt almost soft.

We were the last to arrive at the base, and Wes, for fun, hid behind Baumgart and me for effect.

"Find anything?" Howell called out, looking at us through my binoculars.

"Nah," Baumgart hollered back, "Just some guy."

They all looked up in alarm: Enemy, native?

Wes walked out from behind us with a grin. "Hey guys!"

Everyone shouted, grabbed Wes, shook his hand, clapped him on the back, and asked him where he had come from. Captain greeted him briefly, then signaled me aside.

"Anything to report besides Wes?" He asked.

"I'm sorry, sir, there's nothing on the other side of the island. From Wes's report, he landed on the north shore, and he found nothing there all day yesterday, which was why he was coming down the beach looking for other things. We found about a hundred rotten coconuts, but that's about it."

Captain nodded his head. "I was afraid of that," he muttered.

"Nothing on your end then, sir?"

"Nothing that will let us stay here."

"There was a large island, sir, directly west of us, you can see it from here in the morning. It looks larger and more substantial than this one, if we have to migrate."

"Any driftwood?"

"Uh, no, sir, nothing to speak of."

He nodded, his forehead furrowed, then said, "Thank you, Jacobson, I'll keep that in mind."

"Thank you, sir."

I went to retrieve my binoculars from Howell. I felt too exposed without them today, and there was that outside chance of something I almost didn't want to admit to myself…

Howell was sitting down again, with his leg propped up on a piece of driftwood, watching the rest of the guys swapping stories with Wes.

"Hey, Howell, how's the leg?" I asked him.

"Just fine, sir. I'll be up and around in no time."

"You sure? You don't look so good." He looked grayer than he had this morning.

"I wasn't planning on entering any beauty pageants, sir," he said dryly.

"The country thanks you, I'm sure," I ribbed back. "But seriously, you look paler red than this morning."

"Well sir, I learned an important lesson while you were all out." He pointed at a broad-leafed plant behind him. "That plant collects dew and rain water."

"Really?" That could be a life-saver for us.

"And if you drink from it, you throw up for a good ten minutes."

Never mind.

"I seem to be okay now sir, it passed, and I don't feel any worse than this morning. I'll make it."

"I'm sure," I replied. "Still have my binocs?"

"Yes, sir," he took them off from around his neck. "There you are, good as new, or at least in the same condition you gave them to me."

"Thanks, Howell." He'd been the one watching the strait all day. "You didn't happen to see anything, or anyone..." my voice trailed off as I glanced at Wes.

"Sorry, sir, I didn't."

I sighed, "It was a long shot anyway. I thought maybe it was just possible..." It sounded stupid even as I tried to explain what I was thinking by not explaining it.

"Lieutenant Casey, sir?"

"Yeah, I suppose," I laughed a little nervously at my foolishness. "After we found Wes, I guess I thought if a miracle can happen once, it might happen twice."

"It's not going to happen for Lieutenant Casey, sir, I'm sorry."

"How...how do you...? Are you sure?"

"Yes, sir," Howell said, looking out at the ocean. "I heard you talking to Lieutenant Casey when you guided him back that last time. About the party in Fremantle, you know? I was behind both of you. After a while, Lieutenant Casey kept falling behind, but he was quiet about it, so you didn't notice. He ended up near me.

"He was trying really hard to keep going, but he was in a lot of pain, something was wrong, and he couldn't swim on his stomach. I offered to push him. He was a great guy, and my favorite officer...no disrespect to you, sir," he said quickly.

"None taken, he was one of my closest friends. Everyone liked him."

"Yes, sir, he was the one who personally invited me to serve on the *Flier*.

"Anyway, he let me push him, and I tried, and tried, but we kept falling farther behind..." he paused and took a deep, shaking breath. I knelt beside him in the sand. "He was talking about home and trying to keep *my* spirits up, if you can believe that, but in the end, I just couldn't push him anymore. I...I told him I was so sorry, but I just...couldn't. I was so tired, I didn't think I'd make it. His voice was so quiet by then, I think he was in pain, or maybe even losing consciousness. I don't know. It was so dark, I could barely see him. He said a quick prayer, and put himself in God's keeping. The last thing he told me was... 'It's okay Howell, save yourself.' Then he...I watched him, sir, I had to watch him sink beneath the water."

Howell's head dropped and we both sat silently next to each other. I had known Ed was probably gone, but to hear it like this was just dreadful.

"After that, sir, I just kept going," Howell resumed. "I wasn't going to give in even with my knee after that. Lt. Casey told me to save myself; I wasn't going to disobey his last order."

"I'm sorry I wasn't closer to you, Howell, I would have helped."

"I know, sir, I saw you retrieving Lieutenant Casey several times, while I was helping Ensign Mayer, not that that mattered in the end either..."

There was nothing to say. We both understood, but there was nothing that could ease the pain.

The joyful reunion going on nearby seemed distant now, as Howell and I sat together, remembering Casey, and by extension, all the others.

Later, as the sun was very low in the sky, we gathered on the beach, enjoying the cooling temperature before it became uncomfortably cold. The humidity was dissipating, revealing the large islands to the southwest and east, with smaller ones peeking through here and there.

The captain stood in front of us and said, "It's come to this: If there had been food and water here, we could wait a few days to gain our strength here, but there isn't any. We have only one choice left: to leave. But which way?" He knelt, took a small broken stick and drew a rough map in the sand as he talked. "Balabac Island is southwest of here. We sank about seven or eight miles off its western coast near Comiran." He punctured the sand, the tiny island not even worth drawing an actual "circle." "We know that the Japs have garrisons and outposts on Balabac, which is why we decided to swim north when we had the choice that night. We don't know much about this string of islands here, because they're surrounded by reefs and often are exposed during low tide, which is why subs generally avoid this area."

"We can see Balabac Island over there," Captain said, pointing over his shoulder, "but there are other islands to the east and the west of us, both of which are large enough that we're more likely to find food and water, though there are no guarantees. The large western island is within a mile or two away. The eastern island is a bit farther away, with a string of small islands like this one between it and us." He drew this out on the sand. "According to Jacobson's search party, Wes was the only thing worth retrieving on the western shore of this island." We all chuckled, and Captain continued, "The only thing worth mentioning on the eastern shore is a large pile of driftwood.

"If we take another swim, we may be pushed apart from the currents, so we're going to build a raft out of the driftwood. It can't be too big, or it'll attract the attention of the regular patrols buzzing overhead. But if we hang on to it, while swimming, we'll stay together.

"The only question left is: west, east, or south? The western island is closer, though we'd have to drag the raft to the western shore or raft all the way around this island to reach her. The small islands between us and the eastern island are fairly close together, but we'd have to walk around each island as it came.

"Of course, if we find food or water on one of those small islands, we can rest and recuperate there.

"The western island is also going to be close to, if not bordering, the North Balabac Strait, which means it will most likely have some Japanese forces on it. The eastern island is a complete blank. It may be patrolled by entrenched forces, or it may just be left alone because it does not guard any significant passages or resources that we know of. Of course, it may have no food or water as well.

"Or we could head for Balabac Island, where we know there is food, water, and enemy garrisons that we'd have to avoid.

"We're in this together, so this choice has to be all of ours. Would you men prefer to head for known food and water with enemy forces to dodge to the south, likely food and water with likely forces to the west in one long swim, or several short swims to an island we know nothing about to the east?"

"Sir," Wes said, "after all we've gone through thus far, I'd rather take my chance with the unknown again, than try to play hide and seek with an enemy that knows the ground far better than we will. I'd go east."

"Chances are better that there are native Filipinos there than Japanese anyway," I said. "The Japanese would be on Balabac because it forms one side of both Balabac and North Balabac Straits. If I remember the chart correctly, that western island does guard the North Balabac Strait. The eastern island doesn't guard any critical passage except what native boats probably cruise around here. If there are natives we may find sympathizers, or they may choose to leave us alone entirely." They might also turn us over, but I didn't say that, we all knew that was a possibility.

"I'd rather take my chances with the unknown than the known enemy," Baumgart said.

"Agreed," Russo spoke up.

"Same here, I'll take my chances," Tremaine said.

"I'm not ready to turn myself in," Howell agreed.

It sounds like the crew is decided, Captain," Liddell finished. "We'll go into the unknown."

Captain nodded quietly, looking out to the horizon. "It's too late to begin tonight. We'll start in the morning. If we work fast enough, we can launch as soon as that patrol plane makes her afternoon run."

The sun was just touching the horizon now, throwing long shadows onto the white beach. My family used to have driftwood fires and roast marshmallows this time of day back home. I wondered if my parents and sisters were carrying on the tradition tonight in our stead.

Suddenly, I saw a tremendous explosion throw water high in the air just at the horizon, near where *Flier* went down. "Look!" I yelled, pointing, before ramming my binoculars to my eyes.

The eruption was tall and violent, the water churned into a froth suspended in mid-air for a few seconds before falling back to the ocean to be absorbed. Was it another ship fallen prey to a mine, or *Flier* herself collapsing under the weight of the water?

Captain tapped me on the shoulder. "Jacobson, may I?" I handed him the binoculars as the muted thunder of the explosion, which much have been deafening at the source, rumbled to our ears.

We were silent, crouched there on the beach, watching and listening to the spectacle.

"Do you suppose it was her?" Russo asked.

"Or a mine," Liddell said.

"Did we hit a mine out there?" Baumgart spoke up.

"I don't know. Even at forty fathoms, Japanese mines should have been too deep to catch us running on the surface," Liddell replied. "Could it be a battery explosion?"

"No," I said. "The batteries had already been cleaned for the day when I reported for duty. If they were going to explode, they would have done so then."

"Enemy submarine?" asked Miller.

"We never saw one in the area on radar and no one surfaced to check for survivors or trophies," Tremaine said. "Pope would have heard the scream of a torpedo before it hit, but he never mentioned anything."

"Did we go too fast and get off course?" Wes asked.

"Our radar readings said we were on course." Liddell replied. "It might have been a floating mine, if it broke loose of its chain."

We stood and watched the horizon for several minutes, each lost in his own thoughts, until, one by one, we went to our lean-to and bed.

Before sleeping, remembering the rain squalls I had watched pass by all day, I scavenged dozens of the large seashells scattered around the beach and placed them, hollow-side up, in the sand. Another squall was building in the west and I prayed fervently that by morning, we'd be able to slake our burning thirst.

6

INTO THE UNKNOWN

Even huddled together for warmth, I could barely sleep for shivering. The others tossed, turned, and curled into balls, each struggling to find a position that was relatively warm and comfortable.

Though wide-awake and exhausted when the sky finally began to lighten in the east, I knew I had slept some because I dreamt about my family in Grand Haven.

By now, my mother would have received the letters I had written during *Flier's* first patrol, and that rug and boomerangs that I had sent. I wasn't allowed to tell her 'I'm going out on patrol' in my letters. The censors would confiscate something like that. But I did tell her 'This is the last letter you'll receive from me for a while.' And she knew that meant I was on patrol for a few weeks and would send a letter as soon as I got back. I wondered how long it would be before she suspected something was wrong. Of course, I reminded myself, Ed's family doesn't know about him either, and if none of us make it back…I shook my head. *'Don't think like that,'* I told myself sternly. *'We're going to make it back and I will hug my mother again, and tell Betty Ann about Ed's end.'*

The sun crested the horizon, and we all moved to the sunny edge of the beach, stiffly stretching sore, cold muscles. My stomach cramped painfully, but I ignored it. Though I had heard the distant rumbles of thunder occasionally during the night, nothing had fallen on our island, leaving our seashells as dry as before.

After destroying our shelter and throwing it into the undergrowth, we staggered to the east, following the Captain and Liddell.

The jungle seemed just as impenetrable here as at the eastern end, with nothing that looked remotely useful to eat, or build a raft. At one point, I spotted a small piece of canvas tangled in a low bush. It was dirty and quite tattered, but I grabbed it, hoping there was enough beneath the leaves to make a sail for the raft. It crumbled and fell away at my touch, and despite being as gentle as I could, when I finally extracted the last of it from the bracken around it, I knew that dream was impossible. The piece was too small, and slashed with holes in it everywhere. There was no way we could use this for a sail or anything else, so I dropped it and turned to go, and promptly scraped my feet on a partially buried chunk of coral.

After cursing my luck under my breath, I grabbed that piece of canvas. Tearing it in half, I wrapped it around my feet, tying the ends together in a rough sandal.

I took less than ten steps before I had to stop and rip it off. It rubbed on the sores on my ankles and heel, driving dirt in farther. I re-wrapped it again, carefully avoiding those areas, but after a step or two, I had to stop.

I wrestled with that fabric again and again, wanting some protection from what I knew had to be coming, but no matter what I did, the canvas rubbing on my foot hurt worse than the sand and bracken working their way into my wounds while barefoot.

I left the tattered remains behind and walked quickly to catch up to my crewmates.

The island's beach curved to a point, and just beyond that, we saw a large pile of driftwood washed up against the small cliff that formed here.

"We're going to need vines or something to tie these together," Captain said.

"I'm sure we can find some in the jungle here," Liddell said.

"I'll join you, sir," Russo volunteered.

"I see some nice straight lengths of bamboo, too," I said, pulling aside some strands of seaweed, and yanking the pieces out of the tangle. "These should help make this somewhat easier."

Soon, we were in teams, pulling the long spars of bamboo out of the twisted driftwood and seaweed and dragging them under the shade of the palm trees that overhung the beach. Here, we could build the raft away from the eyes of the morning patrol, and conserve our energy.

It had been over two days now with no food or water, and dehydration was taking its toll. My movements became increasingly clumsy. Sticks and vines slipped through my fingers without the slightest warning, and I sometimes found myself tying the same knots over and over without pulling them tight. My lips were cracked and my tongue swollen, and the constant beating of the waves against the beach was agony. They reminded me of the fresh water of Lake Michigan beating against the shore, but here, I couldn't drink. It was torture.

In the end, the raft was about four feet wide and seven feet long, with a "deck" in the center just wide enough for at least two of us to straddle, and an outrigger frame the rest of us could hang on to while we swam. Captain split two lengths of bamboo halfway down their shafts, and spliced in a number of crosspieces, forming primitive paddles.

Liddell, now that he had pulled down a number of vines, was standing at the edge of the short cliff overhanging the sea, throwing twigs into the water and making scratches in the sand. Since the others were busy lashing together the deck, I checked on him.

"Hey, Jacobson," he said as I approached.

"Hi, Lieutenant, what are you up to?"

"You can call me Jim, if you'd like, Jacobson," he said.

"Thank you Jim, sir," I said. I couldn't help it, the 'sir' reflex was nearly automatic after ten months in the Navy. "You can call me Jake, if you'd prefer."

"Jake Jacobson?" He smiled and shook his head. "I've always wondered about that. Family name?"

I laughed. "Well it is sir, but my first name is actually Alvin, after my father. My family calls me Al, but I picked up Jake in college. It stuck with me when I joined the Navy."

"Well, Jake, tell Captain we've got at least a six-knot current between these two islands." He tossed a small stick into the water and watched it float away, while holding a watch to his ear counting off seconds. "I think it's too strong for us to risk right now. If we leave just before slack tide, not only will the current be slower, but there's a good chance that it will also change directions before we get to the next island. So if we get swept away, we'll probably get swept back shortly thereafter."

"Any idea when that might be?"

"I watched the tides a bit yesterday. I think slack tide will be in four hours or so, but I'll keep checking and narrow the time. Tell Captain that."

"Okay, I'll also tell him where his watch is," I grinned.

"What? You think I slipped this off his wrist when he wasn't looking?" he joked back. "With all the salt and grit stuck to our skin, he definitely noticed when I scraped it over his hand!"

Jim was still throwing sticks into the water when we finished the raft,

The second island, as seen from the launch point of the first. Courtesy of the family of Ens. Al "Jake" Jacobson.

the paddles, and even two poles in case we needed to pole our way across. Now all we had to do was wait.

Time crawled. Insects buzzed loudly around my head while the sea sounded far away. At some point, I must have drifted off, for I woke up suddenly, and found the sand stuck thickly to my skin like a coat. The humidity was almost palpable.

"It's time," Jim said from the shore.

We lumbered to our feet. I carefully climbed down the short coral wall, into the shallows. The shock of the salt water rushing over my feet and into my wounds made me clench my teeth and suck in my breath. It was a good thing, I knew, for the salt to wash my feet clean of dirt and sand, but for a moment, the pain was nearly blinding.

We decided Captain and Howell should ride the first shift, at least until the water was deep enough for Howell to swim without putting too much stress on his bad knee. They carefully maneuvered onto the narrow "deck" and the rest of us seized the outrigger frame. The water splashed around our legs, then hips as we kept hauling the raft away from the old shore. After a few minutes of little headway, the sand beneath us suddenly dropped, and we were free-swimming, grasping the raft frame with one hand, and keeping our eyes fixed on the next beach. It was going to be a long swim, and already, the island was slipping north of us, as the current dragged us back to the sea.

"Listen!" Howell suddenly called. The low buzzing of the plane was almost imperceptible over the sounds of the ocean, but quickly grew louder. Captain and Howell tumbled into the water with us and waited tensely. The tiny dark shape of the plane appeared over the horizon to the southwest, and slowly grew larger. I grabbed my binoculars and scanned her, hoping and praying to see the white star of an American fighter we could signal, but, as we expected, it was the scheduled Japanese Zero. "Enemy patrol," I confirmed, dropping the binoculars and waiting for the right time…

"Wait for it….wait for it…" The Zero came closer while we clung to the raft waiting for the right moment. "Now!" Captain said and we dove under the raft, shielding ourselves and praying the Zero saw only some driftwood in the waves. The shadow streaked over us and departed north without deviating. My heart hammered as we surfaced, but the immediate danger was over.

Within moments, we had the raft loaded again and kicked off once more.

We didn't talk; the salt water got into the mouth when we tried. Swimming while hanging on to the raft was not mentally taxing and I found my mind wandering back to *Flier*, and the first days I had been on her. Then her first kill…

We had been fruitlessly chasing a northbound convoy *USS Silversides* reported to us when we intercepted a different convoy heading south.[24] The glassy sea made a daylight periscope attack impossible so we tailed them from a distance, waiting for night.

Two hours in, Buddy Vogt, sitting on Sonar in the Conning Tower said, "I'm detecting a distant depth charge attack, sir. Three… four… five… they're raining down heavily."

"Is it our convoy under attack?" Captain asked.

"Unknown, sir, but I have not detected any other ships in the area."

"Periscope depth, slow to five knots," Captain ordered, raising the attack periscope only enough to clear the eyepiece two feet above the floor. He crouched, gripping the handles, and peered intently through them.

He quietly counted the ships and smokestacks.

"Twelve depth charges now, sir," Vogt said.

---

[24] These events took place July 3 and 4, 1944.

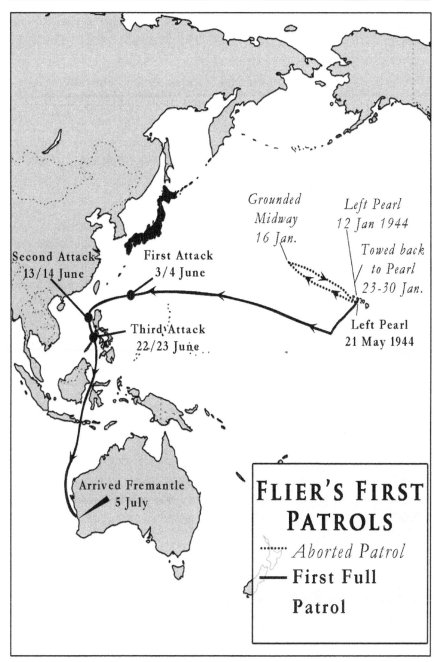

Grounded
Midway
16 Jan.

Left Pearl
12 Jan 1944

Towed back
to Pearl
23-30 Jan.

Second Attack
13/14 June

First Attack
3/4 June

Left Pearl
21 May 1944

Third Attack
22/23 June

Arrived Fremantle
5 July

FLIER'S FIRST
PATROLS

······ *Aborted Patrol*

—— First Full
Patrol

This map shows Flier's first two patrols. Between the aborted and first patrol, she was overhauled at Mare Island, California.

"Thank you, keep me informed," Captain said, shifting slightly from his position.

"Sir?" Liddell asked.

"They're not behaving as if they are under attack, but they're too far away for me to see the ships, only the smoke trails, and they don't look any different than before." he muttered.

Over the next several hours we waited for updates to filter through, hoping that we'd finally engage our first target. Vogt kept a verbal tally of the depth charges. "Eighteen now, sir."

"Twenty-two now, sir,"

"Still twenty-two, sir."

"Final tally, sir: twenty-two. I did not detect any large explosions indicating a damaged vessel."

Captain and Jim took turns on the periscope, raising it up for a momentary glance at the advancing target, then a full sweep of the area, before sending it descending back down. We relied mostly on Vogt's Sonar to tell us what was happening. At one point, we spotted a lone vessel heading north at high speed, too far away to identify or pursue. It was heading in the direction of our convoy, and might have been reinforcements.

After six hours, as the sun set, Captain ordered *Flier* to turn away from the target in preparation for surfacing in the open range. He raised the periscope again, and reported, "Target bearing one–zero–nine." We recorded the position on the chart, while Captain did the three-sixty, when he suddenly said, "Wait…wait a moment…" He peered intently, increased magnification once, then again. "I have a second target, bearing…two–one–zero. Thus far, it appears to be one ship."

We watched both targets carefully, taking readings on heading and position every two minutes. The new target, which proved to be yet another convoy, was approaching faster than the first target, and coming closer.

"Which one, Captain?" Jim asked, pointing at the two tracks of our targets.

Captain looked over the chart for a moment, then, "The new target. It's closer, we have a more favorable position, and that other convoy may already be under attack. I'd rather not run afoul of someone else's prey.[25]

"Change course, turn to heading two–seven–five until the target convoy is at approximately bearing one–six–five. I want them on our port flank. Prepare for surface."

"Aye, sir," Kit Pourciau said, from the helm.

The moon was nearly full and illuminated everything for miles when Captain, four lookouts, and I, climbed onto the Bridge, searching the horizon for our convoy. They were behind and east of us now, nearly ten miles away, and we could see the eight ships, four freighters and four fully-armed escorts, zigzagging in the standard anti-submarine pattern. Whatever cargo they carried was valuable, for this was far more than the standard escort.

A low rumble of thunder reached my ears, and I trained my binoculars on the dazzling firefight from our first convoy over thirty miles away.

With a blinding flare, and several second later, a *boom,* one of our new target's escorts roared back with her big guns, firing in the direction of the original convoy. But then they sped north, toward us, ignoring any further plight of their fellows.

We watched for an hour, as they traveled past us, when the convoy suddenly changed direction, heading straight for us.

"Radar! Watch them, see if this is a zig or a base course change," Captain ordered the Conning Tower.

A zig meant they would zag back in a few minutes, and we'd have to decide on a strategy, but if they had just changed course, they literally were going to sail right into us.

Minutes passed, and they kept coming. Ten minutes passed, then twenty minutes. Then the convoy changed direction, but not back onto their original course. "That had to have been a base course change, sir!" I heard a muffled voice excitedly call.

"All right then. Rig for Dive!" Captain shouted, grabbing the dive

---

[25] Unknown to Cmdr. Crowley, three more submarines were nearby. *USS Pilotfish (SS-386), USS Pintado (SS-387),* and *USS Shark (II) (SS-314)* were indeed attacking a number of ships and multiple convoys only a few miles away, though it is unclear whether they were attacking the convoy *Flier* saw first, or yet another one. *Flier* never saw the other three, and they did not report seeing *Flier.*

alarm and pulling it twice. We all dropped down the hatch and dogged it shut behind us. Moments later heard the waves slapping and gurgling on the other side of the Conning Tower walls.

The lookouts went below, but Captain and I went to our stations in the Conning Tower, where Jim was working on the map table. "ETA?" Captain asked.

"Providing they maintain their current eight-knot speed, they'll be in range in forty-five minutes."

"Good. Jacobson, assist Liddell on navigation and get Howell up here to man the sonar for approach."

The Conning Tower was quiet as we waited, watching Howell peering intently into the SJ Radar Station, and Vogt listening to the rumble and swish of their propellers, tracking the convoy's approach. They were moving fast, and it wouldn't be long now...

"They're changing course, Captain!" Howell called out. "New course is..." it took several minutes for the surface convoy to complete their turn, "The new course is one–nine–two, sir."

"One–nine–two?" The convoy was now heading almost straight south, directly away from us now. Captain quickly raised the periscope and grabbing the steel handles as they emerged out of their well in the floor. He spun around, and swore. "Maybe that wasn't a base course change after all. Keep an eye on them."

Half-hour later, it was obvious our optimism of an early, easy first kill was premature. They were back on their original course, passing south of us over nine miles away. We were going to have to run fast on the surface to catch them.

By the time I went back on lookout duty, they were south-west of us now, almost to our side, steaming safely in the night. Captain and Jim watched them for a few moments, then had a short whispered consultation. I heard the words "End-Around," then Jim went back downstairs, and moments later, *Flier's* props bore down, lifting her bow as she roared north-west, racing the convoy. "Jacobson!" Captain's voice called back to me, "Tell me if they change their base course!"

So we were doing an end-around. *Flier* was going to race ahead of them keeping them on our port side, cut off their course, and wait for them to come to us.

We were so close that through my binoculars, I could make out the details of every ship in the convoy quite clearly, down to the flare of a match lighting a cigarette, and the glowing tips of other cigarettes the sailors clenched in their teeth as they went about their work. Teddy relieved me after an hour, and I went downstairs to work at the map table as we continued our chase.

Flier flew at top speed for three hours. The convoy slowly lost ground, dropping behind us, blissfully unaware they were being stalked.

The moon was setting at 0320 hours when we turned neatly around and settled low to the water, waiting for the convoy to catch up to us. I relieved Teddy on the deck, but a half-hour later, Captain, satisfied that our convoy would cooperate this time, muttered, "Beautiful," then, "Rig for dive!"

We jumped down the Bridge hatch and dogged it shut once again, with a sense of déjà vu, as we waited, listening to Howell's reports as they zigged, zagged, and kept coming on.

My watch said 0447 hours when Howell announced, "Target twenty-one-hundred yards out."

Captain gripped the periscope and swung it around, before giving a low whistle. "Oh, perfect." We waited quietly for the next order. "They've split into two columns, and one is going to pass our bow, and one our stern. If we fire all tubes with proper timing, we can take out all four freighters before the escorts know what's happening. Ready all torpedo tubes, and battle stations."

"*GONG! GONG! GONG!*" sounded the General Quarters alarm. I heard the pounding of the feet below us as men ran to their stations. The floor shuddered sharply as a water-tight door slammed shut, then another, and another. In less than a minute, all was quiet again, and the lights flickered from white to red.

The lack of a moon was an advantage, making our exposed periscope head all but invisible. Captain could hardly keep his voice steady from the excitement as he started to track his targets, two spreads of three torpedoes from the bow and two spreads of two torpedoes from the stern. We counted down, three…two…one…

"Fire one!" Captain called on the intercom, clicking the button clenched in his hand.

"One away!" Chief Gwinn's voice responded over the intercom.

Seconds later, "Fire two!"

"Two away!"

Captain quickly fired all six, watching the bubbling trails stream away to our targets with satisfaction, then he swiftly swung around the periscope to finish final calculations on the stern targets.

"Dammit!" he swore. "The targets are too close to us to safely fire right now, we may miss this shot."

On Sonar, Vogt announced, "Torpedo one hit, sir!"

Captain swung back around, and grinned, "She's smoking amidships!"

I mentally counted down torpedo two's trajectory. *'Three...two...one...'*

"A hit on torpedo two!" Vogt crowed.

'Three...two...one...'

Nothing.

"Miss on three," Vogt reported, then, moments later, "A hit on four!"

"We've got the second ship!" Captain said, pressing his face to the eyeglass. "And she looks like she's dead in the water!" He swung a quick one-eighty, then, "*Send her deep!*"

He sent the periscope shooting down in its well, as *Flier's* deck tilted sharply, heading for safety. "We've got the two trailing escorts coming on us," he announced to no one in particular. He looked around the room and spotted me. "Jacobson, how long have you been on duty?"

"Since 1350, sir," I replied.

"Sixteen hours?! You're relieved."

I dropped down the ladder and headed for my cabin, undogging and re-dogging the bulkhead on the way there. No use arguing with Captain about the fact that he'd been on duty longer than I had.

As I made my way down the narrow passage to my spartan cabin, I wondered what I should do. I'd only heard stories of what a depth charge attack felt like. Officer's Country was quiet, felt deserted. My cabin was empty, my roommate, Herb Miner, apparently still on duty. I sat nervously on the edge of my bunk, waiting. The pressure from *Flier's* long dive was already intense, and I swallowed often, popping and equalizing my ears. The temperature climbed quickly.

Flier's deck finally leveled out gently, then the air conditioning sputtered and died. We'd gone "all quiet," turning off all systems that were not absolutely necessary for life. The temperature rose quickly and the red lights made it seem hotter than ever. Sweat began to pour down my body, so I stripped off my uniform, leaving only my sodden skivvies, as I waited alone in my cabin which seemed even smaller than usual.

Rumble.

Flier barely quaked in the first depth charge attack, too far off to do much damage. I crouched down on the floor, keeping all my joints loose and unlocked as I had been taught, wondering if this was going to be so bad after all.

Rumble. RUMBLE.

They were closer, but still, *Flier* barely felt them.

I waited, not moving, trying to keep so still that the surface boats' sonar, if they had it, couldn't find us. I heard nothing for several minutes.

Click!

"Oh my—" I never finished my whispered prayer.

WHAM!

Flier slammed me into the wall of my cabin and dropped me to the floor. I heard the crash of dishes in the Pantry and someone groan there. I shook my head to clear my eyes of the stars, vaguely aware of the sounds of stocking feet racing down the hallway, as the fire crews checked for damage.

"*Click!*"

WHAM!

I tried to brace my feet against the wall and the bed frame, but *Flier* tossed me like a rag doll, cracking my head against something hard. I groaned, looking up at the ceiling. Photos of Miner's wife and son, as well as my family, fluttered down, landing on my face. Water from the super-humid air condensed on the metal walls, running down to the floor. In the red battle lights, it looked like *Flier* was bleeding.

"Jake!" An urgent whisper sounded in the hallway. "Jake, you okay?"

It was Ed, crawling down the hall.

"I think so," I whispered, rubbing my throbbing skull, "no blood at least."

"Get in the Wardroom, move!" He hissed back, crawling farther down the hall. "Anyone in here?" I heard him whisper in the next cabin.

I belly-crawled out of my cabin, hugging the green linoleum floor, pushing past Ed's legs, when I heard a moan from the Pantry.

"Turner!" Ed's whispered, and he crouched and stepped into the pantry. "You all right, man?" He asked.

"Yes, sir," he muttered.

"Come on, get in the Wardroom with Ensign Jacobson and me."

"Did you get the rest of the china secured?" Ed asked, as they clambered into the room, his face worried. "Another crash like that could lead their Sonar guys to us."

"What's still whole isn't gonna move." Turner said, sitting next to me on the narrow bench.

"Okay you two, listen to me," Ed said, settling in the bench across from us. "The trick to riding this out is to not fully extend any joint, or you'll get hurt. Grab the edge of the table and push your spine into the back cushion, curl your head down and tuck your chin to your chest. Brace your toes against the floor."

We followed his instructions. "Now what?" I whispered back.

"Now's the worst part. Now we wait."

I started shaking in shock. Before, I had never understood the older hands saying how the waiting was the worst, and now I did. Just to sit, helpless, praying that the next one would fall just far enough away to survive one more explosion, one more...

Click!

WHAM!

Flier bucked and rolled, but I pushed back, and rode it out. It wasn't until we let out our breath as she drifted to a stop that I realized any of us were holding it. There was a strange sound above us though: a swishing, bubbling sound.

"What is that sound?" I whispered to Ed, afraid it might be a leak somewhere.

"Just all that water swirling through the superstructure under the deck. Nothing to worry about. If we can hear the swishing, we're still alive."

"*Click!*"

WHAM!

Swish, swish, gurgle, gurgle….

We panted for a moment, then grinned at each other when the red lights suddenly flickered, then went out. We were left in the pitch black, waiting.

"That's seven thus far," Ed's voice whispered.

Nothing I had experienced before had prepared me for this. Ten, then fifteen, then seventeen explosions rattled and tossed the sub around like a tennis ball.

Every part of my body ached, even my jaw from the unconscious clenching. Sweat streamed down my face, dripped off my nose and into my eyes as I stayed curled in my seat. My head throbbed, as I prayed that each depth charge was the last one.

Noises I'd never noticed before seemed painfully loud. The creak of the Wardroom bench, the splash of sweat dripping to the table or deck, the sound of the three of us breathing, but most of all, the ticking of the Wardroom clock seemed to echo horribly in the room. *Tick…tick…tick…* I had quickly given up counting seconds to track the time, but the clock didn't. The relentless sound drove me nuts.

Tick…tick…tick…tick…tick.

Click!

WHAM!

Swish…swish…gurgle…gurgle…

Tick…tick…tick…tick…tick…

After what seemed like an eternity, suddenly, the red lights feebly flickered on again, and I glanced at that infuriating clock. We had been under attack for over one and a half hours. The light at least made us feel a little better, though we didn't relax yet. We watched and waited as ten minutes passed, then twenty, still braced, and still waiting.

Then the white lights flashed on, and the air conditioning rattled loudly, blasting us with a welcome breath of stale air. *Flier's* deck tilted up gently and headed for the surface.

We unclenched everything and sighed, looking at each other with relief.

"Congratulations, you two," Ed said, "You've survived your first depth charge attack." He peered at me and grinned, "You know, I think that tan of yours is gone Jake, you're whiter than snow now!"

"You sure you're not talking about me?" Turner joked.

We laughed in relief as we stood, stretched and cracked back into shape.

Despite being sweat-soaked, I dressed and reported back to the Control Room. Everyone was picking up and putting things back in position, while nursing bruises, aching joints, and bloodied faces. Liddell was sending anyone needing Doc to Crew's Quarters, and put me to work in the Conning Tower with the Captain.

Under the harsh lights, his face looked deathly white, with dark circles under his blood-shot eyes. He looked up as I climbed into the Tower.

"Jacobson, how many do you see?" he said, pointing at the periscope.

I shoved my eyes against the glass and squinted at the dark images, then magnified them twice. Our convoy was fleeing east now, but there were not as many of them as before. I counted quickly, and stood up.

"Seven, sir," I replied.

"That's what I count. We got at least one, then."

I looked down the Conning Tower Hatch. Either Doc was lightning-fast in his work, or he'd been working by battle-lantern through the attack. I saw guys sporting bandages on arms, hands, occasionally around a head, and some limped their way through the Control Room on their way back to their duty stations, checking systems, working *Flier* over. Reports started to pour in over the next few minutes as Captain watched the convoy race away. Despite the pounding, *Flier* seemed to be whole.

"Well, sir?" Liddell called up from the Control Room.

"Something that well-guarded has got to be important…" Captain mused to himself. "I don't know of any other submarines in the area who could pick up the chase…let's finish what we started."

But it wasn't to be. The nervous escorts now ran their sonar almost continuously, and no amount of maneuvering on our part ever let us get close enough for a shot before two to three escorts charged us. We gave up the chase, and headed back to the attack area, looking for proof of sinking and anything that might help intelligence back home.

Even a day and a half later, the water was thickly covered in scorched oil, smothering the waves. Ed, Captain and I stood on the bridge beneath

First Convoy
Flier Found

USS Flier's
Track

USS Silversides
Track

Convoy Flier
Attacked

Convoy Silversides
Reported

1. While seeking a convoy *Silversides* reported, *Flier* finds a different convoy, and a second convoy. First convoy appears to be under attack, so *Flier* decides to do end-around attack on second convoy.

2. *Flier* races ahead of convoy, and sits still while escorts pass. Fires two spreads of three torpedoes. Two hit first, one hits second. Escorts turn for attack.

3. First victim sinks, freighters continue on while escorts attack *Flier*, before leaving area.

◊ Escort   ⊥ Flier

◆ Freighter   ✘ Wrecked Ship

✳ Depth Charge/Explosion

N

W **E**

S

FIRST ATTACK
JUNE 3-4 1944

the lookouts, searching for debris that the deck crew could pull alongside and haul aboard. The life rings were an early find, floating out at the edge of the field, before the oil was more than a few rainbow colored strands. "Bring two of those up," Captain said, pointing at the liferings. "I have an idea for those."

We hauled two aboard, though our victim's name and homeport were written in Japanese figures, so we still didn't know who she had been.

Then *Flier* entered the thick of the field, shattered debris bumping against her hull. We saw six life boats floating aimlessly ahead.

"Cap'n!" one of the lookouts called from overhead. "Just off the port bow, that life boat has something in it."

Flier changed course to draw close enough for the deck crew to grab her with the boat hooks and draw her alongside. Someone jumped down into the empty boat, and grabbed a pile of papers that looked like it had been hastily tied together and wrapped in canvas.

"Anything written on it?" Captain called down.

"Yes sir, it's all in Japanese, but this might be the log book and who knows what the rest are. There's a lot of handwriting though."

"HQ will know how to have it translated. Let's bring that up."

The smell of burnt fuel grew stronger, nearly dizzying, as we plowed farther in. A part of a white pilothouse floated past, with a ship's wheel and other instruments inside. Captain ordered a closer examination of it one, hoping, perhaps for the name of our victim.

"Well whaddaya know, this thing was equipped with New York merchandise," A crewman called up.

"What do you mean?" Captain called down.

"The Gyro is still intact in here sir, and you can see it, clear as day, 'Sperry Marine, New York, New York.'"

"She might have been an old civilian ship before the war, I suppose, or purchased from the USA." Or captured and requisitioned after a paint job.

Flier nudged further into the mess. We started to see bodies floating in the waves, some wearing uniforms. They didn't look like Navy sailors. What was this?

Captain gestured to haul a few bodies out of the water. If something was going on and Japan was shipping a lot of guys back to the homeland,

HQ would want to know.

We all knew from our own military set up that any information would most likely be with an officer. We found two. Each landed with a sodden thud, water from their clothes raining down through the deck, striking *Flier's* metal pressure hull below.

"This one looks like he's in the Army, sir, though I'm not sure what rank." a crewman said, rifling through his sodden pockets for papers, or anything that might prove useful to Navy intelligence.

"This one too, Army officer of some kind," another Flier said, about his man. They removed all papers, notebooks, anything of value, including their canteens. I didn't know if any of the paperwork would still be useful, after so long in the water. We slid the bodies back into the sea. With no way to bury or transport them, there was nothing else we could do.

We came to what must have been the cargo hold. Crates, some intact, others shattered, floated in the muck. A few gently smacked and skittered down *Flier's* sides. The crew pushed and prodded the crates away from us to keep us clear. One crate turned gently after it was poled away, and I saw three bodies curled inside.

Another crate drifted past, and I saw another man laying back, eyes staring. Then another. And another. We just watched, stunned, and realized there were far too many people here, dozens, hundreds even, than was needed to man a ship, even one of her size. Most were wearing uniforms. This was why that convoy had been so highly protected.

"Try to keep them clear," Captain instructed grimly to the men on the deck. "Listen for any shouts, we can take one or two survivors, I think."

But it was quiet. If there were survivors, they never called. We gently nosed out of the debris field, and left it behind.

The rumble of thunder brought me back to the present. The rain squall swept over us, pouring down in thick, fat drops. We opened our mouths to the sky like baby birds, trying to capture a drop or two, but the rain seemed to splatter everywhere but my parched mouth. It was quick and heavy and soon over, crossing to our new island. I thought longingly of the shells we had left out on our old beach, now undoubtedly full, and wished that someone had spread several on the beach on the new island.

We were three-quarters of the way across now, drifting south with the weakening current, when the tide changed, sweeping us north to the lee of the island. We pulled and struggled but the island drifted farther and farther south, as the light from the setting sun began to wane.

"Pull, men!" Captain yelled from the front of the raft.

The sun set, and the island faded from brilliant white and green to a dark shadow in what seemed like minutes. My feet finally struck ground and we slipped and stumbled up the silvery grey beach, dragging the raft behind us above the tide line.

"Get rest wherever you can, men," Captain rasped out. He hobbled up to the edge of the trees and fell asleep quickly.

It was easier said than done. The beach here was littered with a few lumps of broken coral on top of the sand. The rapidly cooling night air whisked the water from my skin, leaving the crusty salt behind. I started to shiver as I pitched some of the coral chunks into the water and burrowed into the still-warm sand, piling more on top of me like a blanket. The grains grated against my skin, but the shallow sandy blanket kept the wind off me, and let the heat seep into my muscles.

But I couldn't stop shivering. Ten minutes later, I'd shaken the coating off, and burrowing deeper only exposed wet, cold sand. I tried to sleep, banks of sand piled beside me to shelter me from the wind, but, what seemed like moments later, I was wide awake, shaking so hard I was nearly convulsing. I struggled to my feet and limped up and down the beach, slapping my arms against my chest, trying to warm myself.

The moon was halfway up the sky, revealing that I had actually slept for quite a while. Under her light, I could see the shadows of several of my crewmates. Most of them seemed to have had the same idea and burrowed into the sand, and promptly shivered everything off, leaving a little wall of sand around the human-shaped trough. One trough other than mine was empty.

I stamped my feet as I walked, trying to pound life back into my numb legs, sucking in my breath through clenched teeth when they came to life again with fiery shock.

"You, too?" I heard Jim's voice rasp. His shadowy figure limped out from under the trees ahead of me.

"You mean the inability to sleep, or the pain in my feet?"

"Does it matter?" Jim said.

"Not really," I said, blowing and half expecting to see the fog of my breath. "If only I could get warm, I'd be able to sleep."

"Same here," he said, blowing into his cupped hands. "I'm trying to walk enough to stop shivering and go back to sleep."

We paced up and down the beachI had no idea what the temperature was now, but it felt colder than it should have been this close to the Equator. We walked back to the huddle of the crew and though we'd finally stopped shivering, neither of us was warm.

"Well, good-night Jake, I only hope I don't start shivering before I can fall asleep."

"Jim? What if we buried ourselves together? Combining body heat with the sand, we may warm up and stay warm for the rest of the night." I said.

"Anything's worth a try, I suppose, though I doubt you're much warmer than I!"

We quietly plowed the sand out of the trench until it was long and wide enough for Jim's frame. We lay back to back, finding neither was warmer than the other. The sand, no longer warm from the sun's heat, felt like we'd buried ourselves in an ice-block. We started to shiver again.

"Come on, Jake," Jim's voice carried a note of amusement. "Shake in unison, or we'll lose our blanket faster than before."

We were surrounded by our sand wall in a few minutes.

"Oh, well, good-night Jake," Jim said, and lay still beside me.

I shivered myself to sleep, and when I woke again, Jim was gone, the moon was low, and Baumgart and Howell were pacing the beach, trying to calm their shakes.

I prayed for the sun's rise. I was already dangerously burnt, but sunlight at least meant warmth.

We were all awake by dawn, but being on the west side of the island, we saw only the colored sky; the sun itself was hidden behind the trees. The effect was the same, however: the air quickly warmed and shimmered with the tropical heat, and I felt my body relax and stop trembling.

"What the hell happened to you, Earl?" Wes Miller exclaimed.

In the light, I could see Baumgart's body was covered in hundreds of red pockmarks from his neck to his feet. "Something kept biting me all night long! I couldn't believe the rest of you slept so soundly!" He looked at us closely, but no one else had the marks on our body. "How——?"

"Where were you sleeping, Baumgart?" Captain asked, with a smile hovering on his lips.

"Over there," Baumgart pointed at a trench that was closer to the water than anyone else's.

Captain, an Annapolis native, walked over, poked the sand at the foot of the trench and grinned. "Ever hear of sand crabs, son?" he said, holding the minute thing in the palm of his hand.

"Oh, hell!" Baumgart groaned, scratching at the welts all over his body.

"Next time," Captain said, clapping his hand on Earl's shoulder, as the rest of us laughed, "sleep as far away from the water as possible.

"Okay, slack tide will be this evening again, so we're going to have to walk to a launch point on the east side of the island. Only question is, long way around," he pointed south-west, "or short way?" He pointed north east.

"Sir?" Howell said, "I *really* don't like the look of those rocks," He said, thumbing toward the northeast.

I didn't either. The beach we stood on quickly graduated from the stones on sand to solely jagged rocks a short distance from where we stood, with another short ridge lifting the jungle above the ocean.

"Neither do I," Wes said. "Trust me, sir, walking on that is horrible and takes forever."

"I vote for the long way around," I said. "We may be able to see an American ship using the Straits and get picked up. Not to mention the coconuts seem to wash up more on the southern side; we might find a good one today."

"Oh, food…" Wes said.

Everyone quickly echoed the long way around idea, and Captain nodded, "Everyone take it easy then, and keep to the shade whenever possible. I don't need anyone pushing too hard and getting heatstroke."

We set off to the south, rounding the point to the powder soft beach. Here in the shallows the coral was covered with a luxurious coat of seaweed that cushioned the feet. Immersed in the cool water, despite the salt sting, my feet felt better than they had in days, but the sun beat down mercilessly on my already burnt skin. My undershirt spared my chest and back, but blisters were forming on my forearms.

Soon, we were taking shifts, some dragging the raft through the soft surf, and others shielding themselves beneath the trees.

I scanned the sky and horizon with my binoculars but never saw a sign of another ship of any nation. We may as well have been at the end of the world for all the traffic we had seen since *Flier's* demise.

Coconuts lay everywhere, but most were obviously split and spoiled. The few that were not were soon smashed open, spewing the sickly-sweet rotten milk over us. We stopped talking, our raw throats in agony, searching for even a swallow of saliva that had long since dried up.

We collapsed on the far side of the island as the afternoon patrol buzzed overhead. We heard it coming a long way away this time, and were well under shade when it passed, but I was starting to wonder if the pilot even bothered to look at these little islands.

"No food, no water, we're never going to survive this," someone grumbled.

"Hey," I said. "If you start talking like that, we'll never get home. Whatever comes, comes, and whatever doesn't, well, okay. The only way we'll get out of this is to keep pushing on." My dad used to say something like that all the time to us. He was no stranger to hard work, purchasing a foundry using his life savings then re-building it after it burned to the ground a few months later. Now it was thriving and making stuff for the war effort.

"Jacobson's right," Captain said. "Just focus on the job at hand, and let the chips fall where they may."

We dozed under the overhanging palm fronds, taking turns watching the current for slack tide, and hauled ourselves out to the surf for the swim when the call came. We held on to the raft, but the water here was shallow, and we had waded nearly a third of the way to the tiny rock between us and the big island before the sea floor finally dropped out from beneath us and we started swimming.

Jim, behind me, poked me in the shoulder, then pointed north. I looked, and saw three dark dorsal fins circling in the water not far away. I did not know what type of sharks lived around here, but I just kept swimming. '*Whatever comes, comes,*' I reminded myself.

It was nearly sunset when we staggered onto the western beach of this tiny third island, and promptly burrowed into the warm sand to try to warm up before trying to sleep for the night. I spent that night much like the previous three: wishing for the sun and warmth, even though it now hurt like hell to move.

I ached all over when I woke the next morning. My hands and feet felt frozen, and my heart pounded with the slightest movement. It was our fifth day since *Flier*, and tonight, we would be on the big island that loomed just east of us. I just hoped it had fresh water near where we landed.

We started around the southern shore without talking about it today. No one was in the mood to talk, and I wondered if I even could. My tongue seemed to have swollen to the size of my mouth, and was bone dry.

This island was rounder, and there appeared to be point on the south-eastern tip which we decided to use as a launch-point. It also kept us hidden from the big island for as long as possible, in case someone was watching.

"Hey, what's this?" Wes whispered and pointed.

Hauled up on the shore was an old dugout canoe, with holes punched in its hull. It was too far gone to be of use, but there was no mistaking that someone had been here not too long ago.

"Survey the area," Captain quickly rasped, kneeling down for a better look, but not touching a thing.

He gave more orders while I searched the jungle for any signs of further occupation of this island. Had natives been here, or had this been a Japanese outpost at one point?

Several yards down the beach, Baumgart grunted at me through his cracked lips. "What do you make of that, sir?"

It looked like a clear path, leading into the jungle. I had roamed many like these in the woods and dunes near home, most of which eventually came to nothing, but we really couldn't afford to take the chance.

The powdered coral beach quickly gave way to hard rock, and the bracken and debris from the jungle was not cushion enough against further damage to our feet. It led upward and certainly looked clearly marked, but

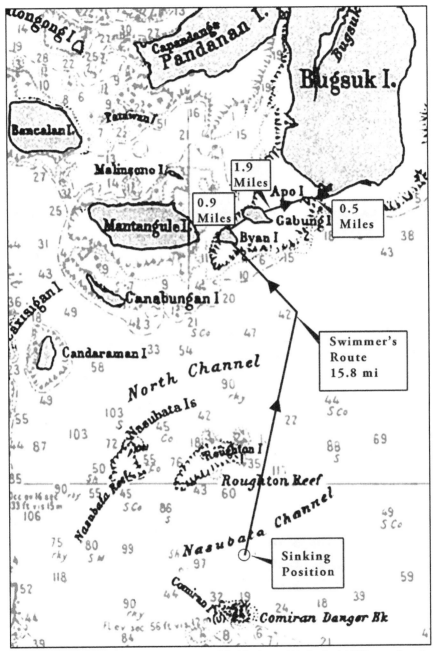

During the escape, the men did not know the names of the islands on which they landed. This map shows the approximate route as later plotted by Jacobson. (Original map from the family of Al "Jake" Jacobson)

after walking a few hundred feet, the path abruptly ended, and Baumgart and I were left standing, surrounded by jungle and the shrieks of monkeys that leapt over our heads.

"Nothing after all, then," Baumgart muttered.

"Given some of the other options, I'll take 'nothing'," I replied.

Everyone had already finished their survey and gathered together when we re-emerged out of the jungle. Captain nodded when I told him what we found, and signaled the group to move to the point. Still, that dugout made us wary, and I know I kept a sharper eye on the jungle than before.

We trudged on, and the sun rose higher. It was almost noon and we were walking through the coconut fields again. With little hope, I grasped yet another seemingly good one, and pounded it against a tree trunk. *Thud, thud, crack,* it opened, spilling milk into the sands. I braced myself for the rotten smell to roll over me, but the milk streaming over my hands and down my legs smelled sweet and clean. "A good one!" I announced as loudly as I could, though still barely a hoarse whisper. "I've got a good one!" I quickly flipped it over to retain what was left of the milk and pried it open, but all of the milk had drained in the sand.

"No matter," Jim said, grinning, "At least it's food, finally. We're almost to the point, we can eat it there."

I cradled our hard-sought prize and stumbled after the group, most of whom were grinning at me and the coconut. It was wonderful to have a bit of luck again after five days.

We reached the point and looked with satisfaction at the big island, our goal for the evening. It was almost mountainous and was covered in dense jungle. I saw birds flitting through the trees and good spots for fishing near the beach. It looked so promising that I...wait a moment. I stared suddenly at one point near the water's edge. It was almost hidden in the trees. I blinked, shook my head and stared again. It was still there.

"What the—?" I heard Jim breathe. I passed the coconut to him in a daze, and grabbed my binoculars, and shoved them against my eyes. "Jacobson?" Captain held out his hands for the binoculars, which I swiftly handed to him.

"You see what I see?" Russo asked no one in particular.

"A house. It's a house!" Tremaine breathed.

7

SIGNS OF CIVILIZATION

The plan had been to wait for slack tide again, but with the evidence of habitation so close by, we didn't want to arrive there while we could easily be seen. We dragged the raft high off the beach and threw it under a bunch of undergrowth, and kept to the shadows as much as possible. My binoculars were passed from person to person as we scanned every inch of the island. I thought I saw some other structures hidden in the trees, but it was impossible to see clearly. The one house was weathered to a silver-grey, and appeared abandoned. Broken branches laid haphazardly on the still-intact thatched roof. The structure itself appeared solid, no sagging lines or leaning walls, so it might have been abandoned only a short while before. Or it might be disguised to look abandoned.

"If we leave during the height of slack tide, and keep low to the water, we'll arrive in the evening, a couple of hours before sunset," Captain announced to us after a couple of hours of watching. "That will hopefully give us enough light to maneuver to somewhere we can set up camp tonight, and still make us difficult to see if anyone is watching. Questions?"

"We're still eating first, right?" Wes asked.

We all laughed. The coconut was smashed against a tree and we scraped the meat off the shattered husk with our teeth. It was hard work for not much gain, but it tasted heavenly after the past few days. I let it roll around my tongue, trying to suck as much flavor as I could from it, hoping that doing so would make me feel fuller.

The afternoon patrol buzzed overhead, and we dozed in the shade, conserving what strength we had. All too soon, it was time to start out again.

Jim, Captain, and I studied the terrain near the house. It sat at the head of a small sheltered bay, the other side made up by a small, jutting peninsula. We decided the safest route would be to land on the opposite side of that peninsula, then hike all the way around the bay to the house. If necessary, we could return to the raft and keep going. It wasn't much of a plan but it was what we had.

Slack tide arrived and we dragged our little raft down to the water for what we hoped would be the last time. The water was shallow, and we had to crouch, while hanging on to the raft.

It took four hours to finish crossing the short distance, fighting the swift currents all the way. The sun was low in the sky when we finally landed. We would have a short time to round the bay and reach the house before dark.

We pulled the raft onto the shore and made our way quietly along. At the end of the peninsula we found ourselves in a coconut grove. Strong, well-maintained trees soared to the sky in neat rows, each absolutely laden with coconuts. Just behind the trees lay the remains of a small village.

A few of the houses, we saw, had been burned to the ground, but most were still standing. The walls, made of bamboo, leaned drunkenly in every direction. Miniature coconut trees blocked doors to these small huts, the thatched roofs starting to collapse in places. Tremaine and Russo swept away a pile of sand, pulling up the tattered remains of a rattan fence which must have fallen down some time ago. The whole place was eerily quiet, but there were no indications of bones or blood or a recent attack.

We quickly separated into pairs and explored, looking for evidence that the Japanese had been here. The rest concentrated their search in the village, but Baumgart and I headed back to the coconut farm. The sand under the trees was soft and silky, and unmarked by footprints.

A coconut dropped from its tree in a thick, green husk. "At least," I joked, "We finally know we have fresh coconuts."

"Oh? Found one that bit you, sir?" he said, grinning.

I picked that one up and looked around. It must have been early in the season. Despite the heavily-laden trees, there were few coconuts on the ground.

We saw no one and no signs of recent activity. The place was so clean that if it wasn't for the neat rows of trees and the ruins of the village, I would have thought no one had ever been through here. Baumgart and I gathered about a dozen coconuts between us, and headed after the Fliers, who were hiking for the main house.

It stood next to a cleared courtyard area backed by the jungle. The

The cistern the Fliers found, photographed many years later. The structures behind it were not there in 1944. Courtesy of the family of Ens. Al "Jake" Jacobson.

windows were empty and dark.

I thought the Fliers would be scattered around the clearing, exploringthe place, but they were crowded around a large cement block. Baumgart and I looked at each other, shrugged, and walked towards the house when we head Howell nearly moan, "Water! I'd forgotten how good it is!"

We dropped the coconuts and shuffled quickly to the cistern. Captain, turning away from it, saw us coming. "Hold up there, guys. I realize you're dying of thirst, but take only a few sips right now. If you drink too much, you may get sick. Take it easy."

Most of the guys were already leaving the cistern regretfully, but Howell continued to drink handful after handful.

Although it was warm, stale and smelled sweetly bitter, the first trickle down my throat felt better than I had ever imagined, and I fought myself not to follow Howell's example. Two handfuls of water later, I forced myself away from the cistern into the house to keep from plunging in face-first.

Despite the light musty smell, the house appeared mostly dry and sound. In many ways, it looked similar to the small village homes, though on a grander scale. There was a shaded porch and separate rooms. The largest must have been the living area, three bedrooms, and another room, littered with paper, which might have been an office. Most doors sagged sadly on broken hinges or had been wrenched off and now lay flat. Tattered shades half-hanged from their window frames, others were missing or lying crumpled on the floor. Some areas of the walls featured darkened rectangles, as though a piece of long-gone furniture had once stood there and protected the wood from the sun's light. Small stripes of paper which must have once been kept in the "office," now lay all over, probably where the last breeze left them. I picked up a couple and saw they were receipts, surprisingly written in English. One was for the sale of a load of lumber, another for several head of cattle, and both were dated 1941. I picked up several more, and noticed that none of the receipts were dated any later than late 1941. Whoever had owned this house must have been a prosperous business owner or merchant, but had vanished right before or after the Japanese invasion.

"Ensign Jacobson?" Baumgart's voice echoed in the empty rooms. "There you are. We're going to crack open the coconuts for the feast now, unless you want to give me your share?"

"Not on your life."

Our dreams of a feast faded as we began the arduous task of removing the husk from the coconut. While cracking open the brown nuts we found washed up on various shores was relatively easy, the thick, fibrous coat on these coconuts thwarted our initial efforts. We tried pounding one against the ground, the walls, and the corners of the walls. Finally, searching the ground, we found a broken rock with a sharp edge. Bracing that against a wall, and taking turns ramming that coconut onto that rock, we finally managed to cut into the fibrous coating and start peeling it back from the nut. It was dark when we finally peeled the hairy brown nut from the husk with a quiet cheer. We quickly pounded a hole in the eye, each taking a swallow of the sweet milk before smashing apart the nut to scrape the flesh from the shell with our teeth. No one felt up to the task of breaking open another one.

"I'll take first watch tonight," Captain said as we entered the house, after our small, welcome, meal. "We'll all have to take turns tonight, just in case the locals aren't gone. Wake your replacement when your time is up." We nodded sleepily, most of us past caring anyway. I claimed a door I had seen earlier, and as I stretched out on it, fell quickly into a dreamless sleep.

A groan woke me suddenly. In the moonlight now spilling through the windows, I saw Howell doubled in agony, his teeth clenched. Captain and Jim woke and were at his side in a moment. "What is it?" Jim asked.

"My stomach is killing me. My head is throbbing, and my hands and feet feel like they're being stabbed with hundreds of needles." He was trying to keep quiet, but the rest of us were awake and alert already.

Howell suddenly rolled over and retched all over the floor, losing most, if not all, of his meager dinner.

"I told you not to drink all that water," Captain mildly scolded.

"Try to rest, you'll be fine by morning," Jim said. "If you haven't taken a turn on watch, I'll take it. Just rest."

He sounded confident, but I wondered if he believed Howell would get better. We had no medical supplies, so all we could do was keep Howell as comfortable and relaxed as possible. He was going to have to pull through this on his own strength.

By this time, everyone was up and surrounding Howell. "Who's on watch?" Captain asked.

"I am, sir," Tremaine said. "I had just gotten up, so I can keep going for a little while."

"Good," Captain said. "Try to keep quiet and let Howell sleep, and the rest of us will try to do the same."

"Yes, sir," Tremaine said, leaving the room.

"I'm sorry to be a bother, sir," Howell grunted.

"You're not a bother." Jim said firmly.

Shortly after, with Howell sleeping fitfully, I lay down, and before I knew it, I was asleep again.

The sky was a pre-dawn grey when I jerked awake. My crewmates were still asleep. I quietly crawled toward Howell. He was sleeping steadily.

I shook his shoulder gently, but he groaned and rolled over. Another shake and he flicked my hand away from him, muttering, "Just five more minutes, Honey."

"How is he, sir?" Baumgart said, walking into the room.

"Well, he thinks I'm his Honey, so he's either blind, or better."

"Oh, that's good," Baumgart said, visibly relieved. "Have you had a turn on watch yet?"

"Not yet," I replied.

"I just got up myself, and am too awake to go back to sleep at the moment."

"Everything in order, then?"

"More or less," he replied.

"Then if you're fine here, I will explore the grounds."

"I'll let Captain and Lt. Liddell know where you've gone. I know Captain would prefer going in pairs, but…"

"We need to know what resources, if any, we have besides the cistern. I'll stay in sight of the house."

"I figured as much, sir. Just didn't want trouble with the Captain."

"Understood."

The land in front of the house sloped quickly down to the beach, where two large launches lay. Each had been fairly large, about thirty-eight feet long, when they were built, but both were now useless. One had been deliberately destroyed, its sides caved in by the heavy blows of an axe. Nothing remained of the engines or props, not even the mounting brackets. The other had never been finished, and nature had taken its toll in the meantime.

There was still room on the beach for someone to land, and we would have to watch this area closely, but the boats were useless to us or anyone else, so I turned to explore the grounds.

There were several square-ish patches of land near the house, now overgrown and gone wild. Those had probably been gardens, when the house was occupied. A gurgling sound caught my attention, and I found a small, clear stream, flowing into the sea. Fish swam lazily in the slow current, and I wondered if we could rig up some nets to catch them. I took a sip of water, and spat it out quickly. Being this close to the sea apparently meant that the water was too salty to drink, but further upstream there might be some possibilities.

When I returned, the rest of the Fliers were up and sitting outside, breaking into another breakfast of coconut. Even Howell was outside, enjoying the morning sun, with his knee propped up again, joking about being accident-prone.

"All right, first things first," Captain said when we finished our tiny breakfast and hearing my report, "we should spend several days here and recuperate before we decide what to do next. We'll need supplies, and between the coconut farm, the fish, and the cistern, we're finally well off when it comes to food and water.

"But this house and the village prove that there were people here not too long ago, and we don't know if they're still in the area, so we'll need to set watch in addition to foraging. Any natives in the area may find us and they may be able to help."

"Or turn us in," Baumgart said.

"Yes, that's a risk," Captain acknowledged, "but we'll need their help if we're to get home. Subs and ships don't pass close enough to this island to signal for help, and we don't know how long it will be before the Allies re-take the Philippines.

"For today, however, we need food and fire, and we'll work in pairs. Howell, once again, you've earned the right to sit on your backside and tend home camp." We all laughed, including Howell.

"Wes is taking the magnifying glass out of the binoculars to use that to light the fire," Howell said.

"Brilliant. Then, Miller, when you're done with that, I guess you can fetch firewood. I'll go back to the coconut grove with Tremaine and gather more coconuts while Baumgart and Jacobson do some more scouting. That leaves Russo and Liddell for the fishing."

At that moment, two native boys stepped out of the jungle. One looked to be barely a teenager, the other slightly younger. We stared at each other for a moment, then the boys began calmly walking toward us. With nowhere to hide, we stood and watched and waited to see what they did next. They stood in front on us, and watched us intently, and quietly.

Captain cleared his throat. "Good morning," he courteously said to the boys. They glanced at each other, but made no response. Captain glanced at us, but met blank stares, no one else having any other ideas. He tried another tack, "Americans or Japanese?"

The taller boy smiled. "Americanos!" he said with a big, white, toothy grin. Then he said, "Japanese," and made a violently quick motion like slitting his throat. He pointed at us. "Americanos?"

"Yes, Americanos." Captain sighed in relief, as we all quickly echoed, "Americanos, Americanos."

The smaller boy, in an apparent effort to be useful, pointed at the cistern and said, "No drink water." Captain asked him why, but both boys looked at us blankly. Remembering our policy of "letting come what may," we just accepted it.

"Food?" Captain asked, miming the motion of eating with his hands.

The taller boy grinned and said, "Rice," while patting his stomach. He motioned us with his hand to follow them back through the jungle, and then disappeared into the woods.

For a moment, we were too astonished to follow. It was all surreal.

"Captain?" Jim asked.

"Well, we've been warned that not all Filipinos are on our side, and to be especially cautious of those who don't speak English, but we don't have many options at this point." He replied.

We all agreed. The prospect of food and friendly faces overcame what would have been our trained distrust.

With a rustle, the older boy reappeared on the trail, looking at us quizzically, then motioned us to follow him again.

"Here goes nothing," I heard Captain mutter to himself.

The boy turned into the woods and glanced back several times to make sure we were following. The other boy was waiting for us at the foot of a giant tree, with a handkerchief wrapped bundle tied to the end of a stick slung over his shoulder. It reminded me of when my brothers and I took off for afternoon fishing expeditions when we were kids. The larger boy, in one fluid move between steps, grasped his own pack off the ground, and vanished into the woods, the younger boy in his wake.

My feet had been sore during my morning exploration, but I had been able to ignore it when moving at my own, slow pace. Now, these two fairly flew through the woods, and we struggled to keep up with them. I felt my feet open again, but bit the insides of my cheeks and tried harder to find the deepest pads of leaves on which to walk, rather than the coarse, broken soil. From the quickly smothered gasps of the others, I knew we all were in for a rough time.

We staggered behind the boys through nearly invisible jungle trails, panting with effort. Occasionally, I felt dizzy, stars floated past my eyes, and I had to rest for a gasp or two before continuing.

The jungle gave way to another clearing, dominated by tall, tasseled grasses. The boys stopped here and motioned us to sit. I gratefully flopped to the ground with a thud, wheezing, and feeling far older than my twenty-two years.

They withdrew huge, curved knives from their belts, but before we could react in alarm, swiftly cut the grass down and stripped the leaves from the central stalks. The taller one held the first yard-long piece out to Captain who took it cautiously. "Eat," the boy said, nodding and smiling. We looked at each other, puzzled. "Eat," the boy repeated, and gnawed on the end of another piece that he was stripping. Captain gingerly licked the end of his stalk and his eyes lit up. "Sugarcane!" He laughed. "It must be sugarcane."

It was sweet and moist, though exceedingly tough. After a few moments, my jaws ached from the effort of chewing it, but I wasn't about to stop. I could feel energy returning to me. After giving each of us a section, the boys sat too, chomping on their own. Half an hour later, they picked up their packs, motioned us to follow them, and vanished into the woods once. We scrambled after them, and after another fifteen minutes or so, entered a field overgrown with tall grasses and wildflowers. Sitting in the middle of the field was a raised platform covered with a roof and open on all sides, like the picnic shelters in parks. Weathered, old fashioned benches with attached desks stood in rough rows facing what must have been the teacher's desk some time before.

The boys motioned us to sit down on the benches and faster than I could have started a fire with matches, they had whittled a spindle and started a fire by spinning it in their hands on a notched chunk of wood. Moments later, they had a steady fire going. The older boy pulled out a small pot from beneath the platform, filled it with water from a nearby stream, and set it in the fire to boil. The other grabbed a small burlap bag out of his pack and poured a pound or so of rice into the water.

That done, the older boy grabbed his large machete and started chopping down broad leaves from a nearby tree. The other pulled a small metal cup from a pack, filled it at the stream, and brought it to us.

"Drink," the boy said, offering his cup to Captain. I could see the water was very muddy and unappetizing and though Captain took it with a smile, he looked at it worryingly. "Drink," the boy repeated, taking the cup back and drinking some himself. He handed the cup back to Captain, who took a cautious sip. "It's all right, I guess," he told us. "Tastes a bit like mud, but I'm not going to complain now."

When he finished, he handed the cup back to the boy, who took it, grabbed another from his friend's pack, and raced back and forth between us and the stream, bringing water until we had our fill.

The older one returned, laden with broad leaves, which he laid near the fire. He stirred the pot with a wooden spoon, said something to the smaller boy, and ladled out hot, steaming balls of rice onto the glossy leaves. The smaller boy scrambled to his pack, took out a bundle wrapped in more leaves, and with a flourish, laid a portion of small smoked fish on top of each pile of rice. The exquisite smell made my stomach groan loudly, and mine wasn't the only one. When the younger boy brought my leaf-plate of food to me, the smell nearly made me dizzy in anticipation.

I pinched some rice between two fingers and threw it in. The hot rice made me cough and suck in air to cool my mouth quickly before it could burn. After that, I resisted wolfing down everything in one gulp and tried to eat slowly, savoring each bite, even carefully stripping the meat from the skeleton of the smoked fish.

I felt myself starting to relax. We had found friends, were eating hot food, were off our feet, and shaded from the sun. Life was looking up again.

A rifle cocked. We froze. A dozen men stepped out from under the shadow of the trees, armed with rifles, machetes, and blowguns, all aimed at us.

The boys stood up next to us and grinned. *"Americanos!"* they yelled, pointing at us.

8

THE BUGSUK BOLO BATTALION

We were betrayed.

There was no escape. The clearing was large enough that we would be shot before we had run more than a few feet. I glanced at Captain, and saw his shoulders sag in defeat. We were done for, and would be carted off to a POW camp.

The apparent leader stood in front of the group, his deeply-tanned skin stretched tightly over sinew and lean muscle. He looked keenly at the boys, who bounced up and down, pointing more animatedly.

"Americanos! Americanos!" They chanted.

His face split into a smile. "Hello!" He said, jogging to the shelter, and jerking Howell to his feet for a handshake. "My name is Pedro Sarmiento, the leader of the Bugsuk Bolo Battalion."

He shook all of our hands while we stared in stunned silence. Was this another trick? The other guerillas, while lowering their weapons, advanced slowly, watching the surrounding trees warily. One spoke rapidly to the boys who replied in their own language, and our guides pointed back into the woods.

"Sit, please, you look tired, and you're going to need energy soon," Sarmiento said, motioning us back to our seats.

"I'm sorry," Captain began, "but what is going on? Why should we trust you?"

"Well, if you give me a chance, I will prove my trustworthiness. As to what is going on, we are Filipinos defending our island, Bugsuk.[26] We have orders to take you to a safe point until you can be rescued."

"How do you speak English so well?" Captain asked, eyes narrowed, apparently debating on whether to trust the stranger.

"I was educated in Manila as a schoolteacher. Before the island was taken by the Japanese, I was the overseer at the plantation near the big house, and the schoolteacher of this school." He gestured proudly at the shelter. "Part of that education is teaching English."

---

[26] Pronounced "Boog-sook".

"How did you know where to find us?"

"We have lookouts surrounding this island day and night. Around sunset last night, a lookout near the big house reported seeing eight men swimming to the island, and it was impossible for him to tell if you were Japanese or American. They sent runners all over the island to gather the battalion." He swept his arms to indicate the armed men around him. "We were surprised you were still alive this morning, so we surrounded the house, and sent the boys to find out who you were. If you were friends, they were supposed to lead you to this place."

"And if we hadn't been?" Captain inquired.

He pulled out his giant knife, which they called a "Bolo" and searched for nicks along its keen edge. "Then they were to go on to the coconut grove, and every one of you would have been killed where you were sitting." I felt the hairs on my arms and neck stand on end. Sarmiento looked up and grinned at our wide-eyed faces.

"Come, Mr...."

"Crowley. Lieutenant Commander John Crowley, United States Navy." Captain replied, giving his name but not our boat's, just as we had been taught.

"Commander Crowley, we've had ample time to attack you if that was our intention. Now please, eat and regain your strength."

Captain stood still for a moment, then looked at us, nodded his head, and seated himself in front of his banana leaf of food. We followed his lead, and I quickly resumed my meal, though it was quite cool now.

We ate peacefully while two of the Battalion patrolled the perimeter, and the rest sat in the shade of the schoolhouse watching us with open curiosity. The boys were now cooking more rice for the guerillas.

"One more question, if you do not mind," Captain said, after a while, "the boys told us not to drink the water. Since they thought we were friends by that time, why would they not want us to drink from the best source of fresh water available?"

Sarmiento smiled and said, "When the owner of that house heard that the Japanese had taken Manila, he took some precautions with his property and business. He hid his tractors and machines deep in the forest, destroyed what he couldn't move, and took his family away to safety. Then, in case the Japanese did come, he laced his cistern with arsenic. Our lookout watched all of you drink from there. That's why we were surprised to find you still alive."

We stared at Howell, who looked shocked himself, then laughed.

"Now look," Sarmiento said, after sending the boys running back down the trail we came up, "we don't have a lot of time. I have standing orders from my headquarters that any Allied survivors are to be brought to Cape Baliluyan on Palawan. We're going to have to walk north across Bugsuk to get to the kumpit I had readied in case you were Allies. It's only about eight kilometers. But we have to leave soon because the Japanese patrol is due to land at the great house shortly."

"When?" Captain asked sharply.

Sarmiento looked at the sky, "If they keep to their usual schedule, they'll check the small islands to the west then land here late morning or early afternoon, so anytime now." We looked at each other in alarm. One day slower, if we had stayed anywhere, we would have been captured. Sarmiento must have misinterpreted this because he quickly added, "Don't worry, they will only patrol about a mile inland, then spend the night at the great house. You'll be safe once we get moving."

Captain brushed his hands together in an attempt to rid them of the starchy rice paste and said, "We're ready to move."

Sarmiento smiled. "Not so fast. You have to finish eating, and so do my men. Besides, I have to wait until the boys get back. They are checking to make sure you left nothing at the house that might reveal your presence to the enemy patrol."

My stomach, so long cramped from the lack of food, now felt grossly full from just the handful of rice and bit of fish. The morning sun was warm and nearly lulling me to sleep as insects buzzed lazily around my head.

The two boys returned and handed Sarmiento a small item. "What's this?" he said, holding a small piece of glass.

"Oh, no," Miller said, as he flipped my binoculars over and looked at them. "That's the magnifying glass from Ensign Jacobson's binoculars. I had just re-assembled them when the boys found us. I must have left that behind."

"Not wise," Sarmiento said, handing the glass to the Captain. "The Japanese may have noticed that and hunted down someone, anyone, to figure out how that got there." His eyebrows knitted in frustration as he attempted to light the pipe in his teeth.

"Mr. Sarmiento—" Captain began.

"Pedro," he corrected.

Captain gave him the magnifying glass. "As a thanks for finding us and very likely saving our lives."

Pedro took the glass, considered it for a moment, then walked into the sunshine and lit his pipe with it in a few seconds. "This is going to come in very handy," he said. "Thank you.

"Now," he raised his voice. "We start." With a few more commands in his native tongue, everyone leapt to work. In less than a minute, the camp was cleaned, brushed, and restored, all evidence of food, fire, and men gone.

Half of the men, including both boys, were apparently locals who lived nearby, and they departed with a cheerful wave. Pedro placed us in the middle of the rest of the guerillas. Three men in front cut a path for us, and those behind guarded our rear and erased our tracks as we went.

"It is not far to the mouth of Bugsuk River," Pedro announced. "If we walk steadily, we should make it by nightfall. Let's go!" He started off, swinging his machete in wide arcs up ahead.

Bugsuk Island was heavily forested and sloped gently uphill, but the wretched coral was always only a few inches beneath the leafy forest floor. I was shocked at how hard it was to walk. I had often hiked all over sand dunes and forests in Michigan. While in Australia, I hunted, rode horses, and went to dances nearly every night. A hike like this would have been child's play, five days ago.

We shambled along, panting and gasping, struggling to walk at a respectable pace on our shredded feet. Pedro and his men tried to hustle us along, but it was soon obvious that we were in too sorry a state to make it to the rendezvous tonight. At our first rest, he spoke to the guerillas in a low, urgent voice. Two left at a run, leaving the other four behind.

"You're obviously not going to make it today," he told us, "so I'm making arrangements for us to spend the night in a little village ahead.

Hopefully, we can start again in the morning and get to the river tomorrow evening."

"Thank you," Captain panted, and we echoed.

"We can't dawdle too much since we need to get at least halfway across the island today to be safe."

It was early evening when we finally staggered into the village. Despite walking eight hours, we only managed to cover two and a half miles. Someone guided the eight of us to a small hut where bamboo mats were laid out on the floor. I was asleep before I was really aware that we had arrived.

"Come on, get up, get up," Pedro's voice intruded what seemed like an instant later. "They've cooked dinner for you. It would be impolite to refuse."

I could smell wood smoke and hear the crackling of a good fire as I limped out of our hut. It was already twilight, the immense tress around us reduced to dark shadows towering overhead. Four bamboo huts surrounded a large central fire, over which hung a steaming cauldron suspended by a tripod. The whole village, which seemed to be about a dozen people, turned out to greet us, and ushered us to sit at the fire with smiles and gestures.

Wonderful smells of chicken and coconut and spices I couldn't identify wafted from that cauldron, and I sniffed appreciably, my stomach growling.

An older man, who Pedro told us was the village leader, sat down next to us, and at a signal, the women scooped the contents of the pot into coconut shell bowls and handed them to us with shy glances.

"This smells like chicken soup," Russo said. "It reminds me of home."

Pedro smiled and repeated the remark to the village leader. He smiled and said something to us, while gesturing for us to eat. Pedro translated the greeting and invitation then added: "Meat is rarely eaten here. It is usually only cooked on special occasions, like when they are hosting honored guests."

The chickens, I suddenly noticed, were everywhere in the village, pecking and scratching at the ground for food. They were tiny, much smaller than anything I'd ever seen, and so scrawny, you probably couldn't give one of these away at home. Yet it was obvious that these birds were treasured by the villagers, and their sacrifice in our honor was greatly appreciated and humbling.

"Please tell them we are very honored by their meal, and we thank them," Captain said.

Pedro translated for us, and soon, the whole village was joining in the meal, talking to one another, and relaxing. We began to relax with them and started talking amongst ourselves and to our hosts with the help of Pedro.

"They woke you?" I heard Jim say to Captain. "I didn't hear a thing."

"Believe me, I resisted the wake-up call, too, but I guess once you join the Navy you're never truly free of paperwork no matter where you go."

"Oh?" I said.

"Yes," Captain sighed. "Pedro needed our names and where we were stationed in order to make a formal report."

Pedro chimed in, "Paper is one of the rarest things on the islands, but I still must submit formal reports to my headquarters."

"Did our Navy train these guys?" I joked.

Thankfully, we were sent to bed again after a dessert of wild honey, with assurances from Pedro that he would post guards around the village to warn us of any incoming Japanese. I slept so deeply that night, it seemed but a moment until dawn.

Pedro was impatient to move on quickly that morning. We gathered yawning in the clearing, several of us bearing the imprint of the bamboo mat on our arms and faces. There was no breakfast to be had but the villagers brought us water from their stream. It was cool and refreshing, if a touch muddy. The hardest thing was getting the hang of the five-foot long bamboo pipes they used as cups. As soon as we drank our fill, Pedro hurried us out with a final wave of his hand to the villagers.

Though the sleep had helped restore my energy, my feet continued to burn with each step. All too soon, I was panting and straining to keep up, and again, we had to rest more often than Pedro was comfortable with.

"Come on," he was urging us. "I've even arranged for a noon meal at another village. If we can possibly get there before noon, that is."

"How much farther?" Baumgart asked.

"Not far. Just another kilometer."

Twenty minutes later after a hard uphill climb, Russo gasped out, "*How* much farther?"

"Just another kilometer," Pedro said, smiling.

We looked at each other, but kept going. We were reaching the top of Bugsuk now and occasionally had to pull ourselves up by grasping trees and vines for support. Colorful birds winged overhead, trilling happily. I wished we were not so hurried or exhausted. It was truly an incredible landscape and I only got to catch glimpses of it when I stopped to gasp at every rest point.

"I thought this village was only another kilometer," I told Pedro after we had been walking for over an hour.

"It is."

"Lemme guess, just another kilometer?"

He grinned, "Exactly."

I rolled my eyes and heard several of the guys groan.

Despite our protests and frequent breaks, we did reach the next village around noon. There were no chickens here, and only one large hut, but they offered us a large pot of blue rice. While surprising to look at, it had only a slightly different flavor from the brown rice. Our dessert was a tasty concoction of more rice, mixed with wild honey into an incredibly sweet paste.

Pedro allowed us to rest here for an hour. Before leaving, the owner of this hut gave him a large basket of rice, which one of the guerillas hoisted onto his back. Pedro and the other guerillas seemed touched by the gesture, and thanked him profusely as we left.

"If you don't mind my asking, why did that village give you that basket of rice? It's far more than we'll need before we get to the boat." I gasped at Pedro at our next rest.

"Our priority is fighting the Japanese, so the villagers often give us food so we can concentrate on that, not growing rice. It's a huge sacrifice for them right now, too, since the last few harvests have been very poor.

"Now come on!" He called out with a grin. "We still have a ways to go, we can't laze about all day!" We answered him with groans.

Five agonizing hours later, we came across a solitary hut on the trail, and the man living there, seeing the guerillas, insisted we stop and share a meal of rice with him. My stomach still felt full from lunch, but he insisted,

"Jungle Scene in the Philippines during WWII" Fili Venetas, Oil on canvas, 1947. Painted by a Filipino artist, this shows a Philippine house similar to those described by Jacobson and the other Flier survivors. Courtesy of Taylor University and the Taylor University Archives: Jose and Consuela Masa collection.

and Pedro accepted on our behalf.

He cheerfully seated us at his cooking fire and served us another meal of rice. We ate, smiled our thanks, and Pedro excused us to resume our march as soon as it was polite.

After another hour of walking, Tremaine, grinning, called out, "How much farther to this boat?"

"Guess."

"JUST ANOTHER KILOMETER!" we sang out. At least now we were going downhill.

The sun was hovering over the western horizon when we broke through the jungle onto the banks of a river. A small sailboat was pulled up on the sand and a tall man with the most mischievous eyes and smile I'd ever seen, bounded off of it. He greeted Pedro and us in his language.

"This is Sula LaHud, one of our best Moro traders." Pedro introduced us quickly. "He is going to take you to Palawan to join the main body of guerillas."

"You're not coming with us?" Captain asked.

"No, I'm needed here. LaHud will take good care of you."

Captain looked unsure of this plan.

"Pedro," he said hesitatingly. "We sure would appreciate it if you could join us. Having someone with us who can translate would be a great help."

Pedro looked at us thoughtfully. "You make a point. While I trust LaHud to get you there safely, I would hate for an emergency to happen and have a language barrier make it worse."

He said something quickly to one of the guerillas, took the basket of rice, and hopped up to the deck himself. LaHud looked only a little surprised and motioned for us to embark.

The ship we boarded had a wooden hull about sixteen feet long, a six foot beam, pointed bow, and square stern, the detachable rudder and tiller currently lifted out of the river. Her smooth hull was flush decked from the stern to the mast, with only enough space forward of the gaff-rigged mast for one or two people. Beneath the deck was the cargo hold and racks on the rigs added even more storage. Everything was Spartan, the only luxury I could see was a framework that would allow a split-bamboo mat to be rolled out for a sun or rain shade. Overall she seemed to be a sturdy little boat, and very suited to navigating the shallow reefed waters around here.

Once we were settled on the deck, LaHud and his boys, Tom Pong and Kim Jong, loaded rice, cooking utensils, rifles, and so many supplies I wondered if she would float when they were finished tucking everything into the various nooks and crannies.

LaHud splashed out to the stern and lifted himself up to the deck in a single, easy movement. With a single order, the boys and guerillas shoved the kumpit into the river, the boys leaping into the bow at the last second. She was caught in the current in a moment, and LaHud swiftly turned her bow out to sea. We were on our way.

I looked at my watch, it said 1800 hours. With a start, I suddenly realized it was Sunday again. A week ago, I was sitting in *Flier's* wardroom, eating stew and fresh biscuits telling Teddy how old he was. And four hours later, everything had changed.

Based on Al Jacobson's description and examples of traditional southern Philippines kumpits and bancas, LaHud's kumpit may have looked something like this.

9

GUERILLA HEADQUARTERS

The sun had just set when we swept into the sea. Only a few yards from shore, Kim-Jong suddenly stood, yelled, and pointed back to the beach. Sailor heeled the kumpit around and headed back. I grabbed the edge of the kumpit, while straining my eyes in the falling darkness, but couldn't see anything or anyone. My crewmates also looked tense, and Pedro seemed alert.

The kumpit slid onto the sand, and both boys leapt out. Kim-Jong ran a few feet and picked up something dark on the water's edge. He waded out to LaHud and handed it to him. LaHud's eyes lit up and he talked excitedly to Pedro while handing the mass to him.

Pedro translated. "It's a type of seaweed," he said handing some to each of us. "A doctor told him that it is good medicine, so he always stops to pick some up whenever he sees it. He says, _They should eat it, it will help them._"

It was difficult to see in the twilight and appeared almost black. It tasted like a bitter sweet pickle laced with iodine. After gathering a mass of seaweed, the boys pushed the kumpit back into the water and deftly climbed aboard.

Moments later, they raised the sail as LaHud quickly maneuvered the kumpit around and off into the darkening sea.

I vaguely remembered, from the charts aboard the _Flier_, that this area was riddled with reefs and large areas that read "exposed at low tide." Several times I saw waves breaking over reefs just feet from the kumpit as it glided past them. There was little chance that the Fliers and I could have gotten through here if left to our own devices, but LaHud obviously knew every inch of these waters.

"You're an amazing sailor, LaHud," I said, visibly impressed, as our boat slid between two barely submerged coral mounds.

"I'll say," Jim said. "I wouldn't dream of navigating anything through this area in the dark, especially without charts."

When Pedro translated, LaHud smiled and shrugged his shoulders, as if to say, 'Ah, it's no big deal.' After that, we all called him 'Sailor' or 'The Sailor' out of respect for his ability.

"If all goes well, we'll be at Baliluyan before dawn," Pedro told Captain. "The reefs and the passages during the low tide tonight are forcing us to go several miles north before we can turn south for the cape. But we should be there and under cover before the morning patrols can see us."

"Wouldn't the Japanese think this is just a fishing boat?" Captain asked.

"Not with this many passengers aboard," he replied. "These boats are designed for only a few people. We'll be searched the moment we're seen."

Sailor suddenly barked a command, and I jumped. So did Tom-Pong and Kim-Jong, who thrust out their oars and pushed the kumpit away from an exposed coral mound that suddenly appeared out of the water.

The kumpit gently slid up the beach at Baliluyan around three a.m. The boys leapt over the side and hauled the boat farther in as armed men swarmed down from the trees, calling greetings to Sailor.

They quickly hustled us off the kumpit and ashore while others pulled the boat in closer and hid it under layers of palms and bracken.

There was a narrow, twisting path under the trees, along which we stumbled. I could feel dirt and leaves underfoot and then wooden planks, and then more dirt. I could barely make out a roofline looming overhead when my hands were grasped and planted on a ladder in front of me. I climbed up and into a hut. The floor seemed to be bamboo or whole branches laid side by side. More hands guided me into a room, and what little light there had been outside vanished. I heard the grunts of my fellow Fliers nearby when suddenly, with a hiss and the smell of sulfur, a match flared and lit an oil lamp. We were in a small bamboo room with a thatched roof, packed full of a number of men.

"Hello," a Filipino greeted us in perfect English, extinguishing the match with a wave of his hand. "Welcome to Cape Baliluyan. My name is Sergeant Pasqual de la Cruz of the USAFFE.[27] These are my men. We man

---

[27] USAFFE: United States Armed Forces in the Far East. In July of 1941, as tensions in the Pacific increased, President Roosevelt ordered the Commonwealth of the Philippines military to be absorbed into the American military with MacArthur as the head. These armed forces were therefore one military with one commander, so there could be no infighting over coordinating two militaries in the

Cape Baliluyan for the war effort." His men quickly introduced themselves by name, before inviting us to sit on the floor near the tables and handing us bowls of rice sweetened with sugar cane. "Can we get you anything right now?" de la Cruz asked.

"Our feet are torn up pretty bad," Captain said. "Do you have any medicine?"

De la Cruz went to a narrow shelf in the corner of the room where he took down a small round jar. Inside was whitish salve full of bugs and dirt. "I'm afraid this is all we have," he said.

Captain politely declined, and I let out a mental sigh of relief. I wasn't sure whether that salve would be worse than the seawater and dirt we'd experienced thus far.

"Tomorrow night, all of you will be transported north to Brooke's Point, where a contingent of US Army Coastwatchers will take charge of you." De la Cruz said, replacing the salve on the shelf.

"And from there?" Captain asked.

"I don't know," de la Cruz replied, "but there are at least three other military men there waiting for rescue. With the addition of all of you, they may be able to convince someone to come and pick you up."

We soon learned that these guerillas were all locals, and had friends and relatives scattered up and down the southern part of Palawan. Their family members helped with food and supplies, and if the Japanese decided to take over this part of Palawan, they could easily blend in and disappear. Before the war, many had been teachers or college students and most spoke enough English that we could talk to each other.

They primarily watched the North Balabac Passage, tracking the movements of ships and convoys. They would then transmit that information north, where it could be recorded and transmitted to GHQ as needed.

Despite their in-depth knowledge of the area, most of them had been cut off from all news of the wider world, as they had no radios or

---

Philippines should an invasion occur. After the fall of Corregidor and the surrender of all American troops on the islands, some of these soldiers took to the forest and continued fighting guerilla-style. Due to their heritage they easily could fade back into civilian life and fight secretly.

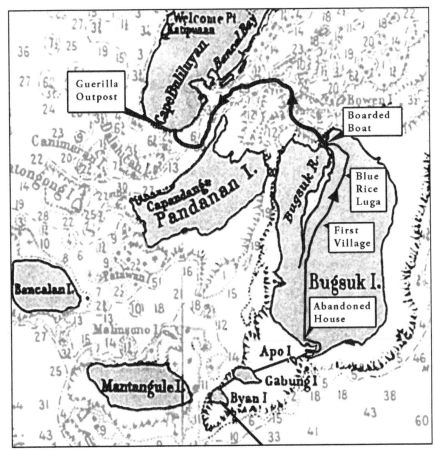

This map shows the approximate route the Fliers took from rafting to Palawan. Original map from the family of Ens. Al "Jake" Jacobson

newspapers since the fall of Manila three years prior. They were eager to hear what was happening in the war, and how things were going. We were more than happy to repay their hospitality with all the news we had heard before leaving Fremantle: the end of the Leningrad siege, the landing at Normandy and the advance of the Allies through Europe, and the failed assassination coup on Hitler. Regarding the Pacific, we told them about the re-taking of Midway, Guadalcanal, the Battle of the Coral Sea, and the most recent battles in the Mariana Islands, including the huge naval battle in the Philippine Sea; the sinking of a massive Japanese aircraft carrier, and the re-taking of Saipan. Everyone cheered and laughed and clapped, excited to hear that the war was going our way after all.

De la Cruz, noting the time, dismissed his men to their duties and sent us to bed. The only place left to sleep was on the tables.

We woke up at around 9:30 that morning, to the sound of men working outside. The guerillas must bunk in closely with each other and their few possessions were neatly stacked in certain quarters about the room. It was strange seeing well-worn classic books carefully arranged on a shelf above machetes, rifles and ammunition.

De la Cruz walked in the room, his arms loaded with piles of clothes.

"Good morning, gentlemen." He heaved the clothes onto the closest table. "I don't know if we'll be able to help all of you, but the men and I scrounged all the spare clothes we had. Figured after wandering around in your underwear for several days, you may appreciate having something..." He paused, and looked over the pile, "well, maybe not nicer, but something a bit more decent to wear."

We sat in stunned silence at their generosity, until Captain said, "Tell your men, 'Thank you very much,' from all of us."

"You're welcome," de la Cruz grinned. "They're all different sizes, so good luck. We found more pants than shirts, and, of course, our shoes and boots long since have fallen apart, so you'll still have to go barefoot. But we hope this helps. I'll be back in about a half hour with breakfast."

We all ended up with a pair of pants when we were done. Mine were light tan, cotton, a little threadbare in the seat and knees, and so large I had to roll up the legs three times. The shirt I found was a size too small, and couldn't be buttoned across my chest, but I felt more human and definitely more presentable.

De la Cruz returned with bowls and a pot full of rice for breakfast. While we were eating, he questioned us in order to fill out his records and reports. We willingly told him our names, ranks, and serial numbers, as trained, but after that, it became a friendly battle of wits.

"Name of boat?" he asked.

"Classified, I'm afraid," Captain responded.

"I thought as much. Submarine though, that much I can tell."

"What makes you say that?"

"Deduction, mostly. We would have seen a surface ship in the area, especially one sinking. You showed up unexpectedly, and we've received no word or record of anyone seeing your ship. So you had to come from a sub, most likely making the crossing at night." He paused, and Captain did not deny his deductions. "You cannot tell me your mission, either, I suppose."

"Sorry, but no, I can't."

"Can you tell me if you were heading out to sea or back to port?"

"No."

"How long you've been to sea?"

"No, sorry."

De la Cruz looked a little frustrated, but understanding. It was the nature of our business. We were trained to give nothing away about our boat, lest the information somehow fall into enemy hands. We trusted de la Cruz, but one never knew. The Japanese could capture him and he could reveal something under torture. It was safer for us and him if he knew as little about us and our now-doomed mission as possible.

De la Cruz glanced at what appeared to be his records, and on top I spied a small slip of paper with our names, ranks, and serials written in miniscule handwriting. Pedro's list. De la Cruz's brow furrowed as he ticked us off one by one on it. He then looked again at Captain.

"The hazards of working in covert and top-secret missions," he smiled wanly. "If you cannot tell me the name of your boat, can you tell me where were you sunk, how long ago, how many got off, do you think there are any other survivors, and did you see any indications of the enemy?"

"I can't say where we were sunk." Captain said. "There were fifteen men that called muster moments afterwards. At least three were definitely lost at sea, and the other four likely were as well. I don't think anyone else could have survived."

"Unless…" I said quietly.

"Yes, Jacobson?" Captain said and both he and de la Cruz looked at me with interest.

Now I had to be careful. "It's just possible sir, that there were other survivors who we didn't see because we missed them in the dark, or…later." I looked significantly at de la Cruz, who took the hint and studied his papers intently. 'Escape Hatch', I mouthed at Captain.

Captain frowned then nodded slightly. Our last reading before she sank was around 250 feet, which was at the extreme edge of the depth we were trained to escape from. It was just possible that guys came up after we left the area. They may have chosen Comiran or Bugsuk...if they survived the ascent.

"It's possible," Captain admitted. "Likely a long shot, but it is possible."

"Well, long shots are our specialty, and it's possible we've already located some more of your crew." He looked at us with a satisfied smile at our open-mouthed reactions. "We know there were at least four submariners taken prisoner and moved to the prison camp at Puerto Princesa. We've heard rumors of up to six submariners in total that survived and were captured, but at least two were killed. I'm sorry. The other four were at the camp until they were transported elsewhere fourteen days ago. Friends of yours?"

"Fourteen days, you said?" Captain questioned sharply.

"Well, the transport of the prisoners was fourteen days ago, yes."

"Our vessel sank only nine days ago." Captain said quietly.

De la Cruz looked at each of us, and sighed. "Damn it. Now I have *another* submarines crew to look for." He jotted a few notes down on his papers and looked up. "All right then. I'll send Pedro back to Bugsuk to search the small islands again for any more survivors. I'll send another group to cover Mantangule and Padanan Islands, and I'll also notify my people on Balabac to keep a sharp watch out."

He called someone at the door of the hut and a moment later, talked to a young guerilla, who couldn't have more than thirteen or fourteen. He took off at a dead run. "All right, but nightfall, half of my teams will be on the lookout, and the other half within a day or two.

"Wait a moment," I said. "Last night, you mentioned sending us north to the Coastwatchera headquarters, but now we're going to Mantangule?"

"No," de la Cruz straightened his papers and stood, "The Coastwatchers were on Mantangule, but moved to Brooke's Point. You'll see it tomorrow at dawn, if we're lucky. Despite being closer to the prison camp, it's actually safer there than the other places.

"So until about 1500, you're on your own. After the afternoon patrol flyover, it'll be safe enough to start out, and we'll even give you some

Cape Baliluyan in 1998. In 1944, there were no houses on the beach, they were all hidden in the jungle. Courtesy of the family of Alvin "Jake" Jacobson.

dinner before leaving."

I felt a little cramped and stiff after sleeping on the table and being scrunched up on the kumpit all night. Seeing that we were going to be put back on the kumpit this evening, I decided to take a leisurely stroll around the grounds. The others just wanted to relax and eat, so I went out myself.

The layout of the guerilla outpost was something I later found to be a standard pattern for most villages on Palawan's shore. The house was made of bamboo and built on stilts about six feet high. The wartime addition seemed to be the six-foot deep trenches that ringed the building. Narrow planks bridged over these trenches, easily removed in an emergency.

There was a sugarcane field, and a chicken coop, and a large cast iron cauldron behind the house, where the guerillas boiled down seawater for their salt. Everything was functional, some things even doubly so. The roof of the house was pitched so the rainwater ran to one corner and collected in a cistern for drinking.

Dinner was a feast. In our honor, they served a thinly-sliced jerky of what they called carabao, a type of water buffalo. It was salty and delicious, but was so tough I could barely tear it with my teeth. The Filipinos, who enjoyed watching our attempts at this unfamiliar food, tore and chewed with a relish. They also served a delicious paste made of coconut and honey, for dessert.

The Zero flew overhead on schedule shortly after 1500, and we all trooped down to the beach. There was another, smaller kumpit next to ours, and despite my years sailing around the Great Lakes, I couldn't help but admire the clarity of the water here. Both vessels looked like they were floating on air, or glass.

The smaller kumpit was for Pedro, who was returning to Bugsuk with Tom-Pong searching for more survivors of either submarine. We would be continuing with Sailor on the larger kumpit. Tom-Pong's position would be filled by another young man named Kong.

"Where's de la Cruz?" one of the guerillas asked. "He said he was going with you."

"I'm right here," he called from a distance back. He and Captain were standing close to each other talking. Captain looked rather disturbed. "We're coming, the tide isn't that quick."

The guerillas launched Pedro's kumpit, then ours. Once again, Sailor steered us so quickly and skillfully out to sea, I almost looked for an outboard motor. For over two hours, the kumpit flew lightly in front of a strong wind. The land raced by smoothly and we settled down for an easy trip.

The calming movement of the kumpit, slicing through the waves, rocking back and forth, and the warmth of the sun relaxed me, and I drifted off into my thoughts. I always had found something comforting and soothing about the motion of a sailboat on the water. It was quiet, perfect.

Flier, under battery power, had been like this, smooth and quiet as a whisper, except for the voices of eighty men talking, the background hum of all the electronics, the beeping of the radar, the crackling of the radio, the various noises from the sonar, and, of course, the creaking of the sub under pressure, which produced a sound like no other.

"I've got a possible target bearing zero-one-five. It appears to be approaching," Captain announced, pulling his face away from the periscope and sending it back down the well.[28] We were heading south along Luzon's western coast, dodging the nearly ceaseless Zeros patrolling over the heart of Japan's Philippine stronghold.

"All stop."

For some reason, the sea was again so smooth, that using the periscope was impossible unless we sat perfectly still. Even so, the strong sunlight could cast a gleam or shadow that might be spotted easily by plane or convoy.

When *Flier* drifted to a slow pause, the Target Acquisition Periscope whirred up through the well and Captain buried his eyes into the eyepieces. "We have...one, two...three...oh boy, this is going to be a biggie."

"Sir." Radioman Paul Barron, at the Sonar station, held the headphones tightly to his head as he spoke quickly. "I can distinguish six distinct prop noises with a background mish-mash of at least three, possibly more."

For a quarter of an hour they approached; eleven freighters and six escorts, bristling with guns and a nearly endless supply of depth charges. The escorts protected the freighters on one side while the shoreline prevented access from the other. That gave us two options. We could attack from the seaward side, shooting the torpedoes through the line of escorts to hit the freighters. While that would give us the most room to maneuver and escape, the torpedoes were unreliable enough that we more likely would hit nothing or the escorts, neither of which advanced the Allied cause. If we wedged ourselves between the beach and the freighters, we would have a beautifully clear shot. However, that left us little room to maneuver once the depth charges began.

"They're coming straight at us," Jim reported to Captain, peeking through the periscope quickly, before sending it into the well again.

"Okay. Three degrees starboard." He picked up the voice-activated telephone and switched the dial to the Forward Torpedo Room. "Mr. Lindeman? Ready all torpedo tubes." He twisted the dial again, this time to the After Torpedo Room, "Mr. Gwinn? Ready all tubes, and be ready for a

---

[28] These events took place June 13, 1944 off of Cape Bolinao, Luzon Island, Philippines.

quick turnaround."

"Angle *Flier's* bow toward the shore," Captain ordered. "We'll target that oil tanker in front. We'll fire all four stern torpedoes at that one and then turn around and aim the bow tubes. Hopefully we can get off all ten shots before they can react." He flicked the "Battle Stations" alarm, and the crew ran to their stations, with two more men joining us in the very crowded Conning Tower.

Because of our close quarters and limited space, Captain was going to attempt an attack while completely submerged, which was much more difficult than the standard, "surface, aim, and shoot" attack that most submarines did. *Flier* smoothly banked and aimed her stern toward the unwary tanker, who was so secure in her escort and protection that she wasn't even zig-zagging.

As we waited quietly for our prey to come in range, *Flier* began to...drift. It was so subtle I didn't realize what was happening, attributing the slight sense of movement to a cross-current. Suddenly, her stern dropped. I grabbed the rail near the Control Room hatch to steady myself as we plunged stern first.

"Lieutenant Casey! What's happening?!" Captain yelled down the hatch.

I glanced down to see three seamen straining at the stern plane wheel, which refused to move. Ed quickly ordered men aft to check the manual controls and control her from there if necessary.

"I don't know, sir," Ed said. "The stern planes failed. We can't fix her here and we're going to try to control it manually in the stern."

"Blow stern ballast tanks to compensate!"

"Blowing stern tanks, aye!" I heard the hiss of the pressurized air as it flooded the stern ballast tanks. *Flier's* stern leveled out, then suddenly shot to the surface.

"Power restored!" Ed announced.

"Flood stern ballast tanks!"

"Flooding tanks, aye, sir!" Commands bounced off each other. *Flier's* stern settled back down, but only for five minutes before the stern dropped again.

"Blow tanks!" Ed's voice was authoritative, disguising the hint of fear I knew was there. *Flier's* stern dropped sharply. I grasped the periscopes to maintain my footing, and heard the shattering of crockery and the yelps of pain as the men stumbled. Once again she leveled out, then began rising to the surface, rear first.

I could feel the pounding of dozens of feet as the men raced from nose to tail using their own weight to try to compensate for *Flier's* buoyancy problem.

Minutes later, she stabilized, and Ed spoke through the Conning Tower hatch. "Power is restored to the stern planes, and they seem to be responding normally."

"Thank you, Casey. After the fight I want you to conduct a full investigation of what happened." Captain's voice was calm, but I heard the ragged edge to his breathing.

"Aye, aye, sir," Casey said.

We were all shaky, and trying not to show it. This was the first time *Flier* had inexplicably failed.

Still unaware of *Flier's* presence, the convoy continued to approach. The air almost crackled with all the pent-up energy. Every few minutes Captain would raise the periscope, quickly glance around, and lower it again in a practiced move. The Torpedo Rooms were packed full of men, each tube loaded and prepared, just waiting for the final orders.

Captain began feeding coordinates, bearings, and speeds to Lieutenant Reynolds, who then inputted the data into the Torpedo Data Computer, and relayed the settings to the Torpedo Rooms, so the torpedo crew could adjust the trajectories.

Crouched at the periscope, which was just barely peeking above the surface, the Captain signaled to Jim, who handed him the remote firing button for the After Torpedo Room. The lights for tubes seven through ten were lit up, announcing the torpedoes were prepped and ready to fire.

"Open up a channel to the Aft Torpedo Room," Captain ordered.

"Channel open, sir,"

"...Fire seven!" He squeezed his trigger, enabling the firing button in the Torpedo Room.

"Seven away!" Gwinn's voice sounded over the intercom.

"Fire eight!"

"Eight away!"

Nine and ten were soon sent on their way and for a brief moment, we could clearly hear the banshee-shriek of their props as they screamed away.

It should only take about two and a half minutes at this distance to reach the tanker, and I instinctively began my own countdown.

"Turn her around!" Liddell ordered the Control Room.

"Yes, sir!" Ed replied.

Flier quickly banked away from the shore and lined up for her next kill.

Captain raised the periscope and ducked reflexively. "Whoa! We went a little too far, the next freighter is only a hundred yards away or so."

"Too close," Liddell said, "How's our sightline on number three?"

"Good enough for a narrow spread," Captain replied, turning the periscope slightly, "but I think we're out of time..."

We were. I heard Reynolds mutter, "...three...two...one..."

There was a pause as we all looked at Barron, clutching the headphones to his head. He shook his head. The first torpedo had missed.

A space of a few seconds...three...two...one...

Rumble...

"Got her!" Barron said, pumping his fist in victory. Moments later, "Two good hits, sir!"

KA-BOOM!

The tanker screamed as she tore herself apart, the shock waves causing *Flier* to quiver and groan. Despite being over a half-mile away, we easily heard that through the Conning Tower walls.

Captain raised the periscope and whooped. "She's going down!" Suddenly, *Flier* herself dove, "ducking" the periscope underwater. "What the—? No!" Captain said, "Periscope depth, our target just went down, not us!"

"Sir?" Barron's voice sounded urgent. "Escorts are closing in on our position fast."

"Belay the last order, DIVE!"

Flier pointed her nose for the depths, and I started to swallow rapidly to pop the pressure in my ears that steadily mounted. The thrumming of the escorts' props started their war beat through the hull, rapidly approaching, and shaking our thin steel skin.

Flier hitched, then slipped again, her stern hauling us down faster than

"Up Periscope" by Georges Schrieber, watercolor 1943. A scene in the Conning Tower under red battle light, as men climb from the Control Room below, work the TDC, look through the periscopes, listen to Sonar, and chart the sub's progress. The tiny Conning Tower often held a dozen or more men during an attack. From the Department of the Navy, Navy Historical Center. Gift of Abbott Laboratories.

we could control. I knew the eighteen or so men who had been reloading the after torpedo tubes would now be pulling frantically at the dive plane's manual levers, trying to force the planes to the right angle.

WHAM!

The first depth charge shook us.

WHA-WHAM!

Flier held, though she wobbled side to side, and her stern seemed to pick back up slowly.

Snapping, groaning noises were easily heard through the hull. Whoever we hit must be sinking.

"All stop!" Captain ordered. "Keep her level!" *Flier's* props stilled, and we waited. After the last depth charge attack, I kind of knew what to expect, and grasped on to the map table and bent my knees slightly.

Already, the temperature was rising, and the sweat started to run down my back.

Barron looked up, panting slightly, his knuckles white as they gripped the headphones. "They pulled away, sir, the convoy is moving away, but the escorts have stopped." A moment later, we knew why.

PING!

The escorts sent out their sonar reach, looking for us, and seconds later, their engines started.

"Here they come, sir!"

I gripped, held on tight, and heard the vibrations of the escorts' props even over the groans of our victim.

Click!

WHAM

WHAM-WHAM

WHAM!...WHAM!

'Six escorts,' I thought, 'God, help us all.'

They worked us over thoroughly, and pulled away again. Barron announced their engines stopped, then they started their pinging. Playing possum wasn't going to work this time.

"If they want to find us, let's let them know where we are. Head port, four-five degrees, full!" Captain ordered.

Flier gripped the water, and laboriously slithered left. Her stern planes were shaky, and tended to slip, but the guys in the back were taking care of us. "They've got a fix on us!" Barron reported.

"Heading!" Captain asked.

"Bearing one–two–zero relative."

"Helm! Turn one–two–zero starboard. Head for that sound. Planesmen, take her down, to two–one–zero feet."

Flier spiraled down, and we passed beneath our pursuers. Nearly a minute later, a dozen explosions sounded behind us.

"All stop," Captain said, and *Flier*'s props stilled. "Mr. Barron, tell me when you hear them start again."

We waited again, as depth charges rained down on our former position. There was silence, then, "Active sonar, sir!"

"Tell me when they start up and their bearing."

Moments later, "Pursuing, at two–one–nine relative."

"Ahead full, bearing zero-four–five to port!"

She turned, and we scuttled out of the way. Barron was driven nearly insane over the next three hours as *Flier* would settle, wait for the active sonar to find us, then quickly shoot beneath, between, beside, or behind our pursuers, hiding our prop noise under theirs. They hit us with everything they had, dropping three to ten at a time, sometimes close enough *Flier* would rock in the shock waves, throwing my balance.

We risked everything in that tiny corner, trapped between the shore, the escorts and the corpse of our victim. Between attacks I had to chart our position and the escorts' courses based only on Barron's reports, and had to make sure we were not about to ground anywhere.

Once, one of the escorts passed just feet above us. She traveled the full length of *Flier* so close, we felt the rumble of her engines and the thrum of her props. Everyone held his breath and watched the ceiling of the Conning Tower, barely daring to breathe, as *Flier* shook in the wash of her huge screws.

She passed overhead, but the thrashing of the water was too loud to hear whether she dropped a depth charge. We waited, trembling, the suspense much worse, again, than the actual attack.

My watch seemed too loud in the tense silence, as it ticked away the seconds, then a minute, then another…when would it come?

Wham

Wh-Wha—Wham

Wham…Wham…wham…

We collectively let out our breath and grinned at each other, the closest we safely could get to cheering. They were giving hell to some empty stretch of ocean behind us.

My head was ringing. I had been crouched in the Conning Tower for nearly five hours. My chart was scrawled with *Flier's* insane circular path, looking more like a child's first drawing than our escape route.

"We're too close to Manila," Captain grunted between his teeth, after another charge went off behind us, close enough to be heard clearly, but too far away to cause any significant damage. "They're only a few hours out and freshly stocked. They're going to give us every bit they've got."

"How many has it been? I've lost count," Earle Dressell asked from the Helm.

"One hundred and five," Barron said from the Sonar Station. He looked worn and pale from the stress.

"That's the largest number of depth charges in one attack I've ever heard of," Buddy Vogt, crouched near the radar screens, whispered back.

"That'll be one hell of a bragging right once we get to port," Liddell said.

We sat quietly, watching the ceiling above as though we could see our chasers in person. We waited for the ping, or for Barron to announce they were coming. He sat, hunched over, listening intently. Suddenly, he sat up slightly, frowning in concentration. Then, a wide grin. "They're moving out, sir." I slumped against the map table in relief.

After another half-hour in which Barron heard no signs of the escorts, Captain finally ordered a very quiet, "Periscope depth."

Flier gracefully rose, her stern planes now behaving, and Captain raised the Attack Periscope and looked around carefully. We waited.

"Take her up, Mr. Casey," Captain announced with a smile.

There was a quiet cheer as *Flier* soared up and broke the surface, suddenly bobbing up and down in the waves. With a nod from Captain, I climbed up to the Bridge Hatch, wrenched the wheel and stepped into the fresh air and twilight sky.

"Phew! What the—?" they heard me yell.

"What is it? What happened?" Several voices called up.

"Would you believe we've been stuck underwater so long that fresh air actually smells bad?!"

Sailor spoke rapidly and heeled the kumpit toward shore. Kong and Kim-Jong quickly hauled the sail down, and within moments, the kumpit slowed to a crawl, forcing Kim-Jong and Kong to row. Sailor, manning the tiller, raised himself onto his knees, watching the horizon keenly. Something large and grey was out there.

"What's going on?" we asked.

"It's a Japanese ship," said de la Cruz. "They are less likely to see us

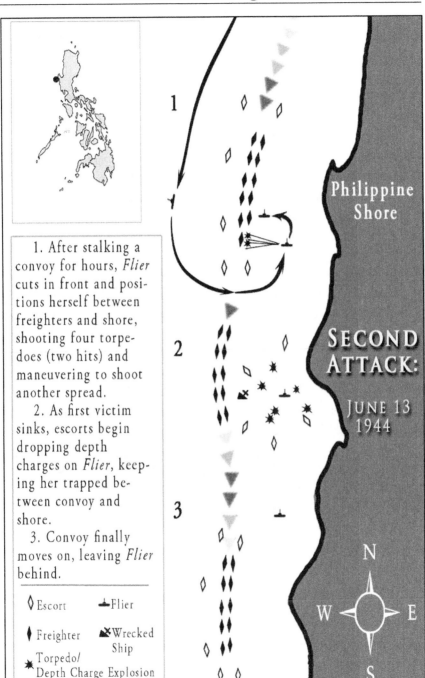

Philippine Shore

1. After stalking a convoy for hours, *Flier* cuts in front and positions herself between freighters and shore, shooting four torpedoes (two hits) and maneuvering to shoot another spread.

2. As first victim sinks, escorts begin dropping depth charges on *Flier*, keeping her trapped between convoy and shore.

3. Convoy finally moves on, leaving *Flier* behind.

SECOND ATTACK: JUNE 13 1944

◊ Escort   ⊥ Flier

♦ Freighter   ✖ Wrecked Ship

✴ Torpedo/ Depth Charge Explosion

N
W   E
S

with the sail down or care about a small fishing boat cruising near shore. Everyone stay low to the deck and keep still so they can't see how many are on here."

My binoculars, now in pieces, were useless, but she was soon close enough to see she was a battleship or destroyer traveling alone. After the fall of Guam and the Marianas, Japan was now fortifying the Philippines, their last great stronghold before their own islands were at risk.

The sun sank behind the island's mountains, throwing us, and then the destroyer, into shadow. She continued on, taking her time, never changing course, but close enough that we could hear her engines clearly.

By the time she finally passed far astern, our fair wind died, and King and Kim-Jong had to keep rowing. De la Cruz and Sailor took shifts with the boys but until Sailor took the kumpit into free water, we couldn't help with the rowing because we didn't know the paths through the reefs.

When Kim-Jong and Kong took up their second shift, Sailor fished out a heavy steel plate, tripod, and cauldron from beneath the deck before settling himself and the new gear at the tiller. He lit a fire on the steel plate, set up the tripod over the fire, filled the cauldron full of seawater and proceeded to cook us a rice dinner. While cooking, he continued steering the kumpit with one foot, and rowed with his other foot.

After dinner, a steady breeze found us, and the sail was quickly raised back into place. I hoped this meant we'd get to Brooke's Point by sunrise.

Sailor and De la Cruz kept watching the wind direction, the stars, and the progress of the crescent moon. Something was troubling them, especially Sailor. Finally, Sailor seemed to say something with a note of finality in his voice, and gestured toward us.

"Sailor says by the time we get to Brooke's Point, it will be broad daylight and well past the first patrol. It's too great a risk. He knows a place nearby where we can probably find food and a good night's sleep," De la Cruz told us.

Sailor turned the kumpit into the mouth of a river nearly hidden by the shadows of the overhanging jungle. Everyone took a turn rowing hard against the current for another two hours. It felt good to be active, but too soon my arms and chest burned from the effort.

We finally pulled up to a pair of huts, and four people scrambled out to the banks of the river. Sailor threw a rope to a young man, and he, with an older man, quickly helped haul us in and secured the kumpit to a tree.

We were ushered quickly into the house, and I was asleep on a bamboo mat before I actually realized it.

10

BROOKE'S POINT

The sunlight streamed through the windows when I woke up. I could smell something fabulous cooking, and ducked my head out of the hut.

Our host, an older man, saw me, smiled, and motioned me to the fire, where Captain and Jim already sat. A pot was happily simmering, as our host's wife stirred and sniffed it.

"Morning," Jim greeted me.

"Morning, sir," I replied. "What's cooking? It smells spectacular." The cook looked up, and I sniffed the air pointedly and smiled widely. She grinned back.

"It's coconut chicken stew," De la Cruz said, crouching down next to us.

De la Cruz then told us more about the family: the older man and woman were husband and wife, whose daughter had just married the young man we glimpsed the night before. Everyone in the small family took time to make us feel comfortable while the rest of the crew woke up and came out to the fire. The stew was delicious and I enjoyed having something besides rice for a meal.

We spent most of the day talking with de la Cruz about the guerillas' work and their history while we waited for the late patrol. After noon, the father began talking to De la Cruz and Sailor, and seemed to be asking a favor of them. They eventually agreed to it and the old man was overjoyed. He clasped hands with both men, then ran to hug his daughter. In moments, all four were talking excitedly and racing around the clearing.

"What's going on?" I asked De la Cruz.

"The hospitality given last night was freely done," he said, as he sat back down next to me, "but in return, it is polite and proper to return another favor, if it is in our power. The daughter and her new husband have relatives near Brooke's Point, and we've been asked to take them in the kumpit. If we could not take them, they would have to go north on foot."

I heard a squawk, and saw the daughter gently bundling two chickens in a large basket before securing the lid.

"We've accepted, but transporting them means transporting her dowry and household goods, too." There was a thud as a large basket of rice landed next to the basket of chickens, which was now surrounded by bundles of clothes, and several pots full of more goods.

"This could get interesting," I mused.

By the time we had lashed and stored all the newlyweds' worldly goods under the deck, on the deck, and to the racks tied to the outrigger spars, we had only enough room left for each of us to sit cross-legged.

"Where's Sailor?" Wes asked.

I looked behind me, and saw De la Cruz at the rudder. "Sailor had to take care of some things, said he'd catch up with us later if he could."

"Aw, gee, I'm going to miss him," Tremaine said.

'We all will,' I thought sadly.

The bride hugged her mother one more time before boarding. Kong, Kim-Jong, and the groom scrambled and grunted and finally heaved the kumpit off the shore with the help of the father. The spars to the floats creaked and groaned as the weight of our extra passengers and their household goods settled kumpit's edges only inches from the water. For a moment, I wondered if I would be shipwrecked yet again, due to chickens and rice!

Our hosts and their daughter waved and called to one another, until we turned a corner in the river.

It was much faster to go with the current this time, but as soon as we hit the open sea, the kumpit, fully loaded, could only lumber along, even with a good breeze behind her

Everyone sat, lost in their own thoughts. Looking around in the daylight, now I could see that where the river ended was in a large bay. To continue north we first had to steer out of the bay, then around a large coral reef before we could head north to Brooke's Point.

A few hours into the journey, just after we finally cleared the reef, we heard a shout, and saw Sailor swimming toward the kumpit. He laughed when he saw just how packed she was and had a bit of trouble hauling himself up to the deck, avoiding capsizing us or knocking any of the bride's dowry overboard.

"I knew I could easily catch up with you later, the moment I saw the sheer size of this dowry that was coming with us," he said through de la

Cruz, "She's a fast little thing, but not when this loaded down!" The bride suddenly looked both proud and mildly embarrassed, while the rest of us, even her husband, laughed.

"I took the opportunity to visit my wife and children who live near here, for a couple of hours," he continued through de la Cruz.

I was glad to see Sailor again. He was a remarkable man, completely at home on the sea, and amazingly dexterous. Later, when I smelled dinner cooking, I looked back and nearly laughed. There sat Sailor, manning the tiller with one foot, rowing an oar with the other, stirring the pot with one hand, adjusting the sail's with a line clenched in his teeth, and with his other hand, he was…sewing?!

I craned and twisted my neck until I could see that Baumgart's pants were missing! He apparently had split his pants out the back and Sailor was fixing them! And yet, for all this, Sailor always had a smile on his face, even through that rope.

Dinner that night was rice pancakes, which Sailor said his wife taught him to make that morning, fried to a golden crisp on the metal plate, near the edge of the fire. Even without butter or any condiments, they were delicious: light and nutty-tasting.

The sun set, and we continued north. Sailor planned on sailing all night and arriving at Brooke's Point before the morning patrol. Weighed down, and with a less favorable wind, the kumpit seemed to crawl at times, though Sailor and his crew maneuvered through the reef skillfully. I tried to twist myself into a comfortable position, but with no room, I think I ended up leaning against Howell while sleeping.

The moon was already behind the mountains when I awoke with a jerk that night.

"You okay, Jake?" Liddell, seated next to me, asked.

"Stiff and cold, but I'm okay, why?"

"You were mumbling in your sleep."

"I was dreaming."

"I could tell. Same dream as me, from the sounds of it."

"Just hard to believe they're gone. A part of me still half-expects them to walk out of the jungle every morning." I said.

"I know, almost like they're just AOL[29], and hoping Captain will be lenient. I can see Barron's grin, saying, 'Sorry sir, just lost track of a few days, again', just like that time he was gone for three days in Cali.'"

"Or remember Chester Payne, running for the boat, with Shore Patrol in hot pursuit, before he knocked them into the water and scrambled on deck?"

"Only for us to learn he was being chased in the first place for fighting with a one legged sailor?" Jim smiled.

"And that was all in my first two weeks aboard. I was so wet-behind-the-ears, I had no idea what gilly could do to a guy."

"I was standing watch once at Pearl with Jim Alls, when we saw this arm reach out of the aft torpedo hatch and set down a pitcher, then another pitcher, then out they came, one, two, three. They just sat there and talked, but as time passed, and those pitchers got drained, they got louder and louder. I was about to say something, when one of them stood up and announced, 'That's it! I'm going home! I'm putting on my blues and swimming home!' The second guy grabs him, hauls him back down to the deck and says, 'Sit down and shut up. You talk some sense into him.' When the third guy says, 'No! I'm going to go with him!'"

"What did you do?" I asked.

"Burst out laughing, me and Alls. They saw us and scuttled back inside so fast they were gone before I blinked."

"Fastest person I ever saw was Harry Ericson, the night he learned not to pinch strangers in dark rooms."

"I don't think I want to know where you spent R&R, Jake."

"The Wentworth, same as you. This was in the Conning Tower."

"Now I'm sure I don't want to know."

"Harry was supposed to go on watch one night, and was wearing those red goggles, and you know how you can't see much in the Conning Tower with those things on when we were running dark?"

"Oh yeah."

"So he's sitting on the floor for a few minutes before going out, when he feels someone sit next to him. I'm watching from the Nav table as he

---

[29] Absent without Leave

keeps looking back at this guy, who won't say a word. Finally, Harry leans over, pinches the stranger's cheek and says, 'And just who are you?' Without missing a beat, the guy pinches Harry's cheek right back and says, 'The Captain, that's who!'"

Jim buried a laugh under a snort and stole a look at Captain, snoring near the mast.

"Never saw Harry move so fast in his life. He was out the hatch and up the lookout deck in a moment." I finished.

"Captain has a sense of humor all right. You hear the one about him and the Tin Can Commander at Pearl?"

"Don't think so."

"It's around Christmas time, right before we left for Midway, and we're out conducting exercises before heading in for the day. We're heading for Pearl's entrance channel, when this surface vessel approaches, and flashes Captain a message to stand down and let them go in first because they're commanded by a Commander. Captain gets the message, and got hopping mad. He scrawls something on a piece of paper, hands it to Signalman Rose, telling him to flash this over there, and proceeded full speed to get there first. Rose showed me the paper later, it said, 'Roger Dodger, you old codger, I'm a Commander too! And it's Me! I'm a comin' through!' and sure enough, we whipped through in front of that tin can."

"Well, just before we got into Fremantle, you know how the guys stayed up all night, showering, shaving, ironing their uniforms?"

"Happens every time. We call it 'Channel Fever'."

"Well, I'm on deck when Captain comes out the morning we're due in port, and he looks up in the rings, and there's three guys dressed in the work dungarees, and one dressed in his dress blues, smartly pressed, his shoes shined, everything perfect. Captain calls up to him, 'What are you doing dressed like that?'

"He calls back down, 'Sir, we're due to dock at 2 pm today, and I don't want to miss the first bus out!' And he was on that first bus out, ready for a good time."

"They were a good crew," Jim said. "Though we had to make a few upgrades. Did you know Baehr was our Commissary Officer before you?"

"He never told me that."

"He might have wanted to forget. Around Thanksgiving, Baehr purchased a brace of fresh turkeys, not frozen. He was so proud of having fresh turkeys for Thanksgiving. Then the day comes and this dreadful, awful, burnt smell comes from the galley. We found the cook was already well into the gilly and had cooked those fresh birds, feathers and all. Cap'n broke him in rank and shipped him shoreside next morning, got Skow in his place."

"Good return on that investment. Remember the Victory Banquet they made the night we got permission to head home two days early? The grilled steaks with the roasted pork and cranberry sauce, and shrimp cocktail?"

"With the Chicken a la King and Mashed potatoes and gravy and buttered corn?"

"On second thought, don't remind me," I groaned. "These people have been so generous with everything they've given us, and I thank them for it. But there's a part of me that would give almost anything for some good food from the galley right now."

"Melvin's chocolate cake topped with chocolate ice cream with a side of coffee."

"Now you're just being cruel on purpose."

"Eh, you'll get some when we get back. And at least I won't have to face Lockwood again. He wouldn't be happy to see me."

"You know Lockwood?"

"Kind of, he knows me by sight at any rate."

"What did you do?"

"Well I wasn't the only one. But we sort of…committed mutiny."

"Get off it." I retorted.

"It's true, sort of. One of those things Dorricott and Elder always said doesn't make it in the official records. My first boat was *Snapper*. We were actually patrolling out of Manila when it was attacked after Pearl. Spooked one of our pilots so bad he actually bombed us the next day, despite sending him the right recognition signals. Thank goodness he had lousy aim. Anyway, our first skipper was okay, we got a kill, but he was rotated out, and we got a new one. He was from the old school of sub commanders, where you don't do anything if you might get seen or caught.

So we sank nothing, only fired from miles away, and wouldn't chase a convoy. By her fourth patrol, we had nothing to show, crew morale was bad, and it didn't look like anything was about to change. So several of us officers got together and told him, 'Either you start chasing something down, or we're taking over. The enlisted men will never know, but you'll follow our orders."

"You're kidding." I said.

"Eight to one, what do you think he did? It was almost the end of the patrol, so we caught nothing either, but we knew what we did was technically a hanging offense. So when we got to Fremantle, we hustled to Lockwood's office, he was in charge of Freo then, told him what was up before Cap could. *Snapper's* record convinced him we might be onto something. He replaced the CO, sent the old one stateside, but the new guy was just the same, and the same thing happened, no scores, no kills, and once, HQ ordered us to find a convoy, gave us coordinates and everything. He couldn't or wouldn't find it. We did our little civil mutiny again, and when we pulled into Pearl, went to brass again. And it was Lockwood, again. He'd been promoted and moved. He saw the same group of us walk into his office, and rolled his eyes, like he was thinking, 'Oh no, not again.' But he was already half expecting us based on *Snapper's* latest reports, and heard us out. Sent *Snapper* stateside for overhaul and replaced the CO again, but said, 'To make sure this doesn't become a habit, I'm splitting you boys up.' That's how I came to the *Flier*, actually."

"Well, I wouldn't worry about Lockwood, Christie's the one we'll face, and in case he's heard of you, I have an in with him."

"Really?"

"I know his driver, and she likes me."

"She?"

"Not like that."

He chuckled and sighed, leaning his head back against the rolled mat tied to the frame. I looked out to sea, watching the endless horizon, which didn't seem to move.

"Look at them." I heard Liddell say.

He was watching the bride and groom, his arms wrapped protectively around her as they slept, her head on his chest.

"They remind me so much of Marion and me. How I miss her."

"When did you marry?"

"Shortly after *Snapper* went stateside, so I guess I owe our old CO that much. You know, if those two manage to stay in each other's company for...nine months, they'll be together longer than my wife and I have, despite the fact we've been married for almost a year and a half."

He just watched them for a while, then said, "Soon, I hope, very, very, soon."

He stared out to sea, as did I, and soon, I heard him snore softly. A moment later, I must have followed suit.

A rooster's crow jolted me out of sleep again just before dawn the next morning. "Can we please shoot the alarm? I'll gladly have it for breakfast." Tremaine grumbled.

"Sorry, can't waste the ammunition." De la Cruz said, laughing. "Come on, it's nearly six already."

"Is that a.m. or p.m.?" Howell grunted.

"You have to ask?"

"Used to."

Sailor shouted at some small sailboats off the port side and heeled the kumpit over to meet up with them. As we drew nearer, I saw that the sailboats were not much more than outrigger canoes with a mast and sail. De la Cruz called them "bancas" and told us that locals often used them for spear-fishing. I watched as a darkly-tanned man leapt with practiced grace over the side, a short spear in his hand. Moments later he surfaced, with an eel neatly speared on the end. Another man surfaced with three fish on his spear.

The fishermen chatted excitedly with Sailor. They were apparently having a good morning, for they had baskets piled high with fish, eels, and squid. The first fisherman I had seen was apparently a good friend of Sailor's and handed him the eel on his spear, to the visible delight of the bride and groom, then retrieved two more good-sized fish, telling us through gestures that it was a gift for all of us. Sailor thanked him on our behalf, and we went on our way again.

The fish themselves looked like a type of mackerel, but the eel I wasn't sure about, until Sailor roasted it over the fire and passed it out, along with more rice, for breakfast. The fish was good, light and salty from the water. The eel, though, was different. Now I knew why the newlywed acted so excited about this. It was fatty, rich, and very good. Sailor didn't have any seasonings on him, and this needed none.

About an hour after that, we heard someone shouting at us, and the sail quickly dropped to the deck again. Another kumpit pulled alongside and its occupant held a quick, multi-layered conversation with de la Cruz and Sailor before getting underway again.

"That was a friend of LaHud's and mine," de la Cruz said as he carefully picked his way back across the deck. "He is coming from Brooke's Point. We asked if there were any patrols ahead, but there haven't been today. We should be there in a couple of hours."

Thick, acrid smoke accosted my nose, making me cough violently. It smelled like a campfire with a tire tossed on for good measure. Kong, rowing in the stern, was taking deep draws on what looked like a cigarette. Russo and Baumgart, denied their smokes for days, looked at the cigarette longingly, and gestured at Kong until he understood that they wanted one, too. He smiled and quickly rolled one for each of them, then held out a third for any more takers. There were none. A moment later, Russo and Baumgart began to cough and retch, heaving over the sides of the kumpit while Kong laughed. He said something, and de la Cruz laughed as well. "He says, 'Funny how two American military men can't handle a little Filipino cigarette!'"

"Cigarette, nothing!" Russo coughed. "I think that thing was made of…" he coughed again.

"Tar, Russo," Baumgart gasped. "That wasn't tobacco, that was some kind of hot tar, or asphalt, or rubber tires or something."

"I could've told you that stuff will kill you," Jim said, smiling. "You couldn't figure that out from the stench?"

"Apparently not, sir," Russo said.

Just as I was starting to watch the skies anxiously for the morning patrol, Brooke's Point finally came into focus. The point itself jutted out into the ocean, forming a small, protected cove. I wouldn't necessarily call it a bay, and it certainly wasn't sheltered enough for more than a few small boats like this one.

Sailor came about, dropping the sail, slowing the kumpit still further, and directed Kong and Kim-Jong to start rowing. De la Cruz picked his way to the bow of the ship, where he stood, searching the jungle for the lookouts that were sure to be on watch. Unless he could secure our entrance, the lookouts might shoot us before we could disembark.

No challenge came as we approached the point. De la Cruz began shouting and calling. Eventually, a sleepy-looking guerilla stood up and recognized us. After confirming that we were friends, he took off to rouse the garrison. De la Cruz and Sailor talked for a few minutes, and then the boys and Sailor rowed for the shore.

"We can land now," De la Cruz told us, "though we probably could have anyway. I think that man was sound asleep when we came in. We should have been challenged first, without my having to call."

The boys gave a final, strong stroke with the oars, and the kumpit grounded in the shallow water. Several of us splashed into the shallows to haul her up onto the beach. So much time sitting cross-legged on the kumpit made me stiff and clumsy.

A number of large, heavily armed men emerged out of the woods. One stepped forward.

"Nice to see you again, de la Cruz," He said in perfect, American accented English. He turned toward us and started shaking our hands. "My name is Captain Nazario Mayor, USAFFE, and I'm the acting Commanding Officer of Section D of the Sixth Military District here in Palawan. I'd like to invite you all to my home, it's only a short distance away."

Captain readily agreed, as did we all, but the bride and groom thanked him in their language, picked up their goods, and departed into the woods. I hoped, as I watched them trudge away, that they didn't have far to go.

Sailor, Kong, and Kim-Jong hauled the kumpit high on the beach away from the reach of high tide, and joined us.

As we walked, Captain Mayor introduced himself. He was a native Filipino, but had grown up in the USA. After graduating from the University of Kansas, he received a commission in the US Army though the ROTC. He returned to Bugsuk with his wife after his tour of duty and started a prosperous business there.

"How is my house, anyway?" he asked us. "I understand from de la

Cruz that you were found there."

"That was your place?" Captain asked.

"It seems like a lifetime ago, but yes. After the Japanese landed, my unit was called to active service, but our transport wrecked off Palawan, and we all had to swim to shore. This place was more defensible than my place, so my wife and I decided to abandon the Bugsuk house, and relocate here. Sorry about poisoning the cistern, by the way. I meant for that to be a gift for any invading Japanese bastard. Is the house still standing?"

"Mostly. You're going to have a lot of work to do when you get back, though," Captain told him. "The trees are taking over."

"That's all right. I'll just re-build, or maybe start all over. Who knows?"

Our feet were still very raw and wounded, and everyone else must have been as stiff as I was as we staggered up the path to Mayor's place. I thought to myself that we must appear very disappointing to the guerillas if they were expecting stellar examples of American military men. Hiking started to help with the stiffness, but the needles of pain shot up my feet and legs, and I tired far too easily.

"Mayor!" A shout came from the forest.

"Ah, wonderful. You received my message." Captain Mayor turned to us and said, "This is Mr. Henry Edwards. He's an American businessman who lived here at the Point until the war broke out. His house is two miles up Addison's Peak, and much more defensible than mine. After we get you fed, we're going to transport you there to await further orders. There are already three more people waiting for evacuation, with the addition of eight of you, we may finally be able to get you out of here."

"Three more?" Captain asked.

"They've been here since last December. George and Bill are from the Army and Charlie is a sailor. You'll meet them soon enough."

Edwards joined the group on the trail and told Mayor, "Corpus is on his way down, too. He should be here shortly, he just had to wait for one of his boys to return to guard the radio up there."

"Good, good," Mayor nodded.

The house, hidden in the trees, stood on stilts like the one at the Cape. Inside, we found a pretty, dark-haired lady cutting up fruit and watching a boiling pot from which emanated all sorts of incredible spicy and sweet

This photo, taken after WWII one mile south of Brooke's Point, shows how Brooke's Point looked during WWII. The mountain in the background is Addison's Peak. Photo courtesy of the family of Ens. Al "Jake" Jacobson

scents.

"May I present my wife, Mary Ann," Mayor said, as she smiled in our direction.

"Pleased to meet you, ma'am," Captain said. He introduced himself and the rest of us while she nodded politely.

"I'm pleased to meet all of you," she said in English, with a touch of an accent. "I will have breakfast ready soon. Please, wash up, and relax, the children will help me."

She called her children in from the woods where they apparently had been playing, and they quickly set the tables for everyone. Mrs. Mayor put on an incredible meal of game, some seasoned and salted fish, fruits and vegetables served over rice with a sweet and spicy sauce, flat breads, and several items I didn't recognize, but all were incredibly good. I probably ate more than I should have.

A discrete cough silenced our conversation and I saw a small man with a slightly worried-looking face finish mounting the ladder to the veranda and stride inside. "Ah, Sergeant Corpus, welcome," Captain Mayor said.

"Captain Crowley, may I present Sergeant Armando Corpus of the United States Army Coastwatcher unit."[30]

Sergeant Corpus was dressed in coveralls, and barefoot. He thanked Mrs. Mayor quietly and joined in the meal, or what we had left of it.

"I brought the cart and carabao," he said to Edwards, "and a boy to help drive them. I hope they will be sufficient."

"I'm sure they will, thank you. I don't think they'd have made the climb to the base in their condition," Edwards said, gesturing in our general direction.

"Which is the base, then?" Captain asked Mayor and Corpus, looking from one to the other.

"This is the guerrilla base. I am the captain of the guerilla movement here in southern Palawan," Mayor said. "We've been independent of the United States Army since the fall of Corregidor. We do the best we can against the Japanese while risking the locals as little as possible. De la Cruz works under me in Cape Baliluyan, and there are other groups all around the Philippines.

"Corpus and his Coastwatchers are with the American military, and have the ability to contact Brisbane. They've been here only a few months, since…May, was it?"

"June. June 8th specifically. Though we didn't settle here for a few more weeks." Corpus said.

"American Intelligence dropped them off on an island called Ramos

---

[30] Unlike the USAFFE, Coastwatchers were an official unit of the American or Australian military forces. Their job was to gather intelligence themselves or from native and guerilla groups in the area and radio this information back to headquarters. They had a nearly 65% fatality rate, because they faced danger from the environment, hostile people, inter-religious or inter-societal conflicts, as well as the enemy. Every radio transmission was a chance for the Japanese to triangulate their position and ambush. In the Philippines, Coastwatchers were recruited from American men of Filipino descent, chosen for both intelligence and the similarity of their facial structure to the natives. Oftentimes, however, having been raised in America, Coastwatchers spoke the native languages badly, or not at all. In times of invasion, their best bet was to hide with sympathetic natives and keep quiet. Due to the expanse of formal education in the English language under the United States rule from 1898 to WWII, many Filipino natives spoke at least some English, partially eliminating the language barrier.

which was good tactically, but bad if you want to avoid capture. They moved themselves to Mantangule, and when we found out they were there, I and a number of guerillas and locals sailed down there to move them here." Mayor said.

"Why?" Captain asked.

"Mantangule is still too hot, too well patrolled by boat patrols. They'd been there nearly a week when my flotilla got there. Personally, I was shocked they were still alive. We got them out of there, but all their gear took another week."

"We have a small shack here near this house where one of our radios is stored in the hopes that it will work someday." Corpus finished. "We do have a working radio up in the mountains near Mr. Edwards' place, which is our main base. Mr. Mayor has kindly let us stay in his 'summer home,' as he calls it.

"As soon as we can, we will send word of you to Australia, unless your mission is too top secret to risk sending word."

"Not that top secret," Captain said. "We'd like to be evacuated if possible. But first we've got to tell them to close Balabac Strait," Captain said.

"We can do that. But with eleven of you now, we may be able to get a plane or submarine here to clear you out. We'll do our best, at any rate. If we get back to the mill before the next scheduled transmission, we'll imbed your message with it, rather than make a new transmission. Cuts down on the enemy listening in and thinking we're broadcasting more than weather reports."

"Have they ever found you here?" Baumgart asked.

They smiled. "Oh, they know we're here, all right," Mayor smirked.

"And they haven't tried to invade and stop you?" he asked in astonishment.

"Only once," Mayor chuckled as he pulled an official-looking book out of the small desk in the corner.

"Ah yes, here we are," he cleared his throat. "'July 26. Japanese gunboat anchored 800 yards off beach and twenty soldiers landed. Enemy casualties: 20. Our casualties: sore trigger fingers.'"

We laughed. "The Coastwatchers gave us their extra arms and

ammunition as a thank you," one of the guerillas said proudly, showing off his Army M1 Garand rifle. "And as long as Kierson gets here soon, we'll have no trouble keeping ammunition coming."

I let the conversation wash over me, feeling completely safe and relaxed for the first time since we were left stranded on the ocean's surface. We were with friends, Americans too, who could obviously take care of themselves, and now we even had hope of rescue someday, rather than living my life out as Robinson Crusoe for the rest of the war.

After dinner, and thanking Mrs. Mayor and her family, we loaded ourselves into the rickety cart that was harnessed to a carabao.

Corpus and Edwards took off on their own, assuring us they would see us when we got to the house. Howell ran up just as we were getting ready to depart for the mountains.

"Sir, I've been looking at their radio here, and I think I can fix it if given time. Captain Mayor said I'm welcome to stay down here with his men to work on it if you will give leave."

"It would be a great help to us if we could get that old thing up and running again, Captain," Mayor said.

"Well, Howell is a great radio tech," Captain replied, "if anyone can fix your radio, he can. He's obviously well protected here with your people, so if he wants to stay, it's all right by me."

"Thank you, sir," Howell said.

"Thank you, Captain Crowley." Mayor added, "We'll send him along as soon as the radio is up and running, unless we can find other things for him to work on."

"We're never going to see him again, are we?"

"I'll take good care of him, and promise to return him in the same condition I borrowed him."

"Yup, never going to see him again."

I waved good-bye to Howell. De la Cruz and Sailor planned to head back to Baliluyan that evening, so we thanked them profusely for all their help and made our good-byes, knowing we would likely never see these amazing men again. After our farewells, the young boy entrusted with guiding the cart to Mr. Edward's place hauled on the carabao's rope and we rode away.

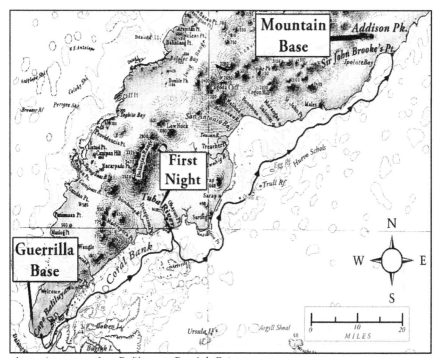

Approximate route from Baliluyan to Brooke's Point.

Though only three miles, it took nearly five hours to reach Mr. Edwards's home. A rainstorm the day before left the jungle dripping and sodden. Every time the carabao found a muddy puddle big enough to muck around in, he thankfully sank to his knees and wallowed happily. The boy, charged with bringing us swiftly and safely to the settlement, would yell, kick and beat the carabao with his crop every time he did this, but he might as well have beaten a stone. When the carabao decided he was rested enough, he got to his feet and moved on without any encouragement. It must have been a heavy rain because there were many mud wallows. We tried not to laugh because the boy was very upset. But it was so very funny.

The panting boy finally led the mud-encrusted carabao into the settlement around dinner time. Two houses and a mill sat in a rough triangle in the cleared land, and stumps from the felled trees still protruded through the forest floor. Like all the others we had seen thus far, these houses also were made of bamboo and suspended on stilts six feet off the ground, with grass-thatched roofs.

Mr. Edwards peered around the side of the mill, wrench in hand, glistening with oil and sweat. "Ah, there you are," he said, "I was starting to wonder." He looked at the boy and the carabao and said, "Oh dear, I'd forgotten about the rain."

He said a few words to the boy, clapped him manfully on the back, making the boy smile broadly, and sent him to fetch the others at the settlement. Soon after, Corpus, along with other men, emerged from the house and the nearby woods.

"You've met Corpus," Edwards said. "This," he gestured to a short, slightly-built man with a big grin, "is Sergeant Carlos Palacido of the Coastwatchers, and the three ruffians behind him are George Marquez and William "Red" Wigfield of the United States Army, and Charlie Watkins of the Navy. The rest of the Coastwatchers are all over the island right now, but they should be returning soon.

"There's also Henry Garretson, a civilian engineer turned guerilla. He's sick with malaria right now, and in bed. Part of the reason I hope you can convince someone to evacuate you is maybe they can also take Harry. His illness is getting worse, and beyond what we can treat.

"I live in the big house here. George, Bill, Charlie and Harry are already staying with us, so we can only take about three of you. The other house belongs to Mr. Mayor, but he only intends on using it if the Japanese ever land here in earnest, so the Coastwatchers stay there for now. It's also where we'll put the rest of you."

"When can we send a message to Admiral Christie in Perth?" Captain asked. "They need to close the Straits before another ship gets in trouble."

"We can only send messages to MacArthur's Headquarters in Brisbane," Palacido said. "However, we can probably have them forward the message if we know who it should go to."

"The message needs to go to Submarine Task Force 71 in order for Admiral Christie to get it."

"We can do that."

"Do you have paper and something to write with?"

"Can't waste what little paper we have anymore. Sorry. Tell me the message and I'll embed it in the next transmission."

Captain thought for a moment, then said, "Tell them the *SS-250* struck a mine and sank in Balabac Straits at 2200 hours on August 13. 50 fathoms of water. There are 8 survivors." Captain avoided giving a name, lest the Japanese intercept.

"*SS-250* struck a mine and sank in 50 fathoms at 2200 on August 13 with eight survivors. Got it. We'll encrypt it, imbed it, and send it out this evening when Sergeant Corpus makes the routine report."

Mrs. Edwards, a native Filipino, was a happy, smiling woman despite her small crowd of children and constant houseguests underfoot. She already had dinner waiting for us, which was coconut sprouts, rice, a citrus fruit she called Kalamansi, and another grapefruit-like fruit. Palacido and Corpus donated the last of their emergency rations to the feast: crackers, cheese, and coffee. They also brought better clothes, soap, sulfa drugs and first aid cream.

After dinner, I took a long bath in the cold stream, scraping and scrubbing off the salt from my skin and hair. I also shaved for the first time since the incident, and covered my feet in the cream, then wrapped them in bandages.

I hadn't felt this good since *Flier* sank, and slept peacefully and deeply that night, more hopeful than ever that I would get home.

11

IN THE MOUNTAINS

The night we landed, Edwards sent a message to a local missionary family, the Sutherlands. Mr. Alexander Sutherland, known as 'Sandy', arrived the next morning, and at Captain's request, conducted a church service in the settlement. A native Scot, Mr. Sutherland had been on Palawan since 1931, administering medicine and dentistry as part of his work. The local people respected him very much.

Mr. Edwards also sent for a woman they taught to give military haircuts, and a native doctor. I wasn't too confident in the local concept of medicine, and had more faith in the Coastwatchers' and Edwards' supplies. I could see from the others' faces they felt the same, but the doc was kind and well meaning, and we had no problem with him changing the dressings on our feet.

Every evening, the compound tuned in to the radio for an update from the outside world. With the generator and mill down, we each had to take turns cranking the hand generator to charge the battery. It was worth it though, to hear how the invasion of France had reached Paris, and our troops in North Africa, finished there, were crossing into Italy, re-taking Pisa. Guam had been re-captured, and two more ships had fallen victim to our submarines stalking the Philippines.

Living in the shadow of the enemy, these nightly broadcasts were the only things reminding the guerillas and Coastwatchers that the war did progress. After days of being cut off from the wider world, I found myself listening avidly for every scrap of information, and understood why this was an important ritual to everyone involved.

The next morning, I woke up feeling better than ever. Two days of rest and good food had done wonders for me, and I was eager to do something useful today while we waited for a response from Australia. Palacido had been on the radio last night, and said there was no message for us, though Corpus looked haunted after looking through the pile of decrypted messages.

"Good morning, Mr. Edwards, Mrs. Edwards," I said, grabbing some of the cooked rice and citrus for breakfast.

"Good morning, Ensign Jacobson," Mr. Edwards said.

"How are you feeling?" Mrs. Edwards asked.

"Please call me Jake. I'm feeling much better, thank you, I'm tired of just sitting around all day. I was never good at doing nothing."

"I only wish I had your problem. I have to head back to the beach today," Mr. Edwards said.

"I thought you were going to try fixing the rice mill again," Mrs. Edwards said, trying but failing to keep the note of disappointment out of her voice.

"I know, sweetheart, I know. But Mayor and I have to take care of a problem with some more bandits. More crop up every month it seems."

"What's wrong with the mill?" I inquired.

"I think it might be the drive belt, but I don't know enough about engines to fix it," Mr. Edwards admitted. "It's driven by a diesel engine that I salvaged from my old home, and I had some help setting it up, but everyone's been too busy to help me fix it."

"I can take a look at it if you like," I said.

"Really?" Mrs. Edwards sounded hopeful.

"Sure. I know a little about engines."

"Being from a submarine I'm sure you're familiar with all sorts of machinery," Mr. Edwards laughed. "When you're ready, I'll show you around and give you access to what tools I have."

The rice mill was a jury-rigged mess, but thanks to my work on *Flier's* diesels for my quals, I thought I could figure it out

"What do you think?" Mr. Edwards said, after showing me the room and the very few tools he had. "You don't have to, and I certainly don't want you to exhaust yourself, but if you think you can fix it, I would be ever so grateful."

"I've got a few ideas," I admitted. "I'll give it a go."

"Great!" Mr. Edwards shook my hand. "I really have to get going down to the beach now, but if you need anything just ask Mrs. Edwards, one of my kids, or the Coastwatchers."

"Sounds good. Say hello to Howell for me."

"I'll do that," he said with a wave, and quickly vanished down the path.

Time passed quickly, and I hummed to myself as I worked on the mill. The other Fliers woke up and said good morning to me as I worked, then disappeared with the other refugees to go fishing. The Edwards kids vanished into the forest to gather fruits and nuts, and before I knew it, it was close to noon, and the compound was quiet and deserted.

It took some doing, but I managed to set the drive belt back on the shafts and get it aligned again. Good thing the belt was still in decent condition, or I wouldn't have been able to do anything. When finished with that, I started tinkering and adjusting valves and timings to see if I could get the engine to run more smoothly.

Gradually, I became aware of someone watching me. I turned around and saw Palacido standing behind me, grinning.

"And here I thought you were dirty and disheveled when you arrived," he joked.

"That bad, huh?" I said, rubbing my sweaty forehead with a grimy forearm.

"Well, if you wish to avoid the wrath of Mrs. Edwards, I would wash off before you dare enter her house."

"It's awfully quiet around here," I said, looking around.

"I think we're the only two left. Mrs. Edwards went off a few minutes ago to wash clothes down where the creek is deep enough. Don't get any bright ideas though, she'll know if you touch anything with those dirty hands."

"Hey, are you busy?"

"Depends on your definition of 'busy'. I'm not volunteering to be a grease monkey if that's what you mean."

"Nah, I've already finished here and was just playing. I was actually curious about something." I glanced around the compound, but still saw no one. "When we first arrived on Palawan, it seemed like we were mistaken for submariners from another submarine that must have sunk not long before we did. Do you know anything about that?"

Palacido sighed and said, "We're still trying to figure this one out. Our means of communication on these islands are good for the technology we have, but sometimes we still have only fragments of information.

"Several days ago, we heard rumors that there were American

submariners sighted on Balabac Island. In fact, De la Cruz had only just returned from his investigation on Balabac a few hours before you arrived at Baliluyan.

"Sometime around or just after July third, there was an explosion and possible submarine sinking near Balabac Island, and several days later, submariners were spotted rafting to Comiran Island. They were captured or possibly killed."

"You don't know?"

"De la Cruz said the stories differed slightly. The general consensus is there were at least six submariners when the Japanese found them, and four were taken to the prison camp in Balabac City. The other two escaped, were shot trying to escape, or were shot after capture, depending who de la Cruz talked to. He was able to get two names: Tucker and Martin.

"There are also rumors of some more newly-arrived submariners up north at Puerto Princesa. It's hard to tell because if you're captured in the company of Filipinos, the Japanese might accuse you of being a guerilla, not a POW, so you would be kept in the prison portion, not the camp portion of the compound, and getting information about who is in the prison portion is much harder. There have been more rumors recently of a submarine sinking around July 27 near Palawan and a few survivors of that one swimming to southwest Palawan and being captured before they could get to us. The call number *SS-273* was mentioned once and *Robalo* another time."

"Are you sure?"

"Yes, why? Do you know these boats?"

"Boat." I corrected. "That number and name belong to the same vessel."

"Are *you* sure?" he repeated my question to me.

"Yes. Last patrol, around June 30, we crossed the path of a north-bound submarine just before we were going to go through our final strait. Found out it was *Robalo*, I learned her name and number that day. At the time, we figured she was on her way out on patrol. Just eerie that four days later they might have…"

He nodded. "We don't know if the submarine in question was crippled in some explosion on the 3rd then sank on the 27th or if there are two submarines besides yours we're dealing with. But after we heard the rumors, de la Cruz, before leaving to confirm them, ordered all of his men to keep a look out for submariners on the Balabac Islands."

"Which is how you found us," I said.

"Exactly."

"I see." It was sobering, and frightening, to think how close we came to swimming to Comiran that night. More might have made it, but we all might have been captured, or maybe worse.

"One of our men is with a contingent of guerillas at Puerto Princesa now, and should be returning soon. Who knows? We may find more survivors of your boat."

"We can only hope, I guess."

After a moment of silence, Palacido mercifully changed subjects and said, "So you have it working again?"

"I believe so," I said hopefully.

"I don't miss the noise, but it is rather convenient, especially because it charges the radio batteries, instead of that generator."

"Well then, let's fire it up and see, shall we?" I said, turning on the engine.

She sputtered, coughed, then smoothed out to a level *thrum*.

"Congratulations," Palacido said.

"Well, that's my chore for the day. What do you have for entertainment around here?"

We have some great magazines, Reader's Digest I believe, and only six years old," Palacido said with a smirk.

"Oh, joy," I drawled sarcastically.

"Hey, you have no cause to complain until you've memorized them all. Just don't forget to bathe before Mrs. Edwards sees you."

As we waited for a response to our situation, I learned more about the guerillas and Coastwatchers stationed here.

The guerillas were an amazingly complex organization scattered in groups all over the Philippines, with over one thousand men on Palawan and Balabac alone. When Captain Mayor introduced himself as a Captain of Section D of the Sixth Military District, it also meant he commanded over eighty men and four officers, who coordinated operations all over Palawan.

The guerillas acted as a first line of defense, they spied on the Japanese, provided connections to the friendly people of Palawan, and even recorded the sinking of Japanese ships which eventually could be accredited to a submarine or two. After the Coastwatcher's arrival, all this information was collected sent to Brooke's Point, where the Coastwatchers would radio the necessary information to Australia and catalogue the rest in case it was needed. The Coastwatchers often patrolled with the guerillas, and helped coordinate large-scale operations as well.

Harry Garretson was a guerilla as well, but was usually in bed with the fevers and shivers of malaria. They had no quinine to cure it, and the Atabrine[31] they did have couldn't relieve his symptoms any longer. As a precaution, the Coastwatchers started us on Atabrine tablets to keep down the chances we'd catch anything. Not wanting to end up like Harry, we took it faithfully.

George, Bill, and Charlie spent most of their days earning their keep by hunting, fishing, and tending the gardens and crops the Coastwatcher started.

We also had heard about a mysterious Finn by the name of Kierson, but he was away on a scouting mission for the guerillas and we had yet to meet him.

From our settlement on Addison's Peak, I could see little dots of coastal kumpits and canoes, and farther out to sea, the occasional massive Japanese convoy or warship. If they thought this side of Palawan was less patrolled by American submarines, they were wrong. I didn't see any attacks, but I wondered who else was out there watching them.

As there was little else to do, I found a large shady tree under which I could read comfortably. The six-year-old Reader's Digests provided a

---

[31] Quinine can be used to treat and cure malaria. Atabrine is a synthetic version, though not as effective. By the dawn of WWII, over 90% of the world's quinine production came from the Dutch East Indies, known today as Indonesia. When the Japanese took over that area in March 1942, the Allies' supply of quinine was interrupted, and they had to rely on Atabrine as much as possible and keep the quinine for desperate cases. Atabrine did not necessarily cure malaria with a single treatment and was used more often to suppress symptoms, especially in an emergency. Without Atabrine, most of the Pacific campaign would have been much more difficult, if not impossible.

surreal form of entertainment as I read about "The Value of the American Wilderness," "The Simple Lives of Farmers,"and"The Public's View of Unions Now."

I was drowsing under my tree the next morning, dilapidated Reader's Digest blocking the sun from my eyes, when I heard, "Hey, Jacobson, you interested in a little hunting?"

I peeked out from under my magazine, and saw George standing over me, a carbine rifle in hand.

"Sounds like fun," I said. "Offering to take me deer hunting?"

"For those piddly little things? Around here, they're the size of a poodle, and they're too far up the mountain anyway. I'm craving a side of bacon."

"Pigs?" I hadn't seen any of those either.

"Boars. And it's too dangerous to go out there alone. Red and Charlie wanted to fish today, so do you want to go hunting?"

"Sure. Beats lying around here all day. I'm sick of reading these."

"You have no cause to complain until you've memorized them all." George said.

"Palacido said the same thing. Is that your motto?" I joked.

"Are you going to make me play, 'Give me an article name and I'll quote you the opening sentence'?"

"You play that?"

"Don't get me started. Come on."

"Where's my rifle?" I asked, getting up and brushing myself off.

"We only have one spare today, so here." He tossed me a thick branch.

"What am I supposed to do with this? Beat it to death?"

"Let's hope not! Come on."

The forests of Palawan were huge and primitive; trees so ancient that ten men would be hard-pressed to encircle the trunks while young trees stretched high, competing for sunlight. The sound of birds and monkeys played to the backdrop of the constant dripping of water through the canopy.

We were soon soaked with sweat and drizzle, and I wondered if it was possible to get any wetter without the help of a body of water. The foliage was waist high in most places, making it impossible to see animals of any kind. We had to find a pig-trail and either stalk them or wait for them to come.

George stopped, fingering the fresh scars on the trunk of an ancient tree when we heard the low, rhythmic grunting of a boar. We froze, then slowly and silently stood up. He was the strangest boar I'd ever seen: a mottled grey, he stood on tall legs with a very long snout, flanked by an enormous mutton-chop beard.

George put his finger to his lips, quietly raised the rifle and took careful aim. The boar suddenly tensed, then ran screaming into the woods just as George got his shot off. "Bugger," he said, "we'll keep going, I guess. There's more pigs in this forest."

We found more boars over the course of the day, each taking turns with the rifle, but several were too far away to get a clear shot, and others escaped through the dense screen of undergrowth. We found a well-traveled animal path, and climbed up a tree to wait, though we quickly fell to talking rather than hunting.

"Heard you're from submarines," he said.

"Yup, best branch in the military." I said proudly.

"I don't know how you guys do that. I'd go stark raving nuts, trapped underwater with no sunlight for days."

"Weeks."

"Weeks?" He asked incredulously.

"For a lot of the guys, it's weeks. Most of the officers go on lookout duty and some of the enlisted, but for most of the guys, once we left, they didn't see sky again until we were back in friendly territory. You lose the sense of days. You're up for four hours, off eight, on four, off eight. You notice its two o'clock, but it takes you a while to figure out a.m. or p.m., not that it matters."

"I couldn't stand that."

"Lots don't." I admitted, suddenly recalling the panel of Admirals and Captains that intensely interviewed all dozen of us from U of M's ROTC unit who volunteered for the Submarine Force. I don't know what I said that convinced them I was a good fit, but only two of us made the cut. Then Submarine School tried to winnow that number down as fast as possible. The real thing was ruthless at separating those who were made for it and those who weren't.

"Think you'll go back now that you've survived your first shipwreck?"

"Well…," this was something I'd never admitted to my fellow crewmen. Sailors tended to be superstitious. "It's not my first. It's my second."

"Second?"

"Yeah, a few years back, my brothers and I rented this rickety old sail schooner named *Sea Girl* to take some friends up north in Michigan. We didn't how strong the winds were that day until we hit Frankfort, a hundred miles north, after only twelve hours, and the car ferry there turned around and headed back to port rather than risk the Lake. We took the hint and pulled in for a while.

"Couple days later, it was beautiful, calm and we took her back out, heading north to this place called Sleeping Bear Dunes and Manitou Islands. Weather kicked up again, and the waves started hitting her directly on the bow and suddenly, her ribs separated from her keel."

"Oh no."

"So every wave that hit the *Sea Girl* wrenched the ribs back and forth and popped the caulking out of everything. Water was pouring in through the seams. Our friends, who weren't sailors of any kind, were hammering the caulking back in while my brothers and I were trying to start the engine, which was thankfully mounted high, and ended up having to drive her onto the beach of one of the Manitous. We were stuck there too until the Coast Guard could come get us."

"Geez. And that didn't warn you off?"

"Hardly. I've been on the water since I was only a few weeks old, I'm not going to stop now. Your turn. How did you and Red and Charlie get here?"

He stretched out on the massive branch and leaned against the trunk. "Not much to tell, really," he said. "Red and I were stationed together at Nichols Air Base near Manila, just a short ways above Cavite."

I nodded. I had heard about the Japanese bombing that base the same day they bombed Pearl Harbor.

"Red and I didn't know each other then, and the day that the Japs attacked, I just kept running around trying to preserve our planes.

Everything was just chaos. I remember seeing the *Sea Lion* sub get blown sky-high with a direct hit. A week later, the entire airfield was evacuated to Mindoro, while MacArthur and the rest of the men started the move to Bataan and Corregidor. So we were spared the Battle of Bataan and everything that happened afterward.

"But when we heard all military personnel were expected to surrender to the Japs when Corregidor fell,[32] a lot of us took to the hills of Mindoro rather than just surrender or let ourselves be captured. About fifty of us managed to get to Panay Island hitching rides on fishing boats. I met Red on the kumpit that took us to Panay.

"We tried to settle in, but the Japs just kept coming, and it was getting harder to hide. Most of the natives were willing to help us, but finding food for everyone was difficult and it only took one to betray us, willingly or coerced. So several of us built a batch of rafts and sailed east until we found Cuyo Islands. They're so small and sparsely populated, we hoped the Japs wouldn't bother to spend manpower on them. It worked for about a year and half. The only sign of the enemy was a naval officer and a civilian who were tried to "recruit" the locals. I personally made sure they went permanently "missing." Apparently they weren't missed all that much, 'cause no one ever came looking for them.

"Anyway, late last year, a couple Japanese platoons landed in Cuyo. Red and I were lucky, we were in the hills when they landed. We had enough time to hide in this hollow under a couple of boulders, while the Japs tried to find everyone. I don't know how many they got overall. I saw about thirty guys being herded into lifeboats as the sun set, including some of the natives that had been helping us. Other people were just murdered outright.

"Afterwards, Red and I resurrected one of those rafts that had gotten us to Cuyo, and we took off east again and landed in North Palawan. We spooked easily at that point, jumping at any shadow, or the crack of a twig. Then one night we stumbled, literally, into Charlie. He was on patrol with the local guerillas, and they took us in.

"It quickly became too dangerous in North Palawan. They call South Palawan "Free Palawan" because we've kept Jap bases out and we are more

---

[32] May 6, 1942

or less left alone. But up north, there is a lot of Japanese pressure and influence, and the danger of betrayal just became too great. So the guerillas shipped all of us down here to wait for pick-up last December. The Coastwatchers arriving this summer has been a great boon, what with the radio and all. But I'm getting bored. All I can do is hunt for food because it's too dangerous to do much else. My white skin gives me away, you see. Hopefully, since you're here, they'll come and get you and we can all get out of here. I might even get my chance to do something against the enemy myself before this war is over."

"Do you know what happened to Charlie?" I asked. He had been quieter, jumpier, but still had a sense of humor, and would quickly join in on card games or conversation.

"Kind of. He doesn't talk much, which I'm sure you noticed, and I don't know if he was always quiet or what. He was in Fort Hughes when the Battle of Corregidor broke out, and one of the POWs at the surrender. He told me that those islands are pock-marked, burnt and all blown to hell now. A pity. They were quite beautiful before the war.

"He was taken to Bilibid Prison in Manila. It's this huge compound that housed only the worst and most dangerous prisoners before the war. Thick walls, iron bars, the whole bit. No one has ever escaped from there. Later, he was marched to the north of Luzon to Cabanatuan. After a few months there, he was shipped to Palawan on a merchant freighter. What little I've gleaned from him about that trip makes my skin crawl. I guess there were not many lights in the hold, and there was only fresh air when they dropped food down in there. I can't imagine how terrifying…he still has nightmares about being 'buried alive' in the ship's hold.

"She docked at Puerto Princesa, which is virtually a ghost town these days. The natives all took to the mountains when the Japanese landed. It's pretty desolate up there. The barracks in the camp are huge, partly transformed into a jail, and metal roofed, so it's got to be hotter than blazes under the sun. He won't often talk about his time in the camp, and I don't blame him. I've seen a little with my own eyes what those prisoners go through, and regret every moment of it.

"Charlie and the other prisoners were told they would be building a road, but what they're really building is a giant set of runways, using nothing

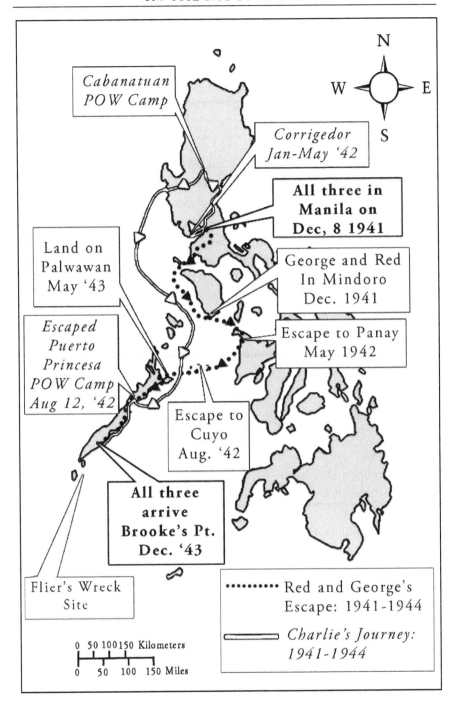

Cabanatuan POW Camp

Corrigedor Jan-May '42

All three in Manila on Dec, 8 1941

Land on Palwawan May '43

Escaped Puerto Princesa POW Camp Aug 12, '42

George and Red In Mindoro Dec. 1941

Escape to Panay May 1942

Escape to Cuyo Aug. '42

All three arrive Brooke's Pt. Dec. '43

Flier's Wreck Site

•••••••• Red and George's Escape: 1941-1944

⬜ *Charlie's Journey: 1941-1944*

0 50 100150 Kilometers

0   50   100   150 Miles

N
W   E
S

but broken-down hand tools. Charlie says that if you didn't work as fast as they thought you should be able to, the guards beat you with sticks as thick as your wrist. They're supposedly experts at inflicting pain without breaking bones, because a man with a broken bone can't work. Those guards would beat you for anything from disrespect to stealing, or just from wanting to break up the monotony.

"So Charlie and another guy, Joel Little, decided to make a run for it. The airstrip is a couple of miles from the prison camp, and the men mostly labor under the eyes of the guards, but they let one or two men at a time go into the woods to relieve themselves. So, Charlie and Little asked permission to go one day, and they did. The guard never saw them again. The Filipinos in that area smuggled him to safety, then let him and Little join the guerillas. Little eventually decided to go with another bunch to Panay, leaving Charlie here on Palawan when we bumped into him. So that's more or less what happened to him.

"No one escapes from Puerto Princesa anymore. Now they count the men into work details of ten. If one man is missing at the end of the day, the rest of the group is executed. No one even tries anymore."

He shuddered, and I silently thanked God that we had thus far been spared that.

A rhythmic grunting broke into our thoughts. The large boar from the early morning was back, rooting among the forest floor. Blood flowed from his shoulder.

"Looks like you didn't miss him after all," I whispered to George.

"And I don't intend to again. Ribs are sounding *really* good. Pity there's no barbeque sauce."

He raised the carbine to his eye, steadied, aimed, and the pig took off into the forest shrieking before he could get off a shot.

"No wonder that old bastard is still alive. He can sense danger from a mile away," I said.

"He's probably tough anyway. Dammit. It's been so long since I've had any decent meat: hamburger, ribs, bacon and eggs. If I never see rice again my entire life, it'll be too soon."

"Well, I promise you, unless the cook on the rescue ship or submarine is a total hack-job, you'll have all that stuff on the ride home. And if he is a total hack-job, I'll cook you bacon and eggs myself."

George cracked up. "You're on, Jacobson."

"What about that?" I pointed at a small, pigeon looking bird that emerged from the undergrowth, pecking among the forest floor.

"May as well," George grunted. "Better than nothing, and I'd rather have that scrawny thing than monkey brains again."

"Monkey brains?"

"Beggars can't be choosers," he said, dispatching the pigeon with a quick shot and puff of feathers. "Charlie's grown to like them, but I just-" he shuddered. "I just can't."

Despite the tiny offering for lunch, everyone was glad for a small bite. Any meat other than fish was a welcome change.

12

SHOT IN THE DARK

The next day, the rest of the Coastwatchers with their guerilla contingents returned to the compound. Corpus accepted their reports and talked to each one briefly, before retiring to their building. They noticed us very quickly, and as soon as official business was over, Palacido introduced everyone. The four returning Coastwatchers were Sergeant Jaime "Slug" Reynoso, Sergeant Ramon "Ray" Cortez, Corporal Teodoro "Butch" Rallojay, and Sergeant Ritchie Daquel, or "Dac". The only ones who didn't seem to have a nickname were Palacido and Corpus.

"Well, this explains what the ladies meant by, 'bring the new Americans tonight,'" Ray said with a grin.

"What's tonight?" Jim asked.

"The Women's Auxiliary Service here is throwing a party for us and the other Americans here at the Point. Apparently, the invite is now expanded to include you all," Palacido explained.

"Does this mean we'll finally get to evacuate some of the civilians from around here?" Slug asked. "With these guys here, there might finally be enough to warrant a submarine or ship or something."

"We'll see, we've heard nothing official from Perth yet," Palacido said.

Captain spoke up, "I thought Corpus said that Perth contacted us two days ago."

"They did, but their message was not about evacuation." Palacido held up his hand to quiet the incoming flood of questions. "I'm afraid that's all I know right now. Sergeant Corpus should update you later tonight.

"Okay, fellas, you're dismissed to make yourselves presentable. We'll leave at 1700."

I started to head for the Edwards' house when I heard Palacido say, "Jacobson, could you wait a moment." I turned to find Palacido standing next to Slug, Captain and Jim.

"What's up?"

"I thought for a moment we'd all go for a walk," Slug said.

We hiked into the woods a ways, my curiosity piquing, but waited until

Palacido called a halt and we gathered in a tight knot around him.

"I thought perhaps, since you are all submariners, I might have a word with you about some things we heard when I was up near Puerto Princesa and the prison camp." Slug said. "Does the name Kimmel mean anything to you?"

I knew Kimmel was the name of the Admiral blamed for Pearl Harbor, but I couldn't see how that could matter now.

Captain, however, said, "Manning Kimmel?"

Slug nodded. "Yes, you knew him?"

"Manning Kimmel commands the *Robalo* but..." his voice trailed off and he looked sharply at Slug. "What do you mean 'knew'?"

Slug hesitated, "We couldn't get accurate enough accounts to make it official, but apparently, the POWs at the camp told some of the guerillas that a submariner named Kimmel was delivered to the camp three weeks or so ago. Last week, after a couple of American aircraft buzzed the Puerto Princesa compound, he was...killed."

"Killed?" Captain looked from one to the other.

"With all due respect, sir, I'd rather not tell you. If the reports we've heard are correct—"

"What the hell happened?" Jim interrupted.

"He, along with several other men, may have been pushed into a ditch and ...set ablaze. At least, that's the story we're getting."

"God..." Captain breathed.

I gasped as my stomach leapt to my throat. '*No man deserves that fate,*' I thought. "What about the others?" I croaked out.

"According to one of our contacts near the camp, Dr. Mendoza, four submarine crewmen were captured and declared to be guerillas by the Japanese. They managed to smuggle a note out of the prison with their names and the number of their boat. Everyone in that section was loaded on a Japanese destroyer on the fifteenth of August. No one could say for sure what the ship's name was, or where she was bound.

"No other submariners have arrived since then, so if more of your crew has survived, they are not there." Slug finished.

Before we got our hopes up, Palacido quickly added, "But you have to know, we haven't found any more Americans roaming these islands, or heard any rumors of any, either. You may have been the only ones to escape your boat. I'm sorry if you were hoping for more."

It was only a slight shock to us. After all, the chance anyone made it out of the *Flier* had always been remote, and swimming to the surface alone would have been nearly lethal.

Subdued, Jim and Captain set off in different directions, no doubt absorbing this disturbing news as well as any man could. We had heard rumors of these horrible camps but I never thought that it could be that bad.

Palacido and Slug watched us quietly for a moment, then turned and walked back to the house, no doubt, to give us some privacy.

I tried not to think that afternoon. Submariners are used to death, we were actually somewhat fatalistic about it. All for one, one for all, live or die we do it together. Being left behind from my own boat was like being potentially amputated. Heck, one of the reasons I'd joined the Submarine Force was because you came back whole or not at all, not wounded or blinded or missing a limb.

Sounded ironic now, as I looked at my sunburnt arms, the blisters now drying and crusting over and my feet finally healing properly, no longer running with pus. And I have gotten off lightly, not like Howell and his knee or...or like Ed.

Still, I had long since reconciled myself to the possibility of dying with my crew on my boat, together. But as a human torch...I shuddered at the thought.

"Hey Jake!" George yelled, startling me. He was hiking up the trail near me along with Red, Charlie, Baumgart and Miller. A basket of fish hung from a pole riding on Baum and Charlie's shoulders. Everyone else carried fishing poles. I composed myself and waved back. "Saw our boar again today," George continued. "Too bad I was only armed with a pole and worms!"

I joined them, and quickly started talking fish, hunting, and anything else to take my mind off Kimmel, and by extension, the price of capture here.

As the sun began to set, we started to gather for the party, the Coastwatchers in their best overalls.

"They promised tuba for drinks, you're going to love it," Dac said.

"What's tuba?" Miller asked.

"It's this great fermented drink the locals make from the sap of coconuts. It's as close to beer as you can find around here."

"Great! I haven't had a beer since my last night in Fremantle," Baumgart said.

"Oh, you poor baby, you want to know the last time I was in a proper bar?" Red scoffed.

The chattering and jibing went on for several minutes. Some of the guys kept looking at their watches. "It's time to go, where are Palacido and Corpus?" Dac asked.

On cue, Palacido walked out onto the Coastwatchers' veranda and down the ladder to the group.

"Are we ready to go?" he asked.

"Been ready," Butch said.

"My, my, aren't we eager? Afraid Conchita forgot what you looked like while you were away?"

"Aw, come on, cut me a break, Sarge," Butch grinned.

"Hey, where's Corpus?" Slug said.

"He said to go ahead, that he'll catch up in a few minutes." Palacido looked slightly worried.

The rest of the Coastwatchers looked slightly exasperated. "He's been down again. Are we going to wait for him?" Slug asked.

"He insisted that we go on without him. Since we're still waiting on Captain and Mrs. Mayor, I'll stay behind and wait. The rest of you go on ahead."

"I'll stay, I promised the Mayor children I'd show them a new game quickly." Ritchie Daquel offered.

"Okay then. Now men, I'm sure the *Flier* guys would appreciate a slower walk to the village since their feet are still healing. Take the scenic route, give them the full tour."

The native village we were going to visit had been the one from where the doctor and hairdresser had come. It was north of the settlement, farther up the mountain, about a twenty-minute walk. The guys kept going on and on about the tuba, which was apparently a village specialty.

I couldn't believe it. I was shipwrecked on a tropical island, about to go to a luau and be served tropical drinks by the local women…it sounded like some of the adventure books I read as a boy.

The crack of a gunshot suddenly split the air and we threw ourselves to the ground on instinct.

"It came from the base!" I heard one of the watchers say. They took off back down the trail at a run, while we followed as quickly as we could.

Everything was in an uproar. Mrs. Edwards's and Mrs. Mayor's children were huddled around their mothers as the women tried to herd them into the house, and Captain Mayor, his face shocked and grim, walked out from behind the Coastwatchers' house, firmly propelling his twelve-year old son forward with a tight grip on his shoulders. Little Robert Mayor's eyes were wide and staring, he looked stunned beyond words.

My blood turned cold. Mr. Edwards, rounding the corner of the same house, saw us clumsily running forward and held up his hands to stop us. "Don't. Just keep clear right now," and in a lower voice, "Sgt. Corpus shot himself while Palacido and Daquel were greeting the Mayors. It's pretty bad."

"Is everyone else all right?" Baumgart asked.

"Physically, yes." He looked over to his wife who signaled that they had everyone inside. I glanced through the stilts holding up the Coastwatchers' house, and saw Corpus's form on the ground, surrounded by the Coastwatchers, some standing, some kneeling. "Palacido told me to tell you that he'll come and talk to you as soon as the women and children are inside where they can't see. Excuse me, I need to tend to my family."

Shortly after Mr. Edwards vanished inside his home, Palacido crept around the corner. We could see him from where he stood, though he was hidden from the Edwards' house. His hands were covered in blood. "We need to bury him quickly in this heat," he said with no preamble. "And obviously, there will be no party tonight. I need someone to tell the villagers why we're not coming."

"I'll go," Red said, indicating George and Charlie as well. "We know the way and the people."

"Thank you," Palacido said. "I wish we knew where the Sutherlands are camping tonight, they've likely moved since we saw him last."

"We saw them earlier today, setting up camp for the night, when we were fishing, sir. I know where to find them," Charlie volunteered.

"Please, I'd like him to conduct the funeral."

They left the clearing at a fast trot, leaving the rest of us standing around awkwardly.

"Daquel and I will prepare Corpus," Palacido continued. "We also need a coffin and someone to dig a grave. There's not much wood around here, so you may have to scrounge."

Soon, I was on the coffin detail, with two Coastwatchers, while the rest were digging a grave in the woods.

The lumber pile was sparse and problematic. Three years after being cut off from the rest of the world, there was not much left. We had to splice and join many pieces creatively.

There was only about thirty minutes of light left by the time we finished the coffin and carried it behind the Coastwatcher's house, where Corpus still lay, out of sight from the children.

He had been bathed and dressed in his best coveralls. His face was at peace, but I noticed his chest had a large hollow in the center. A small man in life, his remains seemed smaller in death. Despite that, he only barely fit in the coffin.

The funeral was quick, though solemn. The women and children did not attend. Sutherland said a prayer over the grave, then we filled it in and covered it with stones to keep it secure from animals. At the end of the ceremony, Palacido picked up a rough cross made from two limbs bound together with a vine, and hammered it into the soil with a shovel. The light fading fast, we turned to leave. On the way out, I noticed this was the third grave here, and, though it may have been a trick of the twilight, I thought I saw a rusty dog tag tangled in one of those cross-topped stone piles.

Dinner, long delayed, was quiet, and Palacido soon excused himself to man the radio for the night's transmissions, and to inform Brisbane of Corpus's death.

I needed some space to think, and strolled around the compound after dinner. After a few turns, I passed the radio shack, still lit by a camping lantern. Palacido sat in front of the quiet radio, massaging his forehead with his hands.

"How are you holding up?" I asked, stepping though the doorway.

"Hmm?" he said, looking up. "Oh, I've just been thinking back over the events of today. Wondering if I could have done something different or seen this coming.

"He had been moody before, told us he felt useless and like extra baggage. He got really quiet again after Perth radioed two days ago, maybe that was what finally did it."

"What did Perth say?"

"Well, we radioed them about your boat going down and included the theory that *Robalo* might have, too, and they radioed back the next night. No word about whether or not they're going to extract you, but an earful for us." Palacido picked up a piece of paper. "They start by essentially asking us why we didn't tell them the straits were mined. We've only been here two months, for all I know those Straits have been mined since the time of Noah. They didn't lay those mines on our watch, that much I know. This last bit was the killer: 'Your mission is to cover that area and advise me instantly of all important enemy dispositions and naval movements. Results thus far are disappointing and immediate improvement in your intelligence coverage and report is desired and expected.'

"I think Corpus might have taken this as blame for the loss of both boats and their crews. I know he'd been depressed since he read that."

"I don't think any of the Fliers blame you," I said. "I know I don't. Our orders told us to stay in deep waters to avoid any possible mines. That's just one of the chances that we take as submariners."

"Thanks," he smiled sadly. "Poor fellow, I guess he just couldn't take it anymore, and needed out."

There was nothing to say to this, and I just stood there awkwardly for a moment. Palacido stood and stretched, saying, "Well, I'll see you and the others bright and early tomorrow. We've got planning to do."

"We do?"

"Yup. Perth just called again. They're coming to rescue you."

13

EVACUATION PLANS

"That far out? Are you sure?" Palacido, Captain Mayor, Captain Crowley, Jim and I were poring over the Japanese charts of the area. The Coastwatchers had gotten them from someone who stole them off a Japanese supply ship that had run aground farther north. That fact alone made me wonder about the accuracy of the charts.

"Trust me, just to float, a fully-loaded surfaced submarine needs at least sixteen feet beneath her, and we'll want to give our rescuers plenty of depth to work with. I saw how far out those reefs extend on our way up here. We'll have to go out at least five miles out," Captain told them.

"We're going to need a large enough boat that can get everyone out there. Is Sailor available?" I said.

"He's off on another trade trip. It would take a while to get him back here, and it sounds like Perth wants you back as soon as possible," Mayor said. "I'll contact Datu Jolkipli and his people. They live a little south of here and have a large collection of boats. Jolkipli's has an outboard motor. We might be able to purchase or borrow it for trade."

"Can we go today?" Captain asked.

"If we leave soon, and the chief lets us have his boat with the outboard motor, we could even be back by dinner time. I'll see what monies I can scrounge up."

"We have some left from our original supplies, too, I can give toward this," Palacido offered.

"Would he trade for its use? I'm sure that whoever rescues us can spare a gallon or two of diesel as a part of a trade if he'll trust we're good for it," Captain said.

Palacido and Mayor burst out laughing.

"What? What's going on?"

"I'm sorry, Captain," Palacido said, tears running down his face. "I know you mean well, but if there's one thing we keep trying to get rid of around here, it's diesel. We all but bathe in it, and we can't trade the stuff away fast enough because everyone else has so much of it, too."

"Where do you get it?" I asked.

"Strange thing about living around here, 50-gallon barrels of diesel fuel marked with Japanese symbols just keep washing up on shore every few days." He looked very meaningfully at me.

"Ah, well, you're welcome."

The day passed slowly. I amused myself carving cribbage boards, which was rather silly because there were no cards. Jim was asleep under a tree, and George, Red and Charlie were trying for that boar again. Baumgart and the other enlisted Fliers were fishing for dinner.

Out of sheer boredom, I tried to make sandals for my feet by weaving some of the local grasses together, but no matter what I did, they rubbed on the still-healing sores.

It was funny, but I had a large family, and my siblings and I were always under each other's feet. Then at college I lived with a bunch of guys at Sigma Phi house. On the submarine, I often wished for a spare moment and space to gather my thoughts or relax. Now, with all the time and space in the world, I found myself aching to do something, anything.

I ended up doing what I usually did these days when I was forced to be still and quiet: remembering *Flier*. How before a shift one evening, Ed jokingly complained that because, once again, I was the Diving Officer while he was manning the periscopes, I was going to "duck" him again. I had been unfortunate enough to duck the periscope underwater the last several times Ed was trying to take bearings on a target or landmarks to assess our position, but I told him it wouldn't happen this time.

"You're going to do it, Jake, it's inevitable."

"You willing to put some money on that inevitability?"

"Easiest money I'll ever make."

So when Ed spotted five columns of smoke that evening, I made absolutely certain the periscopes stayed steadily above water for as long as Ed wanted to take bearings. I think he took more than usual. [33]

---

[33] These events took place June 22-23, 1944 west of Mindoro Island in the Philippines.

We were southbound and this convoy was northbound, probably headed for Manila. They were coming on fast, with several escorts. Because it was so close to nightfall, we decided to wait until dark.

They passed by, letting us count the number of ships: nine freighters and a half-dozen escorts. They were heading north–northwest, staying almost precisely four miles from Mindoro's shore, and traveling at nine knots. On the surface, *Flier* could make more than twice that speed.

Captain decided to do an end-around attack again. By the time we reached our planned position, it was only an hour before midnight. If all went as planned, the convoy would pass between us and Mindoro's shore.

The forward escorts never saw us, whipping past as we sat silently, the freighters lumbering in their wake. We targeted the first two ships of the closer column, sending three torpedoes at each. We then fled out to sea while the torpedoes were still en route. I watched from my position on the Aft Bridge as the first torpedo hit and exploded, shooting water and debris in a blinding flash. Seconds later, the second torpedo hit, and she started to sink by the stern.

Another flash and two geysers of water, and the smaller second ship took two hits. Both ships broke ranks and made a run for the beach.

"Sonar reports two hits on the first target, two hits on the second," Jim said.

The escorts turned and roared back to their charges, passing far astern of us, dropping depth charges in their wakes, thinking we were submerged. It was almost comical.

The smaller freighter suddenly disappeared both from our radar and our sight, though in the night, it was difficult to tell if she sank or had run aground.

The big one drifted helplessly, her engines dead, slowly taking on water in her stern. The other freighters couldn't stop to help her, not with an enemy submarine lurking somewhere about. They sped up, going around the wounded ship, leaving her behind to limp along and take her chances as well as she could.

We raced ahead north, thinking we might get another shot, and sure enough, an hour later, they were positioned perfectly once again. *Flier's* black frame was invisible against a moonless sea and we snuck past the escorts easily, closed in on the convoy, and lined up for a torpedo spread.

I stood on the Aft Bridge, my eyes buried in the Target Bearing Transmitters or TBT, a pair of specialized, water-proof binoculars mounted on a tripod which fed information to the Torpedo Data Computer, or TDC below in the Conning Tower. My job was to center the crosshairs of the TBT lens on our selected victim and hit the trigger mounted on the side of the eyepiece, automatically feeding the angles and bearings to our targets to the TDC which fed the right gyro angles to the torpedoes. Captain and I chose the lead ship for our final spread of bow torpedoes, watching her carefully as she zigged and zagged for about fifteen minutes, hitting the trigger every two. I could hear Howell feed Radar's ranges to the target every time our new angle feeds came in.

With a *THUNK!* and a knee-bending jolt, the first torpedo was away, then another, and another, and the last, *Flier's* bow bobbing up and down in the recoil and from her now-lightened nose. Through the TBT lenses, I watched the spread stream towards our victim, keeping track of the countdown by chewing my wad of gum in rhythm with my ticking wristwatch.

The countdown came and went, but nothing happened. "What the hell?" Crowley said. "*Four* duds?" It wasn't unheard of, but highly unusual, and disappointing.

Boom… Boom Two of our torpedoes exploded against the stern of our large freighter, geysers thrusting into the night sky. Seconds later, we heard the third torpedo strike the ship in the column half a mile behind it.

"What happened down there?" Captain called into the Conning Tower. "Those fish were supposed to hit along the length of that ship, not the stern!"

"We were giving range to the closest ship in the convoy, Captain, isn't that what you wanted?" Howell called up through the hatch.

We looked at the convoy. The lead ship was actually in the far column, but the one behind her was in the closer column, and closer to us. "No, but at least it worked!" Captain called down.

"Aye, sir."

"Reverse course, ready the stern tubes!"

Flier turned, and I focused in on the next largest freighter, but the

"The Kill", 1943, watercolor by Georges Schrieber. Most WWII submarine torpedo attacks occurred while the submarine was surfaced and had lookouts to take bearing and ranges. Jake and Captain Crowley would have witnessed a sight like this from Flier's bridge during this attack. From the Department of the Navy: Navy Historical Center. Gift of the Abbott Laboratories.

escorts found us quickly and charged. They were so close, we couldn't risk diving without potentially getting rammed.

"LIDDELL!" Captain roared down the hatch. "The escorts! What course is the widest gap between them?"

A second later he shouted, "Zero–two–five degrees, sir!"

"Full speed ahead on that course!"

Flier soared above the waves and charged the enemy. We all but waved as we flashed by so fast and so close to one it didn't have time to react or try to ram us. The others didn't see where we went after we vanished behind the bulk of their companion. As we retreated, I watched the first ship we hit settle beneath the waves, the gurgling bubbles swallowing her hull. The other one, though hit, looked like it could continue with the convoy. The escorts, again unable to see us against the black sea, apparently decided it was best to move their convoy out as fast as possible. The cripple from our first attack, now limped along at the rear of the convoy, forcing the whole convoy to slow down and a couple of escorts to stick closely with her.

Crowley wanted to finish off the cripple, but it proved too difficult. They were on high alert now, and every attempt to sneak past them was thwarted. On the surface, *Flier* was faster than they were, and nimbler. Underwater, we had other clear advantages, but working together, those escorts and their sonar kept us from the freighter.

We approached from the south several times, then circled and came at her from the north, but they blocked every maneuver or charge we tried. "Hell with this," Captain grumbled. "What worked once might work again. Liddell, we're going to try to slip between two of them, let me know on the next pass where the largest gap is."

"Aye, sir."

"Captain?" I said, looking through the TBT. The freighter, now over five miles away, suddenly rolled over, and sank.

Captain stared, then said, "Well, never mind, then." The escorts, watching their protectorate sink with probable dismay, apparently decided we weren't worth chasing with the convoy increasingly far ahead and who-knows how many other submarines in the area. They fled the scene, and we decided that the convoy was too far and too fast to catch before we ran into another sub's patrol territory.

"That convoy looks like they may be on their way to Manila," Captain Crowley said to himself. "Raise Commander Krapf of the *Jack*," he told Liddell. "They're behind us, near Manila, and might welcome the exercise."

We later heard that the *Jack* took out two more of that convoy. Of the nine freighters that we spotted, only four arrived...

BLAM!

The explosion blasted me awake, and I was on my feet before I really realized what was going on.

"What was that?" I heard someone yell.

"It sounded like gunfire!" another shouted back.

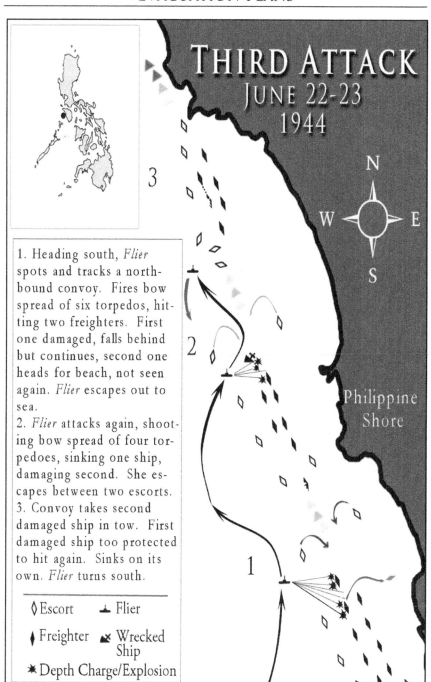

THIRD ATTACK
JUNE 22-23
1944

3

N

W — E

S

Philippine
Shore

1. Heading south, *Flier* spots and tracks a northbound convoy. Fires bow spread of six torpedos, hitting two freighters. First one damaged, falls behind but continues, second one heads for beach, not seen again. *Flier* escapes out to sea.

2. *Flier* attacks again, shooting bow spread of four torpedoes, sinking one ship, damaging second. She escapes between two escorts.

3. Convoy takes second damaged ship in tow. First damaged ship too protected to hit again. Sinks on its own. *Flier* turns south.

◊ Escort   ⊥ Flier

♦ Freighter   ✖ Wrecked Ship

✱ Depth Charge/Explosion

2

1

"Have the Japanese landed?"

Palacido and several people, dropping tools and gardening implements in their wakes, were scrambling to a small hilltop lookout station farther up the mountain. I ran with them, but by the time I limped to the top there was nothing to see: no Japanese ships, no landing craft, not even a fishing boat.

"See anything?" Palacido asked everyone who had a set of binoculars on them.

"No, sir," several men chorused.

That was a relief. To be safe, Palacido sent a few men to scout down to the beach to check for the source of the explosion.

They returned with no answers, and escorting Captain Crowley, who was excited about his trade with the neighboring tribe. He and Mayor purchased a small sailing kumpit and towed it back with the chief's own powered kumpit, on loan for the rescue.

"And all for a little bit of cash and the promise of a barrel of lubricating oil from the rescuing ship," he said.

That evening we sent the plans for the proposed evacuation to Perth. Brisbane contacted Palacido shortly after, formally authorizing him to take command of the Coastwatchers, not that anyone expected differently.

The next day was a flurry of preparations. Just in case Perth did approve of our plans, we were going to try to evacuate the civilians around the base as well. Henry Garretson was going to need a cart to get to the beach because he was too sick to walk. The Edwards family was deciding whether to risk the dangerous ride to Allied land, or stay deep in the jungles of Palawan. Edwards also asked if an invitation could be extended to the Sutherlands, who were desperate to get out. When Captain and Liddell agreed, Mr. Sutherland leapt at the opportunity.

That afternoon, the word suddenly came that a submarine would be standing by at our coordinates on August 30th to pick us up. That left us only thirty hours before evacuation.

Runners informed the Sutherlands that they had to dispose of all their personal belongings in twelve hours and be ready to head for the beach after lunch. Mr. Edwards arranged for a carabao cart to transport Garretson and the few of us whose feet were still a touch tender. Faced with the quick decision, Mr. and Mrs. Edwards decided not to leave, despite the fact that two of their daughters were already attending college in the States.

"It's my home," he said, as a way of explanation, "My wife is from here, and my oldest daughter and her family are here. If something does happen, we can hide with her people, and we speak the language, so we have a good chance at disappearing if worse comes to worst. Besides, we're needed here."

Late that night, as I walked past the radio hut, I thought I heard Captain...singing. I stopped, but there was no doubt about it, he was singing "Sweet Adeline."

Quietly I crept up to the shack, and peeked through the window, trying to keep out of sight. Palacido was smothering a laugh as Crowley trilled, "You're the flower of my heart, Sweeeet Aaaa—deee—liiine!" Whoever was on the other end of the radio was singing along to the tenor part, and both were surprisingly good.

"Thanks, John," the radioed voice said. "I just needed to make sure. It sounded too incredible to believe."

"I understand, Cy. I'd want to make sure myself before I put my..." Captain suddenly stopped, then swallowed hard, "before I put my crew in danger."

There was pause on the other end, then, "We're all set then?"

"Affirmative. We'll hang three lights from the Point Lighthouse when it's all clear and we're on our way." I saw Palacido signal Captain about something. "A question from the men here. Some nearby civilians have requested evacuation too. Would you mind?"

"How many?"

"Six to eight extra people."

"You know the risks, John. I haven't been cleared for a turnaround. This isn't a place for civilians."

'This must be our rescuing captain,' I thought. His orders were to pick us up, then continue on patrol with us aboard.

"Understood. But they've been looking for a way out. They've been trapped here since the invasion, most with a price on their heads."

"Women?"

"And children, too," Crowley said.

There was a pause. "I could confine them to Officer's Country, I suppose. And I'll have to inform COMSUBSOWESPAC. But it shouldn't be a problem if they stay put."

"Thank you."

"Until then." The line went dead.

"You know, Jacobson, you may as well stop skulking in the shadows and come in here," Captain called out.

I walked in the room, trying not to look sheepish. "Sorry, sir, I just followed the sweet sound of your voice." I grinned while Palacido fell over laughing.

"Very funny," Captain said with a crooked half-smile. He turned to Palacido, who was gasping for breath. "Do we have everything?"

"I think so," Palacido wheezed, wiping his eyes. "I can't think of anything else that we need for evacuation. If we leave here no later than noon tomorrow for the beach, we should have plenty of time. Now, if you'll excuse me," he left the room, still trying to catch his breath.

Captain quickly brought me up to speed. If the coast was clear tomorrow, one of the guerillas was going to hang three lanterns in a vertical row from the concrete lighthouse on the bay. Once the submarine saw that, she would surface, and we would motor out to her, the kumpit returning with the lubricating oil the chief had demanded in payment. If something went wrong, we were to try again on the 31st.

"Sir, one more question."

"Yes, Jacobson?"

"Why the concert?"

He smiled. "We're being picked up by the *Redfin*. Captain Austin and I were in the Men's Quartet at the Naval Academy together. Guess he wanted to check my actual identity."

-14-

ENEMY SURPRISE

The sound of paper rustling woke me the next morning. A tall, sparsely built man who looked like a real Robinson Crusoe sat at Mrs. Edward's table and carefully poured a pile of black powder from a drawstring bag onto a sheet of old newspaper.

"No offense, Kierson," Captain was saying, "but you're nuts."

The stranger laughed. "Maybe a little, but how else are we supposed to get ammunition around here?" He had a slight Scandinavian accent.

"Good Morning," I said.

"Good morning, Mr. Jacobson," Mr. Edwards said. "Meet Vens Kierson, world traveler, native Finn, and creator of ammunition from Japanese Mines, among other things."

"Wow!" I exclaimed.

"Don't yell, you'll make me jump," Kierson half-joked. A few guerillas had seated themselves at the table and were packing the powder carefully into old ammunition shells then topping them off with small round pebbles.

"What are you doing?" I asked.

"Sometimes Japanese mines come loose from their mooring chains and float to the surface," Kierson explained. "Some will wash up on the beaches around here. They're supposed to deactivate if they come within a few feet of the surface, but that's not always the case, so dismantling them for the powder charge is still dangerous. But with ammunition so scarce around here, this is how we keep supplying our arms." His calm and educated manner contrasted with his frontiersman appearance. I watched him in fascination, wishing I had met him earlier.

After a large good-bye breakfast from Mrs. Edwards, we began to gather in the clearing. Mr. Sutherland and his family soon arrived.

"May I present my wife, Maise; my son, Alastair; and my little daughter, Heather."

Mrs. Sutherland was tall and thin, her gaunt cheeks showing how long and hard the past three years had been, but had a pretty, smiling face. Her daughter, Heather, who looked about three or four years old, was shy and clung to her mother's threadbare skirt, but Alastair stared at us openly in awe for a moment before blurting, "Are we really going on a submarine?"

"That we are, son," Captain said, kneeling to talk to him as though he was Captain's own son back in Kansas.

"God answered my prayers, Dad! We're leaving on a submarine!"

We looked at Mr. and Mrs. Sutherland and Mr. Sutherland explained. "We've been trapped here for years, it hasn't been easy. Every night at evening prayers, Alastair started praying for something after we finished. Later, he told me that was asking God to send a submarine to rescue us. A ship would be too noticeable this deep in Japanese territory and a plane could crash or get shot down. So, he prayed for the only ship that could sneak in here: a submarine. We've been praying that same prayer as a family now for years. It's finally come to pass."

Henry Garretson slowly climbed down from the house, and got in the cart without help. George, Red and Charlie were ready to go, and Palacido was checking his watch when I heard, "There is still room?"

"Going, Kierson?" Palacido said with a note of regret.

"Yeah, you don't need me anymore, and the guerillas have been telling me I need to go ever since I arrived last night. I think they fear for my safety."

"I can understand that. I'll sure miss you, though."

"I'll miss all of you, too, but it's time for the next adventure."

"So with the Fliers, Sutherlands, George, Red, Charlie, Garretson, and Kierson now, that brings the total to seventeen people," Palacido concluded.

I whistled softly. Seventeen extra people on a submarine with no extra room on a good day, would be tight, very tight.

I fell in next to Kierson during the walk to the beach, and soon learned how he came to be at such a remote place as Brooke's Point.

He had emigrated with his family from Finland when he was a teenager and they settled in the Spokane, Washington area. After a year of schooling, he dropped out to be a lumberjack for Boeing. When Boeing started building airplane frames out of metal instead of wood, he became a diver and worked in Alaska for fishermen and salvage companies. Then he earned enough money salvaging that he was able to travel around the world, and continued his salvage work in Hong Kong, the Philippines, and China, for over twenty years. He was working for the Chinese government when the First Battle of Shanghai broke out in 1932. When that happened, he fought with the Chinese, unsuccessfully trying to drive off the Japanese army.

"Of course, back then," he told us, "we knew that they were hankering for an empire in China, we just didn't know it would go that far. After that incident I had an opportunity to strike out for the Philippines and work in the mining industry, which was great, until the Japanese came here, too. I took to the hills, and with no way to leave, I joined the guerillas." He gestured to Garretson, "Henry and I met while we were salvaging the *SS Panay*.[34] She was bringing us supplies when the Japanese hit her with a torpedo. Thankfully, she hit the floor sitting straight up in shallow water, so we were able to retrieve rifles, gas masks, and ammo, which made up most of the cargo.

"Then we came here, hoping to collect supplies for the guerillas on the Visayas, but ended up staying, partially because of Henry's malaria, and partially because the guerillas here were faced with severe shortages of food and ammunition. I had learned a few tricks in the Visayas that I could put to use here."

"Converting Japanese sea mines into bullets." I said.

"Among other things. I also salvaged grounded ships for cargo, and created a new currency for this area out of Japanese Charts. Since I'm fairly fluent in the local languages now, I trade with a lot of the people around the island for food and supplies. It's a lot easier than leaning on the immediate locals, especially when the last rice harvest was so poor."

"Yes," Palacido said, who had been listening in on the conversation. "What Kierson won't tell you, either, is that when he arrived on Palawan, the guerilla force was unorganized and nearly disbanded. He helped reorganize the group into what you've seen. We're going to miss you terribly."

"Well, I have taught all of you everything I know. You'll make it."

"So, I've been on the western coast of Palawan for nearly a month

---

[34] The wreck of *SS Panay* is today a popular tourist dive site near Sipalay City on Negros Occidental. Located in 135 feet of water, divers on the *Panay* can still see gas masks and boxes of ammunition on the wreck right where Kierson and Garretson and their teams left them.

now. Imagine my surprise at finding an American sailor on the beach, and the guerillas telling me that I was going to be evacuated by submarine in less than twelve hours. I wasn't all that interested in leaving, but they are insisting I have to go. Still, it'll be nice see somewhere else. I have been curious about Australia, and could go back to America, so either way, I am ready for whatever is next."

"I'm sure a good shave would be welcome too," I said jokingly.

He scratched his beard. "The warm water is what I'm looking forward to. You'd be amazed what you can do with a bolo knife, though. It's very effective." I had no problem whatsoever imagining this man shaving his face with one of those machetes. None at all.

It took us a few hours to work our way slowly down the mountainside. Garretson groaned quietly with every bump in the road, and the children, bored with the cart, ran squealing through the trees, called back frequently by the Sutherlands.

My feet were holding up well. Scar tissue looked almost like the coral itself had grown to the soles of my feet, but I wasn't too worried. We were finally going home, and if all went well, I would be able to get a message to my mother before she heard anything about the *Flier's* fate.

Suddenly, Howell sprinted up the path, red-faced, sweaty and panting, with other guerillas at his heels. "Captain…" He bent over, gripped his knees and pulled in deep lungfuls of air. "Captain Mayor sent me…to look for you. A Jap ship has pulled in and anchored two miles off the point."

Palacido looked up sharply at the other guerillas. "It is true," one said. "It arrived over two hours ago. They weighed anchor, but have made no attempts to come on shore via landing craft or any other method, and we cannot tell if they are armed."

"The rest of the convoy?" Captain asked anxiously.

"There does not appear to be any convoy at all. None of our scouts have reported seeing any ships for the past twelve hours. It would seem that this one is alone and without help for at least ten miles."

"Is she in distress?" he asked, furrowing his brow. A torpedoed ship might beach herself, rather than sink, which would explain her odd behavior.

"No damage. She looks brand new, and she's far enough out that she's not caught on a reef or beached."

"She's just…sitting there?"

He nodded. "We are continuing to watch her, and keeping out of sight, but we cannot hang the all clear in the lighthouse now. It is very strange behavior."

"What could she be waiting for?" I wondered aloud.

The guerilla looked somber. "For all we know they are waiting for your submarine to show herself before blowing us all to hell."

Palacido ran ahead with the guerillas, while those of us from the *Flier* tried to hustle everyone along as quickly as possible. We should have learned on the way up, there is no way to hustle a carabao. Even with nothing to wallow in, the stubborn brute still took his sweet time.

Captain Mayor met us with concern in his eyes. "I've got men checking it out, and we've dragged the kumpits under cover, so if we have to try to get you to the rendezvous while she's still here, we can launch from somewhere else."

"I hope your submarine is wise enough to stay out of sight," Mayor said.

"They've probably already seen it," Jim said confidently. "Pity we can't raise them yet, someone might be able to tell us if that thing came down on its own, or if it's a trap and a convoy is waiting around the corner."

"If there is a convoy, I doubt she'll surface or stick around," I said. I didn't say anything, but privately I thought things didn't look good for our evacuation tonight.

As we came down the last few steps in the trees, I saw some papers, only slightly dirty, trapped under a fallen branch. Remembering paper was quite valuable, I pulled them out, and saw a message written in normal letters, but some kind of code. I did see the names "Sutherland" and "Edwards", so showed it to Mr. Sutherland. He took one look at the paper, folded it in quarters and tucked it in his pocket.

"Do you mind if I ask what that is?" I said.

"One of the reasons I'm taking my family out of here." He looked around for Heather and Alastair, but they were a distance away. "It's a reward for the capture of any of us, dead or alive. Fairly substantial, too. There's one of these hanging on the front door of our home in Brooke's Point, if that's still standing."

"I'm sorry," I said. They'd lost so much. Earlier that day, in the mountains, I'd heard Mrs. Sutherland telling Mrs. Edwards that she almost laughed when she received our message to dispose of their household goods. After three years of hiding and bartering for food and supplies, there was hardly anything left, though she was holding a shoebox under her arms, of what, I didn't know.

"God has sustained us, that is enough. He will see this through." Mr. Sutherland replied simply.

The party organized at Mayor's house to wait and watch. We didn't know what to do. Captain and Jim, after talking with Howell for some time about what happened, decided to go and look at the ship themselves, with the help of a guide. The rest of us were ordered to stay put. I chafed at that order a bit, but as the senior officer left behind, the welfare of the party was now my responsibility. Not that anyone would wander off or cause trouble; our main concern was keeping everyone quiet and non-panicky.

Captain and Jim returned within an hour, and with a gesture, told me to meet them outside. "She's still sitting there," Jim told me quietly. "The rendezvous point is some distance off-shore so our sub could still get us, if we can launch and sneak around her in the dark."

"With her sitting there though, I don't know if it's worth the risk," Captain said. "*Redfin* has orders to try again tomorrow night if something prevents rescue, though they were probably thinking more along the lines of rough seas."

"That Maru could move in a few hours," I said.

"It's more of a Truk than a Maru," Jim said. "And we have to face the fact that it might not move today. If she thinks this is a good place to stop and fix something internal like her engines, then they may be here for quite some time. And that's assuming she isn't here specifically to catch the lot of us."

"It might be worth it to go back into the mountains tonight," Captain said, "in case this ship is holding an invasion force for a night raid. If it was just us, that would be one thing, but with the civilians, especially Mrs.Sutherland and the children, I don't want to place them in any more danger than I have to."

"What if we were to cast off farther down the beach?" I asked. "We might not be precisely where the rendezvous is supposed to take place, but we'd be in the area. Even though we won't be able to put the all-clear

The Brooke's Point light, from which the "all clear" was to have been hung. Photo courtesy of the family of Ens. Al "Jake" Jacobson

lanterns in the Point Light, and I'll bet *Redfin* is watching this situation very closely if she's anywhere around. If we used the transmitter to try to contact her, we might be able to complete this tonight. If the civilians are willing to take the risk, I don't think we should just hope that the Truk will move in time. If she doesn't, we're right back here in twenty-four hours, but without a back-up date."

"Jacobson's got a point, sir," Jim said. "The kumpits are small, and close to the water, and despite the nearly full moon tonight, they'll be difficult to see from more than a mile away or so. If, instead of using oars or sails, we tow the small kumpit behind the large motored one, we'll cut down our silhouette, and if we launch far down the beach and give the Truk a wide berth, we'll be nearly invisible. We might find the sub. If we don't, there's still tomorrow."

"Very true," Captain said. He seemed to think carefully, looking up at the sky.

"Are we still going to go for it, sir?" I asked. It sounded like he meant to, but with all the caveats and conditions…

"We don't have to make any firm plans right now. I'll talk to Kierson, Garretson and the Sutherlands. As civilians, they have the right to know all the risks of trying this, and see if they want to continue. Not to mention, we may still get lucky. That ship might move before sunset."

To a person, all the civilians in the rescue party agreed to risk pickup that night despite the extra danger. With an invasion looming, this may be their one and only chance to escape.

Mrs. Mayor made dinner for us in grand fashion, while her daughter played with the other children. The Mayors never questioned leaving. They had been born here and intended to defend their home.

The mountain covered the forest in shadow as the sun sank into the west, and still the Truk sat. The eeriest thing about her was the reports of the lack of men on the decks. If it hadn't been for the fact the guerillas and Howell watched her come in and anchor, I would have thought she had run aground and been abandoned.

Late in the afternoon, we decided to try to contact the *Redfin*. We couldn't use the lighthouse to help her find us, so we had to hope she was looking for us on a radio frequency.

"Here goes nothing," Howell said, fiddling with the radio. "November-

Whiskey-Golf-Charlie, do you read? This is November-India-Tango-Whiskey."

November-India-Tango-Whiskey; *Flier's* Navy-assigned code name. After tonight, I would probably never hear it used again.

Every few minutes, Howell called as we hid in the trees and watched the sky flame red in the hidden sunset, then begin to darken. If we could contact her now, we would at least know she was waiting for us if we decided to risk the boats.

One hour passed, then two. She wasn't replying but it was early yet, she might be on an unusual frequency, or not risking an answer this close to an enemy ship.

"It's time," Jim said, watching the waves. "We'll need at least an hour to get out to the rendezvous point. If we're going to do this tonight, it needs to be now."

The Fliers grabbed and hauled the kumpits to the waves, making sure the towing cable was securely fastened to the small kumpit in the rear. Howell and Miller hefted the radio into the front kumpit, along with a shielded lantern. Robert Mayor climbed the slim mast like a little monkey, tying the antenna to the top to give us the furthest reach possible. Another, less reliable radio was left behind with the beach party, so they could keep in touch with the boats.

The Sutherlands hugged and bade the Edwards, Mayors, and the guerillas good-bye. Kierson and Garretson roughly shook hands with everyone. George, Red and Charlie talked to some of the guerillas in a low voice. For those of us who had spent little time here, this was a chance to go home. For the rest, they were leaving home, possibly never to return.

Those of us from *Flier* were assigned to the motorized kumpit with Palacido, and some locals, while Butch and several more guerillas took the towed kumpit with the civilians. Both boats were equipped with oars in case the motor died, since we didn't want to have to use the sails tonight. Jim, Baumgart, Russo and I gripped the sides of the beached kumpit and shoved off into the waves, leaping aboard as soon as the water splashed around our knees. Butch, Kierson, and Mr. Sutherland did the same for the one behind. I looked back at the beach. With the enemy so close, no signal fire had been lit, but in the dim light of the rising moon, I took a last look at the guerillas, the Mayors, and the Edwards family waving from the beach. They were soon lost to sight.

Palacido started the motor and followed the edge of the island south for a mile, putting distance between us and the ship before turning for the rendezvous point.

The ship causing all the trouble was a typical wooden Sea Truk, sporting two masts, and evidence of a diesel engine within. She had an open deck between the pilothouse structure and the forward mast, and another raised deck between the forward mast and the small bowsprit but no one patrolled, no one was on watch.

The wind whisked by our faces as we moved slowly around her, and we strained our eyes looking for the men who should be there. After the last time the Japanese attempted to invade this area, one would think these sailors would be on extra watch duty in case the guerillas stormed and killed them. But there was no one, no lights, no movement, nothing. And that scared us worse than seeing hoards of the enemy might have. She might be harmless, she may be unarmed, but she almost certainly had a radio and could call for backup.

The hour passed slowly. Howell discovered quickly that the radio on the beach broke down again, severing our link to the guerillas. We were on our own and were going to have to find *Redfin* without help, if she even showed up at all. Anything could have happened since we last spoke: the ship might be the last of a convoy that had been attacked, *Redfin* could be on the ocean floor…I forced that thought from my mind roughly. The most likely answer was that *Redfin* would not reveal herself with the enemy so close. She may even miss us in the dark.

Howell began to call out quietly for the *Redfin*. He alternated between voice, and then the CW Keying,[35] because he was unsure after the failure of the radio on the beach if the voice transmission was working at all.

The rendezvous time of 2000 hours came and went. There was no sound besides the waves and breeze, and no new shadow on the moonlit water to announce *Redfin*. Howell called again, and again, and we each took turns cranking the radio generator lever which powered the set.

Two hours passed. Howell's voice started to rasp, but there was no

---

[35] CW (Cable and Wireless) Keying is similar to a telegraph, using clicks on a radio frequency to spell out a message.

response. What happened?

"*...ang-Whis-...not hear...difficulties...W keying better...*"

"They're there!" Howell whispered excitedly. Several of us quietly cheered and pumped our fists in victory. In the confusion, the antenna fell off the mast and clattered to the deck.

"I'm switching to CW keying, sir," Howell announced. "I think that's what they were requesting. Perhaps sending a light signal would help them find us if this doesn't work."

"I'll do it, Sir," Russo volunteered, grabbing the lantern and using the shields to signal out to sea, first to the east, then to the north, then to the south, then back east. Wherever *Redfin* was, she would see us.

"And I'm going to need someone to hold the antenna as high as possible in order to get any range on this," Howell continued. There were fewer volunteers for this task. Clinging to the mast while holding that antenna up and trying to maintain balance in a narrow boat of shifting people wasn't a picnic. My arms soon ached, and we had to take turns holding the antenna, resting, cranking the radio generator, resting, and back to the antenna. *Redfin* was out there, but where was she? Another hour passed, but no more messages.

The civilians in the other boat shifted restlessly. I could hear Mrs. Sutherland shushing her son, and a Filipino guerilla crooning a soft lullaby to little Heather Sutherland to keep her from crying. We kept up the routine, Russo flashing the message, Howell clicking away, and the rest of us doing what we could while we waited.

Midnight came. The moon long ago had passed its apex and was sinking in the west, throwing us into its light. I began to wonder how long we would stay out here before giving up for the night and trying again tomorrow.

Suddenly, the radio started to click frantically. Howell frowned in concentration, then gave a quiet yell of triumph. "Russo! Stop signaling! They see us, and they're on the way!" I wanted to yell, laugh, but had to settle for a grin. That ship was still there, still quiet.

It was 0043 hours, August 31. We had been signaling for nearly three hours.

The first thing I saw was the moonlight glittering off her wake. *Redfin*, painted black, faded into the night sky, but the silvery arrow of her wake steadily moved closer. The rumble of the engines grew to a growl. She bore down onto us, and for a moment, I had a glimpse of the frightening aspect our victims might sometimes see, but *Redfin* turned and banked to our port side, her deck guns fully manned and trained on us.

"Captain Austin!" Crowley called out, but the engines downed out his hails. "Captain Austin! Cy!" He yelled, waving his arms over his head, heedless of the enemy now nearly three miles behind. *Redfin's* engines stopped, then reversed, arresting her forward momentum and tossing us around in the backwash.

"Crowley!" I heard from the figure on the Bridge, "You're a sight for sore eyes! Stand down!" He ordered his gun crew. "Take her down to the water!"

There was a loud hiss of air releasing from the ballast tanks, as we all screamed and shouted with excitement and joy. I threw a mooring line to one of the submariners flooding onto the deck and he tied us to one of *Redfin's* cleats. We were so eager to get aboard that when a hand was held out to me, I didn't hesitate or ask permission to come aboard. I just grabbed it and vaulted onto the deck.

Captain Austin jumped down from the Bridge. He was tall, slightly balding, but walked with the confidence of a leader. He held his hand out to Crowley, who grasped it and shook it, then they thumped each other on the back in a rough hug. "Boy, am I ever glad to see you, Cy!" Crowley said.

I helped haul the second kumpit alongside and give a hand to the civilians and children on board. Alastair's eyes were as big as saucers. "Is this a real submarine?" he asked in awe.

"It sure is, little man," the *Redfin* sailors laughed. "And we've got your own room ready for you downstairs."

Mr. Sutherland stepped onto the deck. "Thy way is in the sea, and thy path in the great waters." He said quietly.

I looked at him, and he smiled. "Psalm 77:19, a verse that hasn't left me ever since Alastair first told me about his submarine prayer. I told you, God would see us through."

"Evening, Captain Austin," Palacido bounded onto the deck. "Been a while, hasn't it?"

"Sergeant Carlos Palacido, as I live and breathe. How on earth did you get here? I recall dropping you off about a hundred miles south."

USS Redfin, taken around 1944. Official Navy Photograph

"It was too hot back on Ramos. It's nice to know the ol' *Redfin* is holding together well. She looks just as pretty now as she did then."

"Wait a minute." I looked at Palacido. "*Redfin* was your disembarking submarine?"

"Sure was. Never thought I'd see you again, with all the hundreds of boats in the ocean."

"Small world, I guess. We've got your lube oil ready, anything else you need?"

"Everything. Look, I know you're still on patrol, but whatever you can spare — food, arms, ammunition, clothes, anything would be very appreciated."

"Well, you're in luck. We received orders two hours ago to run straight for Darwin the moment we're clear. Navy doesn't want to risk the civilians. So I think we can load you up nicely, we'll just re-load there."

He gave a couple of quick orders and the civilians were hustled up to the Bridge and loaded into the sub. Moments after they disappeared, more sailors began flooding out, bearing cases and cans of fruit and vegetables, and bags of flour, yeast, and ground coffee. Butch and Palacido laughed as we bucket brigaded and packed the two kumpits. Out came four rifles, two .30 caliber machine guns, ten Colt pistols, three carbine rifles, and nearly 25,000 rounds of ammunition of different calibers. Then the men of the *Redfin* started to dig deep, bringing out clothes and shoes, including a brand new pair of size nine-and-a-half shoes which Palacido promised to give to Mr. Edwards; cigarettes, playing cards, toilet paper, pencils, writing paper, three bags of medical supplies including the crucial atabrine and even quinine to combat malaria, and items still kept coming. Tears and laughter were rolling off the men, as they packed the kumpits higher and higher, and the boats settled lower and lower into the water. By the time the crew of the *Redfin* had given most of their spare clothes, radio tubes, soap, and typewriter ribbons, the kumpits' edges were only a couple inches higher than the water surrounding it. "It's Christmas in August!" Butch crowed. "I can't wait to see their faces when we get back to shore."

"Sir?" One of the lookouts up in the rings called down to Austin. "That ship has not moved, and I still have yet to see any sign of life whatsoever."

"That is so strange. Is she one of yours?" he asked Palacido.

"One of ours? No, she's one of theirs."

"She's flying no marking of any kind we could see, and I had to consider that you might be on that ship. I actually signaled her two hours ago in case that was your boat. She didn't respond."

"No one can see what's she's doing, even up close." Crowley said. "It's more than a little suspicious."

"We won't be able to move as fast on our return journey, either," Palacido said. "I don't understand it. If they ever were going to attack, now would be the time."

"She's definitely not abandoned, either," Austin said. "We watched her come down from the north and anchor there." He paused for a moment, studying the silent vessel. "You know, I'm sure she's chock full of good equipment you could use. And my men could always use some gunnery practice."

Palacido grinned. "Sir?"

"Just don't forget to capture any crewmembers that make it to shore, you wouldn't want them running loose in your territory."

"Yes, sir!" Palacido gave a smart salute. "And thank you."

A sailor was hauling one last container to the deck. "The battery acid you wanted, sir," he said, and handed it to Butch who loaded it onto the second kumpit.

"Coleman?" Palacido peered at him in the darkness. "Is that you?"

"Palacido! Well, how are you?"

On the left, the peso all the Coastwatchers signed before disembarking the Redfin., entrusting it to Redfin Larry Coleman. Signatures from top to bottom are Daquel, Reynoso, Rallojay, Palacido, Corpus and Cortez. On the right, another peso signed by the Brooke's Point evacuees, From top to bottom: Tremaine, Russo, Miller, Charlie Watkins, Howell, Red Wigfield, George Marquez, Harry Garretson, Baumgart, Jacobson, Crowley, Vens Kierson. Coastwatcher peso image courtesy of Larry Coleman USS Redfin sailor, Peso on the right courtesy of the family of Lt. James Liddell, USS Flier XO.

"We're doing well. Still have that signed silver certificate I gave you, or did you spend it already?" Palacido said as he hefted the acid down to the kumpit.

"Nope, still have it, safe and sound."

Captain Austin stepped in. "Thank you, Coleman. I need you to inform the Sutherland family and any of the other civilians in Officers' Country that we're going to be firing the cannon over their berths, so don't be frightened." Austin turned to the Bridge while Coleman said a quick, "Aye, sir!" and wished Palacido and Butch luck before swinging up to the Bridge and plunging back down the hatch. A moment later, the gunnery crew, who had been helping haul people and supplies around, swarmed back to the guns, swinging them towards the Truk. I suddenly felt homesick.

"You'd best get clear, Palacido, and good luck to you," Austin said. "I'll wait until you're well out of the way, but you'd best move as fast as you can."

"Thank you, sir," he said. I was one of the few people left on the Bridge. Most of my crewmembers had already taken their leave and gone below. I shook Palacido's hand before he jumped into the kumpit, and threw him the mooring lines attached to *Redfin*. The outboard motor sounded quieter now, as they slowly plowed out into the darkness.

The moon had set behind the island, and the Truk was all but impossible to see as she blended in with the dark shadow of the mountain ridge of Palawan. The gunnery crew's pointer and trainer, unable to see their target well, were cranking the muzzle to match the bearings the lookouts overheard called down to them. A second crew was loading the 20 mm on the Bridge deck with repeating rounds, and aiming carefully.

As I climbed up to the Bridge, it all felt sadly familiar. *Redfin* was a close sister to *Flier*, even though there were subtle differences. It was surreal in a way to be aboard another submarine, so like her and yet, not nearly the same enough. A hand grasped my shoulder. It was Captain Austin. "Your name?" he said.

"Ensign Alvin Jacobson, sir." With no uniform, he had no idea who I was or whether I was a civilian or military.

"Thank you. Please join your crewmates down below, Ensign. You'll find them in the Wardroom." I suddenly realized until we reached Darwin, this was my new commanding officer. Dropping down into the Conning Tower, I was met by the smells of sweat and oil that brought back memories. But men I didn't know were peering into the radar screens like Vogt and Pope once did. Where Madeo or Dressell or recently, Kit Pourciau under their tutelage, used to stand at the helm, someone else stood, waiting for orders.

I slid down into the Control Room that was gleaming with polished

"Clear for Action" Georges Schrieber, watercolor, 1943. Gun action on a submarine deck was difficult and dangerous. Some sub commanders preferred to never use it unless there were no other options or as a last resort. From the Department of the Navy, Navy Historical Center. Gift of Abbott Laboratories.

brass and steel. It was all there: the Helm station, Trim Station, Periscope Wells, the Navigation Table, just like the one I'd spent hours leaning over. I shouldn't have expected differently, but with no familiar faces, it just seems so jarringly alien.

I wanted to look around, but knew we had to be debriefed by Captain Austin before, or rather, if we'd be allowed to explore freely, and I stepped through the bulkhead heading for the Wardroom.

The Sutherlands had been placed together in the Chief's room, the only cabin with four beds. I saw the sailor called Coleman in there with them, patiently answering Alastair's many questions, while reminding the family that the gun would be right over their heads.

George, Red and Charlie had been billeted in the XO's room, with three bunks, while Kierson and Henry Garretson were in the two-person cabin I had had on the *Flier*. All these people, as non-quals, were going to be restricted to their cabins for the next few days, except for escorted visits to the restroom, or Wardroom, all in an effort to make sure they were out from underfoot in case of an emergency. Even with the orders to report directly to Darwin, we were still a week out.

I found my crewmates in the Officers' Wardroom, just as the *Redfin* thundered and shook. "*Boom! Boom! Thunk! Thunk! Thunk!*" The four-inch and 40 mm tossed the *Redfin* about so much that it was difficult to get to my seat. I could hear George and the other guys yelling in triumph and giving high-fives, while the children, who I expected to be frightened, were laughing. Alastair was even yelling, "Get 'em! Kill 'em!"

Redfin surged forward, rocking violently under the kickback of her guns. For ten minutes she kept up the barrage, knocking dust from the cork-covered walls and rattling the clocks. We held on, braced against the wall and the strut under the table as she shook and roared. Suddenly, the men in the Forward Torpedo Room sprang to action, folding and stowing racks, checking and pressurizing torpedo tubes, sliding the next torpedoes on their skids into place, ready to take their position in the tubes the moment the current occupants were fired. I felt the tense silence I was used to, of the men waiting for the orders on range and bearing that were due to be radioed in moments.

"Stand down," Austin's voice came over the boat's intercom. Moments later, as the torpedo room was being put right, the engines roared and *Redfin* turned smoothly out to sea.

-15-

REDFIN

Redfin's stewards, Henry Hoyt and Otis Morgan, brought us coffee, and I still couldn't taste the difference, though I wondered briefly if this was the stuff I'd personally given away in Freo. I told Hoyt and Morgan about George's hankering for bacon and eggs, and they laughed, saying that they would fix that craving right now if the civilians were willing to stay up for it. After the excitement of the night, there was going to be no sleeping for hours, so an early breakfast of bacon, sausage, eggs, toast, juice and coffee was fixed, and the smell wafting down the passage as they cooked and delivered a deluxe breakfast, was utterly mouthwatering. George even defied orders and snuck across the two feet of passageway to the Wardroom to thank me, saying it was everything he had missed.

Captain Austin and some of his officers came to see us about an hour after the firing ceased. Captain Crowley thanked them again for rescuing us, and introduced us all in turn.

"It was only what you would have done if the circumstances were changed, John," Austin said. "And now, allow me to introduce my XO, Commander Charles Miller, my COB William O'Hara, more commonly known as "Jeep," and Lt. Mitchell, Lt. Reinhardt, Ens. Helz, Lt. Taylor, and, oh, yes, I'm sure you'll get to know this one quite well: our Doc, Bernie Ross."

Ross stuck his head in for a second and waved. "If you guys are good for a while, I'm gonna check on the civilians."

We were, and Ross left, as did a number of the junior officers, back to their stations.

"Well, I can see that Otis and Henry put you right at home. I'm glad."

"Did Perth tell you anything about what happened to us?" Captain asked.

"A bit. I'll wager you're the reason the Balabac Straits are now closed until further notice. We were on the western side of Balabac and were specifically ordered to travel all the way around the northern tip of Palawan to get here. I think you are the first submariners to come back home."

Crowley looked down at the table. I knew he was thinking of the men under his command who were never going to come home. Because he had survived, there would likely be an investigation on his return to determine if he was somehow responsible for the deaths of his men. I knew there was no way he could be held responsible for that mine or whatever had taken us down. Still, knowing you were not responsible didn't stop you from constantly going back over the infinite "What ifs" that inevitably rose in your mind.

"Were you able to sink her?" I asked Captain Austin.

"No," he said, smoothly transitioning to the new topic. "She was manned though, all right. Within moments of our first salvo, she hauled anchor and fled south. She must be really shallow-bottomed. She stayed in the shoals where the water can't be more than a few feet deep. I couldn't get any closer, and we only managed to hit her once or twice at that range. The first flash actually blinded most of my gunners, and they had to work from shouted commands from the lookouts, so their aim wasn't as good as it usually is. I had hoped she'd head for deeper water and I could fire a torpedo at her but she never strayed from the shallows. Pity, I really wanted to take her down for the Coastwatchers."

"Yes, well, I was worried that you wouldn't appear at all with that thing there," Crowley muttered.

"I almost didn't. Seems recently, my job has been a multi-million dollar ferry. I pick you up this patrol, dropped those Coastwatchers with all their gear off last patrol, and the rendezvous on the patrol before that was a total disaster. I was really suspicious about this pick-up because of that."

"What happened?" Howell asked.

"I was assigned to pick up about six Australian agents at the tail end of my first patrol on *Redfin*, near the Sibutu Passage. I looked, saw the security signal, responded, and received acknowledgement of my signal from the beach. Everything seemed in order. They couldn't get their hands on a boat, so I sent Ensign Helz with a small landing party to shore in a rubber boat. Cross currents pushed them four miles north of the rendezvous point, so they were almost on top of Dent Haven Bay when they got close to landing. Helz signaled back into the trees, hoping the agents had followed their progress north and were close by, but this time got the wrong reply.

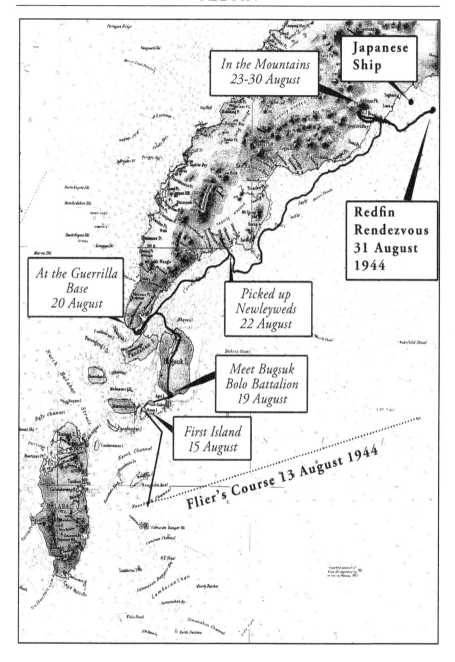

The full journey of the Flier Survivors from 13 August to 31 August. The survivors covered more than 125 miles.

He tried again and got a different, and still wrong reply. I saw this from the sub, and grew suspicious, but word was these guys were being systematically captured and tortured by the Kempeitai[36], and were desperate to get out. Helz decided to make a cautious landing, asking another seaman, Carinder, to cover him with a rifle. No sooner do they step away from their raft than a Japanese soldier runs out of the woods and tries to run Carinder through with his bayonet. Turns out, a Japanese station was there on the bay. More and more Japs start to fire from the woods while my men are held down behind a rubber raft. Helz and the Carinder managed to get back, and they launched their raft back into the water, bullets whizzing all around them. Some said I should have retreated immediately in case the Japs had radioed for help and *Redfin* had been captured, but I couldn't do that. It took nearly seven hours to recover them, none the worse for wear, but all the time our position could have been reported. We never saw hide nor hair of the purported Australians. It might have been a trap."[37]

"No wonder you were suspicious. It gets more dangerous every year out here," Captain said.

"I was surprised at how well you remembered 'Adeline,' I must say."

"We sang it to the point that it would run through my head for days. I couldn't forget it if I wanted to," Captain smiled. "I felt rather foolish singing, especially with Jacobson here listening in." The enlisted men snorted into their napkins, doing a lousy job of smothering a laugh, and he continued, "but it was worth it if it got you out here."

"I'm glad."

"Captain Crowley, can you tell me, is it true, the rumors about the *Robalo*?" Cmdr. Miller asked.

---

[36] Kempetai: Military Police of Japanese Army. They carried out interrogations and sometimes torture of prisoners, and were quite feared by the Allied POWs.

[37] It wasn't a trap, just the third in a series of unfortunate attempts. *USS Redfin's* rescue attempt was the third rescue attempt which had gone awry for various reasons (*Guitarro* and *Haddo* also trie d earlier). *Redfin* returned to Freemantle, picked up the Coastwatchers and departed in the company of *USS Harder*. *Harder* and *Redfin* parted ways a few days later, but strangely, on the day *Redfin* dropped the Coastwatchers off in the Philippines, *Harder* was picking up the six men from this Coastwatching contingent in Borneo. This time, they made it home. *Harder* also took out four destroyers in that same patrol before returning to Fremantle, where *Flier* and *Redfin* were already in port.

"Depends on what you heard."

"That she's overdue, with all that implies."

"She's gone." Captain admitted quietly.

Miller's face fell, as did most of the officers' faces. "Know someone?" Jim asked.

"One of our guys, Kimball Graham, was transferred to the *Robalo*. We were hoping it wasn't true," he said sadly.

"I'm sorry." There was nothing else that could be said.

"Come on, guys," Austin said, "we need to get back on station and let these guys find a place to rest. With the civilians taking over Officers' Country, you'll have to hot-bunk[38] it wherever you can on the way home.

"Now, I know that you're all qualified, and as of today, you're members of my crew, but we have a rhythm here that works well, so I won't need your services unless it's a battle situation. Please try to stay out of our way, but enjoy the Mess Hall, the movies, anything we can offer. Officers," he said addressing Jim, Captain and me, "you are more than welcome to join us when we partake of meals, though it may be a little crowded. After Doc Ross checks you out, feel free to make yourselves comfortable wherever you can. Is there anything else I can do?"

"No, thank you, Cy, and...thank you, again." Captain said.

"No problem, John, it's just-" he stopped and looked. "What happened to your Academy Ring?"

Crowley looked self-conscious as he looked at the paler band of skin on his bare left ring finger. "All the heat and changes in pressure on *Flier* got to me. I took off my ring that last night, left it in my cabin. I was going to put it back on after my shift, but..."

"Sorry to hear that."

"Not half as sorry as Louise will be when she finds out."

"I think your wife will glad you're coming home to her and the kids."

"Yes, but that was not just my Academy ring, it was my wedding band!"

Redfin's Doc was very unhappy at the state of our feet. Mine were

---

[38] Hot-bunking: A common practice in modern nuclear submarines, though not on WWII boats, hot-bunking is where two or more people share a bunk, and sleep on alternate schedules. Therefore, one person gets up, and the other goes to bed while the bunk is still "hot."

starting to heal over all right, though they were still raw and tender in some places. Some of the guys' feet were red, raw, and scabbed over with pus more than blood, but after a thorough antiseptic wash and bandaging, which stung horribly, Doc assured us all they would heal well with no more than scars to remind us of the last two and a half weeks. He also prescribed quinine, just in case we had been infected with malaria.

I walked back down the hall, listening to the conversations going on. The Sutherlands were putting their children to sleep in the bunks in their cabin. Though they hardly compared to real beds back home, the Sutherlands had been sleeping on bare bamboo floors, and thought the new digs were heavenly.

"'I will lay me down in peace and sleep: for Thou oh Lord makest me dwell in safety.'" They said in unison.[39]

"At least no one will be sneaking into our place tonight." Alastair said, snuggling under his blanket.

"No," his father answered him, tucking him in, "not anymore. We're safe here."

A couple of hours later, Cmdr. Miller, who was on duty, sent a message to the Fliers. They were passing the southern end of Palawan, and if we wanted, we were invited up to the bridge.

It was just past dawn when we stood there, saying a silent good-bye to our loyal boat and friends. Due to the danger, *Redfin* was miles away from the site we had been at, and Palawan was just a smoky mass on the horizon, the smaller islands invisible. We all stood in silence out of respect for the fallen until Palawan faded.

The trip home was uneventful. *Redfin* stayed on the surface as often and as long as she could, only diving to avoid a patrol plane or convoy. The civilians were thrilled with the motion of the boat, tossing in the waves, perfectly still underwater, and the peculiar groans and rushing noises when she dove and surfaced.

The crew adopted the children, making them toys from various items around the sub, even a pair of sandals for each of them, woven out of

---

[39] Psalm 4:8, which the Sutherlands said every night before sleeping. When they woke up, they recited Psalm 3:5 : 'I laid me down and slept: I awakened; for the LORD sustained me'.

Philippine
Sea

Redfin's Position August 23:
Redfin told to avoid Balabac
Strait and head for Brooke's
Point. They are not told why.

Redfin's
Rescue
August 31

Redfin attacks
convoy
20 August

Balabac
Strait

Java Sea

Redfin's
Return
September 7

Redfin clears
Lombok
13 August

Lombok
Strait

Darwin

Redfin leaves
Exmouth &
shoots Mildura wreck
August 10

Exmouth
Gulf

**Redfin's
Return**

Indian
Ocean

Redfin leaves
Fremantle
6 August

Fremantle

——— Track of
USS Redfin
6 Aug-
7 Sep 1944

Redfin's stock of leather.

Dinners were events. The Wardroom was packed, even with the children sitting on someone's lap, and rang with the conversation and story swapping about things that happened on Palawan, and what was happening in the wider world. Mrs. Sutherland divulged that what had been in the shoebox she carried aboard was her last pair of shoes, which she'd carefully saved because she didn't want to go home shoeless in case of rescue. Despite being clad in a patched dress made from an old tent, she was still determined to wear shoes like a civilized Scotswoman.

"I guess God has a sense of humor about a lady's vanity, because my feet have swollen so much in the past year, I can't fit into them at all!" she finished with a laugh.

The next night, she was delighted to find a pair of silk stockings next to her place at the table, donated by a *Redfin* sailor who had been intending to send them to a girl back home, where silk was scarce. Mrs. Sutherland had never had a pair before. In gratitude, she repaired a tear in the *Redfin's* large battle flag, already sporting eight miniature Japanese flags.

Tremaine came down with malaria three days after coming on board, and had a rough time of it, but Doc Ross soon got him on the mend. Even Garretson was feeling a bit better.

I spent my time playing cards, visiting with our friends, or sleeping wherever I could find an open bunk. I didn't write to my family. Whatever I sent would be censored, and perhaps forbidden. It would be weeks before they began to worry, though, and by then I would know what I would be allowed to say.

After passing Timor Island and returning to the free ocean, Captain Austin allowed the evacuees and crew time on the deck to get fresh air.

I was dressed in gifted clothes, like the rest of the Fliers, and had even been able to beg a shower and shave the night before. A *Redfin* sailor even gave us all haircuts.

The breeze blowing across my face felt heavenly. Alastair and Heather Sutherland, cooped up so long in their cabin, raced squealing around the deck, frightening their mother. Submarines, after all, don't have deck rails.

One of the crewmen of the *Redfin* had a (technically contraband) camera, and took a picture of Captain Crowley and Captain Austin together

Seven of the eight Flier survivors on the deck of the Redfin. Back row left to right: Lt. Jim Liddell, Cmdr. John Crowley, Ens. Al Jacobson. Front row left to right: QM3c James Russo, MoMM3c Wesley Miller, MoMM3c Earl Baumgart, CRT Gibson Howell. Not pictured: TCR2c Don Tremaine (ill with malaria) Photos courtesy of the family of Lt. James Liddell.

on the Aft Bridge, which led to more photos to commemorate our rescue. Tremaine was too ill to come on deck, but Garretson was finally well enough to stand with the Brooke's Point evacuees photos. We looked respectable and healthy, the sunburns healing, and, aided by the excellent galley crew of *Redfin*, everyone quickly began regaining the weight we had lost.

Australia came into view the morning of the 5th of September, and *Redfin* pulled into Darwin on the early morning of the 6th. Darwin had been attacked by a Japanese air raid less than a year ago, and still showed the evidence, much like Pearl. Hulks of ships sat heavily in the water, and the dusty town was in a state of repair, or disrepair in places.

No crowds, bands, fresh fruit or milk greeted our arrival as they often did in Fremantle or Pearl. *Redfin*, with orders to continue on patrol once they dropped us off and re-loaded, did not fly her battle flag or brag rags. Instead, we were met at the dock by several Marines and a convoy of cars. The Sutherlands, Kierson, Garretson, George, Red, and Charlie were quickly loaded into the first cars and driven away. I never saw them again.

With a quick farewell to the *Redfin* and her crew, the other Fliers and I were escorted to a pair of jeeps and driven to the base at Darwin where a hospital corpsman checked us over thoroughly. They pronounced us all temporarily unfit for duty and needing R&R until our feet healed and all threat of malaria passed.

Rumors of *Robalo*'s fate buzzed around town. Nothing official had been said, but she was now six weeks overdue, and people talked. We didn't say anything, though. There was enough time for the truth to come out, after their families had been informed.

Captain, Jim and I went out to the docks late in the evening to see the *Redfin* off. Her orders were to resume her patrol that night. When we pulled up, Captain Austin was checking off the last of his stores, reading systems checklists, and greeting his crew as they straggled in, dusty and sweaty from an impromptu afternoon baseball game.

"Permission to come aboard," Captain called across to Austin, who smiled at us. "Permission granted," he called back. We stepped across, pausing on the deck to salute Old Glory which waved proudly at the stern of *Redfin*'s Bridge.

"Come to see us off?"

"We can't stay that long. Admiral Christie has chartered a plane to Perth for us, and it's leaving soon. Still," Captain held out his hand to Austin, "Happy Hunting. I hope to see you again."

"God willing. Good luck, John." He shook hands with each of us in turn, and we disembarked. *Redfin's* engines roared beneath her, offering her own good-bye before she disappeared into unknown regions of the Pacific.

The Brooke's Point Evacuees. Standing, from left to right: Liddell, Crowley, Baumgart, Howell, Miller, Henry Garretson, Russo, Mrs. Maise Sutherland, Heather Sutherland (held), Alastair Sutherland, Alexander "Sandy" Sutherland, Vens Kierson. Kneeling left to right: Jacobson, George Marquez, Bill "Red" Wigfield, Charlie Watkins. Not Pictured: Donald Tremaine. Courtesy of the family of Lt. James Liddell

Al Jacobson at work on USS Ling in 1945. Photo Courtesy of family of Alvin Jacobson.

"…a pair for two and a run of three for five means that I have one-hundred-twenty-one points, and I win again!" Mary said gleefully.

"I knew I never should have taught you this game," Muriel Jacobson said wryly. "You sure you're not a cribbage shark or something?"

"Guess you're just a good teacher," Mary grinned and shuffled the deck. "Another hand?"

"What time is it?" Muriel asked, looking around for the clock in her friend's living room.

"Looks like about 4:25, or thereabouts," Mary pointed to the clock hanging over the radio.

"I think I'm good for one more hand, then. Mom will want me home to help make dinner for Papa. It doesn't take long now that Edna Mary and Marilyn are back at college, and David is in the Army Air Force."

"Oh, so he did get in?"

"Sure did, and Mom's more worried than ever."

"Well, I hope they all come home soon."

"Me, too."

Mary dealt the cards again, and the 4:25 newscast began on the radio. Both girls ignored it and concentrated on the game, until…

"We've just received news that the *USS Flier* is overdue and presumed lost at sea with all hands," the announcer read methodically.

Muriel froze, her eyes widened. She began shivering like a leaf.

"Muriel, are you going to play a card or what?" Mary said playfully, looking up. Muriel's face was now white.

"Muriel?" Mary ran around the table, "What happened? Are you okay?" She touched her friend's shoulder in concern.

Muriel uttered a single, strangled gasp, fled the table and crashed through the back door, leaving her friend behind.

She dashed through the backyards of her neighbors, tears streaming down her cheeks. The families of sailors were encouraged not to talk about which vessels their family members were on, so Mary hadn't known that Al was on the *Flier*, and that Al was…was…Muriel couldn't yet bring herself to think it.

She pounded through the back door of her house, and screamed, "Mom! *MOM!*" Edna Jacobson ran out to the back hall to catch her nearly-hysterical daughter.

"What is it? What happened?"

"It was on the radio, Mom, they said Al's submarine went down with all hands!" she cried.

"Muriel, Muriel it's okay, it's okay," her mom gripped her shoulders hard. "Look at me, Muriel. It's okay—"

"How can it be okay? Al's..."

"He's alive, Muriel. I got the letter yesterday!"

It took a moment to register. "You got a letter yesterday? Did...did Al get reassigned and we didn't know?"

"Come over here and sit," her mom said, leading Muriel to a chair in the sunroom. She pulled a letter from her apron pocket. "I only found out yesterday and I'm sorry I didn't tell you, but your father and I were given strict instructions not to say anything to anyone until it was announced on the radio. I didn't think the notice was going to be today, though."

Muriel took the proffered letter with shaking hands and read aloud, "My dear Mr. and Mrs. Jacobson, Your son, Ensign Alvin Emmanuel Jacobson, Jr. United States Naval Reserve, who was aboard a ship the loss of which will be announced in the near future, is safe and well." She started to cry in relief, sinking into her mom's embrace. For a while, they simply sat like that, comforting and being comforted. Eventually, Muriel was able to continue.

"'The circumstances of his rescue are such that information concerning it should not reach the enemy, and it is requested that you do not divulge any reports that may come to you concerning his experiences, or disclose the name of the ship in which he served. The Navy department shares in your pleasure over the safety of your son. It is hoped that he will communicate with you in the near future. Sincerely yours, L. E. Denfield.'

"What happened?" she asked her mom.

"I don't know. I haven't heard from Al yet, but all things considered, I think I can live with the mystery for now." She sighed and stood up. "I had better call your sisters at school. I don't want another case of hysterics if they hear about this the way you did. If you need time to recover, I can handle dinner myself."

"I'll be okay, I think, just give me a few minutes," Muriel smiled weakly.

"All right," her mother turned to go, then turned back and said, "I love you."

"I love you too, Mom."

Muriel took several deep breaths and felt much calmer. She'd go back over to Mary's after dinner and try to explain if she could. The world was all right again. Her big brother, the one who wrote her letters from the front on blank Japanese Deck Logs and teased her from thousands of miles away, was still alive, somewhere.

The tree outside the sunroom swayed in the breeze and Muriel started to laugh remembering the stories about Al and that tree. He had climbed it when he was around ten years old to peek in at Mom in this room, and fell and broke his collarbone. Papa then forbade him to climb it again, but soon after his collarbone healed, Al placed a refrigerator box under the tree, climbed the box and fell again, re-breaking his collarbone. Al argued with their father that he shouldn't get in trouble, because technically he had obeyed. He hadn't been climbing the tree.

Perhaps it was that stubbornness, determination and creative recklessness that had gotten him through whatever had happened, and maybe one day he would tell her about it.

Suddenly Muriel decided her mom was right, she could live with the mystery for now. Knowing that Al was all right, somewhere, was enough. As she went into the house to help her mom with dinner, Muriel said a quick prayer for her brothers, wherever they were, and for those families of the *Flier* that might not be receiving the letter they had gotten.

"Gentlemen! The war is *OVER!!!* Japan has surrendered!" Commander Molumphy's voice roared over the intercom.

I yelled as loudly as the rest of the men on the *Ling*, my new submarine. We had cleared Panama Canal just a day prior, on our way to the front. Scuttlebutt said we were headed to Japan itself in the final stages of preparation for the invasion, but now the war was finally over!

"To celebrate, we are going to fire every last shell on this blessed boat at that little scrap of rock off our portside!" Molumphy continued. "Gunnery Crews, report to your stations!"

It took us a couple of hours to fire every shell out of the *Ling's* guns, and the next day, the reason was obvious. We docked at a Panamanian port and loaded the ammunition lockers with as much alcohol and liquor as would fit, and received express orders to report directly to New London Navy Base as fast as possible.

In the year since *Flier*, much had happened. After the *Redfin* left Darwin, we were loaded on a plane and flown to Perth to collect our pay, find clothes that fit, and order new uniforms.

Baumgart had friends in Perth and went to stay with them. Captain Crowley spent most of his time with Admiral Christie going over the details of the incident. The Navy flew the rest of us to a remote gold-mining town called Kalgoorlie. Admiral Christie thought that this would be the best way to prevent our story from spreading to the other submariners. After all, the submarine community was small, it wouldn't take long to realize a number of Fliers were back, but the rest of them, and the boat, were not. The only thing in Kalgoorlie was the gold mine and the horse track, and since it was horse racing week, the mine was completely deserted.

In the peace and quiet of this small town, I finally allowed myself to remember my friends: Ed, Reynolds, Pope, Hudson, Clyde, Doc, Tommy, See, Dag…there were far too many who hadn't made it. Why had I?

More news kept trickling in. Now the *Harder* was missing in the Philippines. The invincible Sam Dealey and his crew had likely been lost in a depth charge attack near where we had danced in circles between the escorts, the shore, and our victim's wreck. Because of our adventure, the Navy refused to accept the loss for nearly six months, and stretched its intelligence networks to the breaking point looking for any trace of Dealey and his men. In the end though, the Navy had to accept the undeniable.

After a couple of weeks, the Navy brought us back to Perth for the official investigation into the *Flier's* loss. It was held at the same berth to which *Flier* had been tied, but the old *Orion* was gone, replaced by her sister, the *Eurayle*.

This time, not only was Captain being investigated for his possible part in *Flier's* demise, but so was Admiral Christie, who commanded the Fremantle-based submarines and drafted the orders to go through Balabac Straits. Because of what we had learned about the *Robalo* while we were in Palawan, her fate was attached into this investigation. All of us except Captain, who was an interested party inside the courtroom, sat outside in the passage during the two days of the inquiry waiting to answer any questions they had. They talked to me for all of ten minutes. All they wanted to know was my name, rank, where I had been the night *Flier* went down, what I thought had sunk the *Flier,* and whether I had properly adjusted my eyesight before lookout duty. No one cross-examined me, or indeed, any of the other survivors, though they talked with Liddell and Howell longer than with the rest of us.

In the end, the loss of both boats was ascribed to the risks of war. We had operated as safely as we could with the best intelligence available, but sometimes that simply wasn't enough.

The ban on Balabac Straits was not lifted for the remainder of the war.

Every *Flier* crewman on the second patrol, living and dead, was awarded the Purple Heart, and Captain was awarded the Legion of Merit for leading the escape. Liddell, Howell and Russo also received commendations.

After the investigation, I was sent home to Michigan to be with my family for thirty day leave. The Navy, knowing the story of our escape would boost the public's morale, but not wanting to reveal the Coastwatchers, who were still behind the lines, encouraged us to talk about everything up until when the guerillas found us. My family kept a scrapbook of those articles. Some of them made up some interesting stories about how we must have gotten back. Sadly, at first some newspapers reported that most, if not all of the *Flier* crew survived, falsely raising the hopes of their families.

My mother insisted that talking about everything that happened to me would help me work through it, and as she was an excellent short-hand secretary, she also wrote down my adventure. I didn't tell her specific people's names or places where we went, but committed that information onto another sheet of paper, locking both up when we were done. She was right; living through it again and talking about it removed some of the nameless horror.

Donald See won our bet on The Game that fall. OSU, in their first ever undefeated season, beat U of M, 18-14 and for perhaps the only time in my life, I didn't mind too much. See had been eerily right, he was still right there on the *Flier*. I wrote his mother and told her a little bit about See on the *Flier*, including our bet on the game. I hoped that brought her some comfort.

I also wrote to Betty Ann, telling her about Ed, his life and death, and hoped that too, would give her what little comfort there could be.

Coming back from leave, I was given the option to leave the Submarine Force and transfer to the surface fleet. The Navy didn't want me in submarines if I did not feel ready to return to serve on one of *Flier's* sisters. But they were short experienced officers, and I wanted to see the war through to its end, so I accepted an assignment in Boston, where the new sub, *USS Ling*, was undergoing her last trials before her commissioning. I even got to do a little bit of U-Boat hunting before heading to Panama.

Both my brothers survived the war. Charles and I were assigned to Boston for a few weeks before our discharge, and did we ever have fun painting the town red.[40]

Charles and the *Boise* had traveled the world during the war, working in the Med and the battles of Guadalcanal, the invasion of New Guinea, and the Battle of Leyte Gulf. They even hosted MacArthur on a tour of the Philippines when the re-invasion was finished. Charles had had his share of close scrapes too. At one point, during heavy bombardment in the Guadalcanal campaign, he had to leave his station to deal with an emergency, and an enemy shell blew it apart seconds after he left, killing one hundred seven people, but leaving him unscathed.

David became a bombardier, and flew dozens of missions over Nazi Europe, including the firebombing of Dresden. My mother, convinced that forcing me to work my way through my memories had helped me, sat with

---

[40] True story. Due to a lack of parking, Boston started to paint its "no parking" curbs yellow. Jake and Charles painted the curbs near their place red. When the city re-painted those curbs yellow, Jake and Charles re-re-painted them blue. It got enough attention to show up in the Boston paper, though no one knew who was responsible. Jake kept a copy of the article in his scrapbooks.

The Jacobson family reunited outside their Grand Haven home after WWII. From left to right, Alvin Jacobson, Sr., Charles Jacobson, USN, Edna "Sissy" Jacobson, Alvin "Jake" Jacobson, USN, David Jacobson, USAAF. Courtesy of the family of Ens. Alvin "Jake" Jacobson.

them and made them talk through their experiences, too. Her advice proved to be ahead of its time, as talking about wartime experiences is now one treatment for Post-Traumatic Stress Disorder.

I returned to the University of Michigan that fall and finished my degree in one year. I hadn't been studious before the war, but now college seemed simple compared to what I had been through. I joined the Adventurer's Club and took a backpacking trip through Canada with some buddies of mine over Spring Break. You'd think I'd learn. The canoe tipped over, lost all our gear, and we ended up trekking through unmapped wilderness for days until a trapper found us, and guided us back to civilization. Some of my friends were really worried on that trip, but I wasn't. To me, it felt quite familiar, if a lot colder.

After college, I worked for the Crane Company in Chicago before returning to my father's brass casting business. He made me start on the foundry floor and work my way up the ranks, like anyone else.

I finally met the "gorgeous girl" Ed promised me at my sister Muriel's wedding, nearly a decade after *Flier*. I guess you can't rush perfection. Mary was kind enough to marry me in 1955, and we soon had three beautiful children and a nice home near my family. From the outside, it appeared as though I'd left my WWII memories behind me.

But the *Flier* never really left me. Sometimes the aftereffects were strange. While I had no problem with eating rice, the smell and taste of coconut made me sick. I refused to go anywhere without a knife. It was the last thing out of my pocket at night, and first thing I grabbed in the morning, even before my wallet.

Sometimes, Mary would wake me in the middle of the night and tell me I was muttering, "Keep swimming, just keep swimming," in my sleep, but, still bound by *Flier's* Top Secret classification, I couldn't tell her why.

My feet healed, but remained deeply scarred.

For years after the war's end, various family members of my lost shipmates would write me heart wrenching letters. They seemed to ask, "Why you and not my husband, or son, or brother? Why couldn't our loved one escape, too?" I wrote back to them, giving what comfort I could, and prayed the letters would help bring peace.

Decades later, after most of the WWII records of the Submarine Force had been declassified, I received an invitation to speak at a Rotary Club meeting. Mary, who now knew about what I had been through, convinced me that others needed to hear stories from actual WWII veterans, and that my children especially needed to hear my story, to keep the memory of *Flier* alive. I had never been as nervous as I was telling that story with my son in the audience.

Before beginning my talk, they warned me sternly that the Rotary Club meetings ended at 1:30 sharp, not a moment later. By the time the closing bell rang, I wasn't finished telling my story. However, no one moved a muscle; they stayed, skipping work and errands, until the end of my tale.

The men of the *Flier* didn't see each other again until 1994, the 50th anniversary of the *Flier's* loss. Five of us — Crowley, Liddell, Miller, Russo, and I — were able to go to Annapolis, the home of Crowley, to visit together for the first and, as it turned out, the last time.

We caught up with everyone else's life. Captain Crowley and Jim had both been assigned to be CO and XO of the brand-new *USS Irex*, and their reputations apparently made some of her crew very nervous! Some even tried to transfer off, requests which were promptly ignored. The *Irex* was in the Canal only a day behind the *Ling* when Japan surrendered.

The Flier Survivors at the 1994 reunion: From left to right: Al Jacobson, James Liddell, John Crowley, Wes Miller, and James Russo. Earl Baumgart, Gibson Howell, and Donald Tremaine were not able to attend. Photo courtesy of the family of Al "Jake" Jacobson

We wondered what happened to the Coastwatchers, if they got out, but no one knew.

We pored over charts of the area, and decided that though Captain Crowley had originally stated that we landed on Mantangule Island (and so the record reads to this day), we really had landed on the much smaller Byan Island.

A year later, most of the records of the *Flier* became declassified, and, because I was now retired from my company, I was free to do something I had wanted to do since 1944; search for the *Flier* and bring closure to the families left behind.

I did find the niece of Palacido in California. She told me all the Coastwatchers who were left after Corpus's suicide survived and made it back home. Palacido was alive and well and a baker in Laguna Beach. She sent me a copy of his report he submitted to the military about his time in Palawan. It was a very interesting look at what happened to them after we left. They sheltered escapees from Puerto Princesa, established lookout stations all around Palawan, and had several close calls. Once, Palacido was at the supposedly deserted Japanese station on Balabac Island, only to wake up and discover the Japanese guards were back-with reinforcements! He fled with only the clothes on his back, leaving their good radio behind.

While behind enemy lines and after finding a Catholic priest, Butch married Conchita, and Ray apparently followed with another local girl.

All five were awarded the Bronze Star for their efforts in the war.

The death of Cmdr. Crowley in 1997 spurred me to overhaul my memoirs and go back to the Philippines with my now grown son, Steve. We left from Grand Haven and landed in Manila. There, we were greeted by Dr. Nellie Abueg, President of the Palawan Historical Society, and her husband Congressman Alfredo Abueg, who helped us make arrangements.

So much had changed in the fifty plus years since I had been on Palawan. It is still one of the most remote, pristine, and beautiful islands of the Philippines, but modern development had radically changed the jungle I had known. I visited the memorial erected at Plaza Cuartel, on the site of the POW camp in Puerto Princesa. The Japanese massacred more than one-hundred fifty prisoners there, and I said a silent prayer for those who died. It was the mercy of God alone that kept me and the other Fliers from this fate. I prayed for the *Robalo* sailors, including Kimmel if he had been there, and tried to find more about what had happened to them.

Brooke's Point, a three-hour drive south on good roads, was vastly different. The only houses I saw in 1944 were Mayor's house on the beach, and the Mayor's and Edwards' houses inland. Today, it is a town of 40,000 people. The mayor of Brooke's Point was the granddaughter of Mr. Edwards, who survived the war, along with his whole family.

Rio Tuba was two hours farther south on a not-so-good gravel road. In 1944 there were only two houses here, but now it is another major port shipping nickel mined out of the mountains nearby. They even have a full-time Coast Guard station and large department store.

From there, we chartered a boat and re-traced my journey on the smaller island.

We landed on Byan Island, and I recognized the beach where we landed that afternoon in 1944. It looked so familiar I almost expected to see the seashells I laid out fifty years ago. Where we cast off in our raft from Byan, there is now a shipbuilder who builds 50- to 60-foot yachts, and a housing development for employees. They have a deep well to get their water.

Jake at Brooke's Point in 1998. It had developed from a small, war torn village to a thriving community of 40,000 people. Photo courtesy of the family of Al "Jake" Jacobson

We passed Gabung and APO, the second and third islands we'd landed on before docking at Bugsuk. The abandoned house site is now the village of Sebring. The house is gone, but the cistern is still there, and the water is now safe. The Mayor family returned after the war and their descendants built a beautiful home about 100 yards away from the old house site. They welcomed Steve and me to stay with them for the night.

The most emotional and difficult time, though, was returning for *Flier's* last position. When we arrived at the coordinates where Captain Crowley and Jim figured *Flier* went down, the surroundings didn't look right. The landscape I admired just before *Flier* blew was etched in my memory so clearly, even decades later. The captain of our boat took us south until finally the silhouettes matched what I remembered in those last moments high on the Bridge.

Once again, I could see the land on three sides of us: Comiran Island off the port bow, Balabac dead ahead, Palawan a faint shadow to the north. Byan was hidden by the exposed tops of Roughton and Natsubata Reefs, proving we had been pushed around them by the currents, and hadn't swum in a straight line.

Some people tell me that we should have swum to Comiran Island to preserve more of our shipmates, but the rumored fate of the *Robalo* crew and the POWs at Puerto Princesa convince me that we made the right choice and that God was watching out for us that night.

The captain of the chartered ship told us that native fishermen and divers have seen *Flier* on the few days a year when the ocean is crystal clear. She apparently sits straight up on the ocean floor, her bow buried deeply in the bottom. No one approaches her, for she is very deep, nor could anyone tell me if the escape hatches were open and others might have escaped.

I stood there on the bow of that ship with my son and wrote down the GPS coordinates of this site, about a mile from the official coordinates. Perhaps someday, I would be able to come back with the equipment to find her, but for now, it was enough to know she was at peace.

Alvin "Jake" Jacobson died on October 16, 2008, after years of declining health, before he was able to find the *Flier* himself.

In April 2009, his son Steve and grandson Nelson Jr., along with experienced divers Mike and Warren Fletcher, and YAP Films, a documentary company, went to Balabac Straits looking for *Flier* and *Robalo*.

Triangulating a likely resting area for *Flier* by combining the last known path and Jacobson's coordinates, the search team used side scan sonar to map the ocean floor until they found a "hit" that looked like a wrecked submarine in the area Al marked eleven years earlier.

When they dropped the guide line down, the divers discovered that their weighted bags had landed on the *Flier* herself.

She sits upright listing slightly to starboard, in 330 feet of water, surrounded by a beautiful bed of white sand and rock. After six decades underwater, she is encrusted with corals and is home to dozens of species of fish. The Fletchers called her one of the most beautiful wrecks they had ever seen. [41]

A massive hole has caved in her starboard side, where the Control Room and Crew's Mess meet, directly beneath Jake's seat that night. The blast also may have removed shield plating from the bridge, exposing the Conning Tower Pressure Hull from which Jim Liddell, Don Tremaine,

---

[41] A documentary about the discovery of *Flier* was made using footage taken on these dives. The title is Dive Detectives: Submarine Graveyard.

Charles Pope, Paul Knapp, Jim Russo, and Art Howell escaped.

The lookout deck, where Wes Miller and Earl Baumgart stood watch with Gerald Madeo and Eugene Heller still exists, but the rails they leaned against are wrapped around the periscope shears. The periscope heads themselves are missing, cut off just above the shear structure.

The aft escape hatch Al always wondered about has not yet been explored. The forward escape hatch, however, is open.

But there were no other recorded survivors of *USS Flier.*

The Navy, after studying these images, declared this to be the wreck of *USS Flier* on 1 February, 2010.

The National Memorial Service for *USS Flier* was held Friday, August 13, 2010 at the Great Lakes Naval Memorial and Museum, on the 67th anniversary of her loss. Family members came from around the country to honor their lost loved ones, including a welcome member: James Alls, who stood for his replacement Donald See during the Lost Boat Ceremony.

The formal ceremony took place aboard *USS Silversides, Flier's* sister sub and the one who gave *Flier* her first tip on a convoy in 1944.

Like all sunken warships, the *Flier* is considered a war grave by international law, and is not to be disturbed. The men of the *Flier* will be left in peace.

WHAT HAPPENED AFTER

THE SURVIVING FLIERS

Lieutenant Commander John D. Crowley went on to have a long and successful career in the Navy. After being CO of *USS Irex*, he served in the Submarine Force in the Korean War, then the Pentagon, finally retiring at the rank of Captain. He and Liddell remained good friends, and their families frequently visited one another. He and his family lived in Baltimore, Maryland, where he died in 1997.

Lieutenant Jim Liddell, concerned his wife would hear of *Flier's* loss before his rescue, sent a telegram to her the day they got to port: *"Darling am well and safe/Hope Dad is better/received mail/love to all."* When he met her again for his leave, he told her the whole story of *Flier* from beginning to end, then rarely spoke of it again. By the end of the war, Liddell, a reservist who had been activated before December 7, 1941, was qualified as a prospective submarine commander, and likely would have been awarded his own boat had the war continued another six months to a year. His duty done, he requested separation from the navy and, in light of the length and honor of his service, was granted it quickly. He returned home to his wife and later became a salesman for a company in Lancaster Pennsylvania. When his product line was put up for sale, he purchased it and formed his own company with several partners. It was later named after his last boat, the *Irex*. He and his wife Marion kept scrapbooks of his WWII adventures, as well as copies of the Deck Logs and War Patrol Reports in their library. His son revealed that one strange side effect of the *Flier* escape was Liddell's intense dislike of rice for the rest of his life. A beloved husband, father, and grandfather, he died in Lancaster in 2001.

Earl Baumgart was assigned to the Minesweeper *Falcon* for the rest of the war. After discharge in 1946, he returned to Wisconsin where he became a police patrolman and then a police-fire dispatcher until he retired in 1977. Married twice (his first wife died of brain cancer) and with two sons, he lived in Milwaukee until his death in 2005.

Wesley Miller served on the Submarine Tender *Orion* and was discharged after the end of WWII. He reenlisted as an officer after he completed college in 1950. This time, he went back aboard submarines on

CREW OF USS FLIER (SS-250)
OFFICERS

John Crowley, 35
Lt.Cmdr., CO
Springfield, MA

James Liddell, 26
Lieutenant, XO
Forth Worth, TX

John Casey, 24
Lieutenant
Baltimore, MD

Paul Knapp, 26
Lieutenant
San Francisco, CA

William Reynolds, 24
Lieutenant
Industry, PA

Herbert Baehr, 33
Lieutenant, j.g.
Flint, MI

Alvin Jacobson, 22
Ensign
Grand Haven, MI

Philip Mayer, 22
Ensign
Beverly Hills, CA

Herbert Miner, 32
Ensign
Escondido, CA

Photos of Liddell and Jacobson courtesy of their families. All others All others courtesy of Charles Hinman and On Eternal Patrol

USS Sterlet patrolling the West Coast, then the ammunition ship *USS Paricutin* in the Korean theater, before leaving the military for good as a lieutenant in 1952. He returned to Washington state, where he married and had a family while working as the head of maintenance for a large school district. He rarely talked about his military experiences or the *Flier*, though he attended the *Flier* reunion of 1994. He died in 2000.

James Dello Russo's family was informed of *Flier's* loss, but not his survival. Their first notice that he was alive and safe was when he walked through his family's door with thirty days leave. He didn't talk much about his experience on *Flier*, and suffered vivid dreams and would frequently wake up screaming. After the war, he wrote to and visited many of the families of his lost crewmates. Never married, he lived with his niece for many years. According to her, it was probably the fact that, as a youth, he loved to swim out to the channel islands that dot his native Boston harbor, which saved him from drowning that night. He died after a battle with cancer in 1997.

Arthur Howell was interviewed about the Flier's escape on CBS' March of Time radio spot in December 1944. He returned home to his wife and three children in East Moriches New York and worked in a radio repair business as well as became a member of the fire department. Due to the illness of his wife, he was unable to come to the *Flier* reunion of 1994. He died in 1997.

The author was unable to discover the fate of Donald Tremaine following his experience on the *Flier.*

James Alls, left ashore suffering a broken jaw, went on to become a Photographer's Mate and served on *Hammerhead* and *Kraken* during WWII then *Pilotfish* and *Blackfin* until he left the Navy in 1948.

One of the most difficult experiences for him regarding *Flier* happened shortly after the war while he was serving in the *Kraken*. As they pulled into Portsmouth to participate in Navy Day celebrations, a man went from boat to boat asking if anyone aboard served on the *Flier* or knew anyone who had. Alls introduced himself, and discovered he was talking to Waite Daggy's brother. The brother invited Alls to his family home for dinner where he met a number of Daggy's relatives during that time, and talked to them about Daggy's life on *Flier*, including his surgery at Midway. It was a

MOTOR MACHINIST'S MATE

William Brooks, 35
Poquonnock Bridge, CT
Chief Motoe Macinist

Edgar Hudson, 28**
Nashville, TN
Chief Motor Mac

James Snyder, 26
Traveler's Rest, SC
Chief Motor Machinist

Alexander
Abrahamson, 26
Chicago, IL

George Banchero, 23
San Jose, CA

SURVIVOR

Earl Baumgart, 21
Milwaukee, WI

Ervin Borlick, 28
Chicago, IL

Edwin Canady, 25
Lumberton, NC

Robert Cushman, 20
Bridgeport, CT

Waite Daggy, 21
Castle Rock, WA

Peter Daros, 21
Springfield, MA

Fred Fender, 22
West Toledo, OH

All photos courtesy of Charles Hinman and On Eternal Patrol.

difficult, and emotional meeting on all sides.

Following discharge from the Navy, Alls and his wife moved to southern New York state, where they had two children, before relocating again to Washington D.C. where Alls worked multiple jobs in real estate, insurance, and machinist fields until his retirement in the 1980s.

The scars from the *Flier* however, remained. He had frequent dreams of *Flier's* lost crew asking him what was taking him so long to join them. But during the Memorial Weekend of *USS Flier*, he was able to describe a lot of these men to their relatives, many of whom had never met them in person, as well was tell stories about what life was like on *Flier*. To those family members, Alls' survival was a gift. He later met the family of Donald See, and got to learn more about the young man who took his place. His stories were part of the inspiration for this second edition.

THE SURVIVING FAMILIES

Due to WWII secrecy classifications, the families received a very difficult letter to read. The following is a transcript of the telegram delivered to the home of Mrs. Violet Klock, mother of *Flier's* Chief Radioman, Walter "Bud" Klock. Bud's wife, Velma, was living with his mother:

14 10 44 [14 October 1944]
<Address redacted> (N. ST. PAUL MINN)=
"THE NAVY DEPARTMENT DEEPLY REGRETS TO INFORM YOU THAT YOUR SON WALTER JOSEPH KLOCK RADIOMAN FIRST CLASS USN IS MISING FOLLOWING ACTION IN THE PERFORMANCE OF HIS DUTY AND IN THE SERVICE OF HIS COUNTRY. THE DEPARTMENT APPRECIATES YOUR GREAT ANXIETY BUT DETAILS NOT NOW AVAILABLE AND DELAY IN RECIEPT THEREOF MUST NECESSARILY BE EXPECTED. TO PREVENT POSSIBLE AID TO OUR ENEMIES AND TO SAFEGUARD THE LIVES OF OTHER PERSONNEL PLEASE DO NOT DIVULGE THE NAME OF THE SHIP OR STATION OR DISCUSS PUBLICLY THE FACT THAT HE IS MISSING=
VICE ADMIRAL RANDALL JACOBS THE CHIEF OF NAVAL PERSONNEL."

Other families received a similar letter, rather than a telegraph.

All submarine families in WWII, when their relative's submarine was overdue or missing were sent a telegram or letter like this as soon as the Navy suspected the submarine was not coming home, several

MOTOR MACHINIST'S MATES

Joesph Grimshaw, 27
Indian Orchard,
MA

Harry Holtyn, 22
Buffalo, NY

Oliver Kisamore, 22
Andover, OH

James LeRoy, 26
Ely, MN

Vernon McLane, 27
Happy Camp, CA

Wesley Miller, 21
Portland, OR

George Phillips, Jr., 19
Rchester, NH

Michael
Ricciardelli, 23
Upper Darby, PA

Paul Vest, 22
Chicago, IL

James Alls, 17
Washington D.C.

James Dello-Russo, 17
East Boston, MA

Earle Dressell, 22
S. Hadley Falls, MA

QUARTERMASTERS

James Alls photo courtesy of James Alls. James Dello Russo photo courtesy of his niece. All others courtesy of
Charles Hinman and On Eternal Patrol.

weeks after she was reported due back. This was the reason for the Sailing List that Walter Dorricott and Jimmy Elder prepared for *Flier*. The lost submariners could not be declared dead, however, because the fates of most submarines were unknown. In *Flier's* case, since some had survived, it was possible that others had. It was also possible that those who disappeared in the night had not died, but been swept to other islands, where they may have been captured or discovered by other people.

John Crowley and James Liddell, after their family leave and before assignment to the *Irex*, were brought to Washington D.C. where they wrote to the families of the *Flier*, trying to explain what happened, but due to the classified nature of submarine service, had to still be vague. Below is a partial transcript of the letter Cmdr. Crowley sent to Mrs. Violet and Velma Klock, dated October 28, 1944:

"...*Due to the nature of submarine warfare requiring operations deep in enemy controlled waters and the circumstances under which our ship was lost, it is not possible for me to describe the action to you, nor the circumstances surrounding the rescue of survivors. This is necessary to provide maximum protection for your own son and those of his shipmates who may yet be able to make their way home, and to safeguard the lives of other boys on our submarines who are now bravely seeking out and destroying the enemy.*

"*While there is a possibility that Walter may yet be found, it is only fair for you to know that the situation is not so favorable as numerous newspaper accounts would lead one to believe. However, the Navy does not give up hope for many months unless the fact of death is proven beyond any possible doubt, and I share this hope with you.*

"*Words can but poorly express the sympathy of Walter's other shipmates and myself in your sorrow. As you know, he commissioned the ship with me. His work was always of the highest calibre [sic] and I considered him to be one of our most stable and trusted men...All of Walter's personal effects, which I know you would prize most highly were lost with the ship...I regret I can tell you no more, but if there I any other way in which I can be of assistance to you please do not hesitate to write me.*"

Some families did. Walter Dorricott's wife asked Crowley for a map of where *Flier's* resting place was, but the Navy did not permit it at that time.

TORPEDO CREW

Kenneth Gwinn, 40
New Castle, IN
Chief Torpedoman's Mate

Victor Anderson, 23
Keego Harbor, MI

Ronald Cosgrove, 20
Corning, NY

Thomas Donovan, 29
Hornell, NY

Clyde Gerber, 23
Slayton, MN

Sol Kantor, 21
Brooklyn, NY

George Laderbush, 21
Portsmouth, NH

Richard Lambert, 16
Warren, OH

Boyd Lindeman 29
Corpus Christi, TX

Joseph Nicholson, 29
Lynn, MA

Lucius Wall, 26
Minco, OK

D
I
E
D

A
T

M
I
D
W
A
Y

James Cahl, 21*
South Holland, IL

All photos courtesy of Charles Hinman and On Eternal Patrol.

Others formed family networks. With the Navy and survivors unable to say much while the war continued, they contacted one another looking for information trying to discover whether or not other family members had received different information, trying to put details together. The families of the Ohio Fliers quickly found each other and wrote back and forth to one another, in addition to the survivors. In a series of letters written in January 1945, the families of Walter Kisamore and Donald See corresponded, looking for more information. These letters referenced contacts being made with the Pope family and Al Jacobson and Gibson Howell. By this time, these families at least, knew that only that those on the bridge or conning towers had survived, information which was not yet publicly acknowledged.

The survivors wrote to the families too, though what information they could share was very limited. In a poignant letter to Lt. John "Ed" Casey's mother, Howell spoke of Casey's end, in heartbreaking terms.

News traveled slowly in 1944. Some of the men from *Flier* had brothers and other relatives in other branches of the military all over the world. Some wouldn't know about their family member's death until they returned home. Albert Ricciardelli, stationed in Papua New Guinea, wrote a letter to his big brother Michael (whom he called Nick), a Motor Mac on *Flier,* in October 1944, two months after *Flier* sank. He welcomed Nick's new wife to the family, and told Nick about his own recent marriage. Albert even drew a submarine on the envelope for his big brother. Today, it shows marks of bouncing around the USA before returning to Albert, unopened. Oliver Kisamore's family received an even stranger note. Oliver wrote his family a postcard from the Panama Canal when *Flier* passed through in December 1943. It was postmarked "Dec. 4 1943" in Christobal, Panama, but for unknown reasons, not passed by the Office of Naval Intelligence until September 4, 1945. The Kisamore family received this postcard, in Oly's handwriting, a year after they'd been notified of *Flier's* loss, but before the Navy could have confirmed his death. All the postcard says is:

> *"Just a few lines to let you know I am O.K. Hope you fellows are too. Is it ever warm here. I'm pulling out soon. I'll write you when I reach my next destination. Love, Oly"*

It wasn't until after the war, when the rolls of POW names were collected and cross-referenced, that the Navy could change the lost *Flier*

ELECTRICIAN'S MATES

Mason Poole, 29
San Antonio, TX
Chief Electrician

Thomas Bohn, 18
Easton, PA

William Cowhey, 29
Duluth, MN

John Cowie, 24
Syracuse, OH

Harry Ericson, 27
Brooklyn, NY

Frank Falowski, 22
New York, NY

Joesph Kucinski, 22
Rutherford, NJ

Harvey Myers, 23
Fairmount, WV

Charles Parker, 25
Philadelphia, PA

Jarrold Taylor, 23
Odessa, TX

S U R V I V O R

Arthur Howell, 30
E. Moriches, NY

James "Buddy"
Vogt, 22
St. Paul, MN

RADIO TECHNICIANS

Howell's photo courtesy of Liddell family. All other photos courtesy of Charles Hinman and On Eternal Patrol.

crew's status from "Missing in Action" to "Killed in Action", closing a door on the hopes of many.[42]

The following is a partial transcript from a letter sent from the Secretary of the Navy, James Forrestal, to the family of *Flier* crewman Ervin "Paddy" Borlick of Chicago dated 1 February 1946:

> "...On the night of 13 August 1944 the FLIER was cruising on the surface through a pass between islands in the Philippine group. Suddenly there was a tremendous explosion in the water alongside. All personnel on the bridge were temporality stunned by the force of the explosion and no word was received from below decks in the twenty or thirty seconds before the submarine went under.
>
> "Immediately after the sinking, personnel were seen in the water. However it appeared that only those who were stationed on the bridge or in the conning tower managed to get clear of the vessel. There were islands in the vicinity, some of which were occupied by the enemy and others by the friendly guerrilla forces. The eight men who were the only known survivors of the blast swam about 12 miles and finally landed on an uninhabited coral atoll. Several days later they succeeded in making contact with friendly guerilla forces on another island who immediately instituted a search of all islands in the vicinity not occupied by the enemy. This search proved fruitless, and to date no further information has been received by the Navy Department concerning your son.
> In view of the length of time that has now elapsed since your son was reported to be missing and because there have been no official or unconfirmed reports that your son survived or was taken prisoner of war, I am reluctantly forced to the conclusion that he is deceased...I extend my deepest sympathy to you in your sorrow. It is hoped that you may find comfort in the knowledge that your son gave his life for his country, upholding the highest traditions of the Navy."

From 1948 to 1960, the remains of those who lost their lives in the Pacific were gathered and, providing the family did not specifically request they be repatriated to the US, were laid to rest in the Manila

---

[42] Many lost submariners were also declared dead around this time. Those whose submarines never returned and whose cause of loss is still unknown, were finally declared dead, though those letters could not include the cause of the loss, or even a concrete date of loss.

SEAMEN

William Bivens, 18
Chicago, IL

Christian
Christensen, Jr., 19
Watsontown, PA

Charles Clawson, 23
Los Angeles, CA

Charles Courtright, 20
Franklin, NJ

Walter Freeman, 19
Havana, FL

Eugene Heller, 31
Floyd, IA

Edward McCoy, 18
Newark, NJ

Vernon Moench, 19
Kansas City, MO

Chester Payne, 19
Tulare, CA

Kit Pourciau, 18
New Orleans, LA

Walter Dorricott, 24
New London, CT

James Elder, 21
Ottawa, KS

YEOMEN

All photos courtesy of Charles Hinman and On Eternal Patrol.

-265-

American Cemetery and Memorial in the Philippines. For those who were lost or buried at sea, their names were inscribed on the Tablets of the Missing at the same cemetery. Each man lost on *Flier* has his name engraved there.

It would be over twenty years before *Flier's* official records, her deck logs and war patrol reports, would be declassified, still more before the final paperwork could be released and the survivors allowed to speak openly.

There is no way to describe the "typical" reaction or survival of the families who lost a man on *Flier*. Some families drew closer, others were shattered. There were children who never met fathers, wives who remarried, others who didn't, parents who erected photos of their lost sons, but rarely talked about them. Others did. Many siblings named their sons after their lost uncles. A number of *Flier* spouses lost contact with the families of their husbands, leaving cousins who are still discovering each other's existence nearly seven decades later.

USS FLIER COMMENDATIONS

The *Flier* was awarded one battle star for her successful patrol, and during the war, was given credit for the four ships her crew claimed they sank.

However, after the war, the Japanese claimed they had no records of any ships or convoys being Mindoro or near Cape Bolinas on the dates *Flier* named. The only ship they were given credit for sinking was the ship on the very first attack. Their victim's name was *Hakusan Maru*, a 10,380 ton ship that had been built as a luxury passenger liner and converted into a troop ship. During the war, she ferried troops all over the Pacific, from those bound for the invasion of Kiska and Attu, Alaska, in the north, to New Guinea in the south. Several times, ships in her convoys had been attacked and sunk. On 2 November 1943, while anchored in Rabul, *Hakusan* was bombed and severely damaged by American Mitchell bombers. A repair ship was brought in to make her seaworthy again. On 31 May 1944, she departed Saipan with thirteen other ships, bound for Yokosuka, Japan. Two days out, *USS Shark*, on a tip from *USS Silversides*, sighted *Hakusan's* convoy and sank her companion, *Chiyo Maru*. The next day, *Flier* found them, and destroyed *Hakusan*. The rest of the convoy made it to Yokosuka safely. As

RADIO CREW

Walter Klock, 27
St. Paul, MN
Chief Radioman

Paul Barron, 21
Hollywood, CA

Bernard Fite, 21
Philadelphia, PA

David Nordhof, 23
Holland, MI

FIREMEN

Elton Brubaker, 18
Palatka, FL

Gerald Madeo, 20
Waterbury, CT

Victor Murawski, 19
Amsterdam, NY

Donald See, 19
Columbus, OH

GUNNERY CREW

Charles Pope, 27
Greensboro, NC
Chief Gunner Mate

Joseph Galinac, 24
Steelton, PA

SURVIVOR

Donald Tremaine
Gilroy, CA

All photos courtesy of Charles Hinman and On Eternal Patrol.

Jacobson would later say, he felt sorry for the men on the ship, but it would have taken a good sized Marine unit to take out those soldiers if they had gotten where they were going.

A postcard depicting the ship Flier sank, Hakusan Maru. In the 1920's and 1930's she was a passenger liner, carrying people and mail from Japan to Europe in luxury accommodations.

Her resting place has not yet been found.

USS Flier was credited with severely damaging, though not sinking, *Marifu Maru,* during the June 13 attack off Cape Bolinao, which had to be towed to Manila, where she was considered to be a complete loss, and her CO and crew transferred other vessels.

The ship attacked during the June 22 attack south of Manila, according to records, was the *Belgium Maru.* Whether she was sunk or severely damaged depends on which records one finds. Her wreck, if it exists has not been found or identified.

Very few submariners were happy with the post-war submarine records as the American and Japanese navies finally settled them. In a post-war interview, Cmdr. Roy Davenport, who was awarded five Navy Crosses for his immensely successful submarine patrols, claimed that the post war records sometimes claimed he did not sink ships he watched go down,

SHIP'S COOKS

Clyde Banks, 21
Cincinnati, OH

Alvin Skow, 20
Luck, WI

James
Westmoreland, 28
Atlanta, GA

BAKER

Melvin Getchell, 20
San Francisco, CA

BOATSWAIN'S MATE

Gale Hardy, 29
Denver, CO

SIGNALMAN

Robert Rose, 23
Hickman, KY

STEWARD'S MATE

John Turner, 25
Powder Springs,
GA

PHARMACIST'S MATE

Peter Gaideczka, 29
Pearl River, NY

All photos courtesy of Charles Hinman and On Eternal Patrol.

while other times, he given credit for sinking a ship on a day he did not attack any. Wartime records were quite messy, and the fact that the Japanese were in retreat for nearly three years may have contributed to the differences between what skippers claimed to have destroyed on patrol, and what was acknowledged later.

THE WRECK OF THE USS FLIER

The wreck of *USS Flier* was discovered in April 2009 and confirmed by the US Navy on February 1, 2010.

At 330 feet deep, a round trip dive required each diver who explored the *Flier* to bring multiple tanks filled with various gasses, and, due to safety restrictions and decompression time, only allowed them twelve minutes of exploration time. Professional divers Mike and Warren Fletcher, who lead the team and have traveled the world diving, had never gone that deep before. Such a depth will hopefully, protect *Flier* in the years to come.

Due to the extreme depth and difficulty of the two dives, *Flier* was only explored and documented from bow to Conning Tower. From that point to the stern remains, as of this book's publishing, unexplored and undocumented. It is still possible that the after escape hatch, like the forward, could be open.

In 1944 and until his death, Al Jacobson believed that the *Flier* hit a mine somewhere in her forward compartments, likely in Officer's Country, as did a lot of the other survivors. The wreck survey shows that the blast site was actually almost directly beneath him, and close to the waterline. The bend of the metal surrounding the blast site proves the force that destroyed *Flier* came from outside and not due to an internal, mechanical failure. It is likely *Flier* hit a floating mine, something that they couldn't have prevented.

Flier was identified through a combination of her position, a comparison of the configuration of this wreck with *Flier's* last weapons and antenna configuration, as well as certain details. Her dive planes, for example, were in the "up" position, proving that she was on the surface when she sank. Her bow has broken off, also showing she sank quickly, with enough force to crush and sever it. These details match the description of her final moments given by her surviving crew.

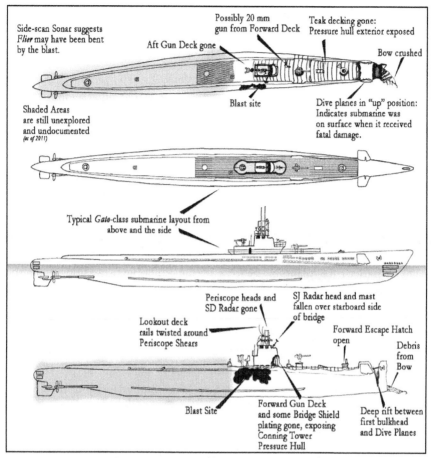

Side-scan Sonar suggests *Flier* may have been bent by the blast.

Aft Gun Deck gone

Possibly 20 mm gun from Forward Deck

Teak decking gone: Pressure hull exterior exposed

Bow crushed

Shaded Areas are still unexplored and undocumented *(as of 2011)*

Blast site

Dive planes in "up" position: Indicates submarine was on surface when it received fatal damage.

Typical *Gato*-class submarine layout from above and the side

Periscope heads and SD Radar gone

SJ Radar head and mast fallen over starboard side of bridge

Lookout deck rails twisted around Periscope Shears

Forward Escape Hatch open

Debris from Bow

Blast Site

Forward Gun Deck and some Bridge Shield plating gone, exposing Conning Tower Pressure Hull

Deep rift between first bulkhead and Dive Planes

This diagram, based on the footage returned from the dive on Flier's wreck, shows how the wreck differs from Flier when she was whole and the damage she sustained. Her wooden deck has all but disappeared, the upper portion of her exposed pressure hull now littered with the remains of the teak, the deck supports and other debris, which were not drawn in this diagram. The aft section of the wreck, as of this printing, is unexplored and undocumented. Its condition can only be speculated about.

Flier is protected against salvage by an international agreement that all warships lost in action are the sovereign property of the nation whose flag they served under. *Flier* is unlikely to be disturbed.

THE REST OF THE EVACUEES AND COASTWATCHERS

George Marquez eventually retired to California, where he kept in touch with Larry Coleman of the *Redfin*. Charlie Watkins returned to Miami by the end of 1944, but his trail went cold there.

Larry Coleman of *Redfin*, also found Palacido in Laguna Beach, California, and returned the Silver Certificate with the signatures of all the Coastwatchers to him in 1995. Palacido never married and ran a popular bakery until his death in 2000.

After medical exams, the Sutherlands were interviewed about the Philippines. Sandy Sutherland's hobby was cartography, and he had carefully studied the various islands all over the Philippines and knew which beaches and harbors had steep or shallow grades, were suitable for landing troops, tanks, or mooring deep-drafted ships. That information became vital as part of the planning process of the Philippine invasion. After the interviews, they tried to return to their native Scotland. Due to the war and travel restrictions, they made it as far as South Africa, where they had another son in 1946. After a brief visit to Scotland, they returned to Brooke's Point in 1947 and resumed missionary work. Sandy Sutherland died of cancer in 1976 and was buried, as he requested, in the Brooke's Point cemetery on the shore of Sulu Sea. Maise Sutherland and the children continued to serve in Palawan for years. Occasionally, the evacuation had unusual side effects for Heather and Alastair. Neither really remembered it, though their parents frequently told them the stories. Years after the rescue, Heather Sutherland was quite startled when she re-met the guerilla who sang her that lullaby in the kumpit while waiting for *Redfin*. He was the postmaster, and had seen her in his office, but hadn't caught her before she left. He chased her down the street telling her she had to remember him, he was the one that held her on the banca while they waited for the submarine to arrive.

Heather and Alastair now live in the USA. A number of their relatives still live in Palawan.

This author was unable to discover the fates of the other Brooke's Point refugees or Coastwatchers.

USS REDFIN

The *Redfin* completed her fourth patrol and three more after, commanded by Austin and then *Redfin's* former XO Charles Miller, who was promoted after Austin went stateside. Every single one of her six patrols was given a battle star, signifying a successful patrol. *Redfin* finished the war credited for six ships sunk for a total of 23,724 tons of shipping destroyed. She was decommissioned in 1946, then re-commissioned in 1953 as a radar picket submarine and served through the Korean and part of the Vietnam wars. She was decommissioned in 1971 and sold for scrap the next year, the fate of a number of gallant submarines.

To this day, the crews of the *Redfin* gather together annually, to remember their boat. Three men, Charles "Red" Schwertfeger, and Larry Coleman, who were on *Redfin* when she rescued the Fliers, and the late Jack March, organizer of the Redfins, were instrumental in helping research *Redfin's* role in this story.

THE FATE OF THE ROBALO

The story of what happened to the *Robalo* and her crew has never been fully settled.

In the transcripts of the investigation into the loss of *USS Flier* and *USS Robalo*, Captain Crowley stated that de la Cruz told him the *Robalo* sank 40 miles west of Balabac on 3 July, with at least four people washing up on Comiran Island. Two were captured and at least two others escaped, were shot while escaping, or were shot after being captured. The names of the survivors, according to de la Cruz, were Ensign Tucker and a sailor called Martin. De la Cruz also said he was able to discover *Robalo's* last port of call was Darwin in late June. These details convinced command that this story had merit, because those names and facts could not have been known by either Crowley or de la Cruz through normal means.

Ensign Samuel Tucker and Signalman Wallace Martin, along with two other men, Quartermaster Floyd Laughlin and Electrician's Mate Mason Poston, who were captured in an unrecorded location, were transported to Puerto Princesa and imprisoned together as guerillas rather than POWs. According to Filipino guerillas in northern Palawan, on 2 August, the day

Flier left Fremantle, they dropped a note out their window, which was picked up by an American POW and made its way to the guerilla forces. The note contained at least these men's names as well as the name, or according to some sources, the hull number of the *Robalo*.

According to intelligence from the people of Palawan, the prisoners were loaded on a ship on or around 15 August and never heard from again. Al Jacobson records in his memoirs that the prisoners were placed aboard the *Takao Maru* and were signed for by the ship's captain, Aida Sakutaro, with the intended destination of Manila. He does not identify where he obtained the information, but it is the author's and his family's opinion that he likely obtained it during his trip to the Philippines. Al Jacobson was a careful researcher all his life, especially as concerns this story. Inquiries have been made in Palawan regarding this record, and at the time of publication, were still awaiting verification.

Eventually the US Navy formally ruled that the *Robalo* may have sunk on 27 July just two miles west of Palawan Island, with Tucker, Martin, Laughlin, and Poston landing together on Palawan Island, not Comiran. The original suspected cause, Forward Battery explosion, was revised to a mine strike.

During the war, Admiral Christie told the Kimmel family that Manning Kimmel had gone down with his sub, to spare them the story that Al Jacobson heard, a story that had also reached Christie's ears. In the end, whether Kimmel went down with his boat, had been taken prisoner, or died in August, would not have mattered. The entire Puerto Princesa camp was slaughtered on December 10, 1944. Apparently afraid the invasion of the Philippines was coming to them, and of what would happen if they were found with so many Prisoners of War in such poor condition, the Japanese guards herded all the POWs of Puerto Princesa into air raid shelters, dumped aviation fuel over them, and set them on fire, shooting and torturing those who managed to break out. Only eleven men escaped, six of whom were delivered to Palacido and the Coastwatchers at Brooke's Point for pickup.[43] When the Americans liberated Palawan in March of

---

[43] For more information on this horrible tragedy, read <u>Last Man Out: Glenn McDole USMC Survivor of the Palawan Massacre in WWII</u> by Bob Wilbanks

1945, they found three large mounds of partial remains which were exhumed and sent to St. Louis Missouri, where most are buried together in a mass grave. [44] (A few who could be positively identified were buried according to their families' wishes.) The number and identities of some of the men who died that horrific day are still debated. What is known is that no *Robalo* sailor was ever returned to the US after the war.

The hunt for *Robalo's* resting place continues.

JAPANESE MINES

After the war, the Navy learned that the Japanese had invented a new type of sea mine. The old mines that American intelligence knew about could only be laid in waters a few hundred feet deep, so submarines were always ordered to stay in water at least five hundred feet deep whenever possible. Despite a Geneva Convention that required all mines to have a failsafe which would deactivate them if they broke loose of their moorings, this device often failed. In fact, during two war patrols, submarines *Atule* and *Dace* recorded using their deck guns to explode floating mines they encountered, a common tactic. In *Dace's* case, one mine detonated after shooting it with their 20 mm anti-aircraft gun, throwing shrapnel onto *Dace's* deck.

How effective these mines were is a matter of debate. Though mines are believed to be the cause of loss for at least six submarines[45] as well as *Flier* and *Robalo,* they also inadvertently sank a number of Japanese ships as well. The floating mines ended up being a hazard after the war, and even when the Russian Submarine *Kursk* sank in 2000, there were many who initially believed a rogue floating mine from WWII may have been the cause.

Naval Intelligence always suspected that Balabac Straits had been mined. An examination of Japanese records after the war proved that Balabac was mined at least twice, once using the old mines in 1941, and again in 1943 by the *Tsugaru Maru. Tsugaru* laid the new Type 93 Model 1

---

[44] The site of the Massacre is Plaza Cuartel Park in Puerto Princesa and contains a monument to those who died.

[45] USS Runner, USS Pompano, USS Capelin, USS Scorpion, USS Escolar, USS Albacore, and USS Kete.

Deep Sea Contact Mine, which could be laid in water nearly 3,500 feet deep. *Tsugaru Maru* was sunk by *Flier's* sister *USS Darter* on 29 June, 1944.

Darter herself would end up resting near *Flier* and *Robalo*. She grounded on a shoal west of Palawan on 24 October, 1944. Her crew was saved by the submarine *Dace*.

The loss of *Robalo* and *Flier* spurred the development of the FM Sonar device used specifically to detect mines in enough time to change course. The chilling gong that sounded when it found a mine was nicknamed "Hell's Bells," and was a submariner's worst nightmare. However, it did save many submarines toward the end of the war.

WORLD WAR II SUBMARINE STATISTICS

The Submarine Force lost fifty-two boats in WWII, and 3,700 sailors. Of these, four subs grounded with no casualties, one was scuttled following the Japanese attack on Manila, and thirty-eight sank with their entire crews. Eight submarines, including *Flier*, had some survivors, totaling 199 men. Of these, 191 men were captured by the Japanese, some dying in prisoner of war camps. Only those men from the *Flier* were able to elude the Japanese and return home to serve again.

The resting places of the grounded subs *USS Darter, USS S-27, USS S-36* and *USS S-39*, have been known since the dates of their losses. The other forty-eight subs remained lost until 2005, when the *USS Lagarto* was discovered in the Gulf of Thailand. Since then, the resting places of six subs, including *Flier*, (*Lagarto*, in 2005, *Perch* and *Wahoo* in 2006, *Grunion* in 2007, and *R-12* in 2011) have been found. There are active searches for a number of other lost boats, raising hope that the final locations of more submarines will come to light in the coming years.

USS Flier, 20 April 1944

AUTHOR'S NOTE:

This book has been an interesting journey. I first learned of Mr. Jacobson while I was transcribing board meetings at the Great Lakes Naval Memorial and Museum of Muskegon, Michigan. Mr. Jacobson was one of the nominees to fill two vacant places on the Board of Directors, and the man who nominated him quickly told the *Flier's* story. As the curator and exhibit designer of the museum, I remember thinking "I have got to interview him, this story is amazing!"

It would be another six months before I met him, but in the meantime, the museum director gave me the memoirs Mr. Jacobson had written in 1944. After his trip to the Philippines in 1997, Al had re-typed the 1944 memoirs, re-inserting the names and locations, and adding information that had come to light afterward. In many ways, it was a bare-bones account, but full of little gleams of adventure beyond anything I had read before, in the amazing voice of a man who had lived the impossible.

Like most Americans born two generations removed from WWII, my education about it was somewhat limited, and it mostly concentrated on the European Theater, pausing just long enough to mention Pearl Harbor and the atomic bomb.

My grandfather had served under General Patton in North Africa, Italy and Germany, but refused to talk about it, so WWII was a bit taboo for me. Though I had very little interest in WWII until I landed my job at the museum, I quickly grew to admire and respect these men who pulled some truly outrageous stunts during WWII. Those who returned rebuilt America during a time of unprecedented prosperity.

When I finally met him in his office, Mr. Jacobson told me that he had been contacted by several authors in the past few decades since the story had been declassified, but nothing had ever been published beyond some small articles or short accounts within larger books on the Pacific front of WWII. He was now the only survivor of the incident still alive, and wanted the men lost aboard the *Flier* to be remembered long after he was gone. He agreed to work with me, and over the next two years, answered many questions, was interviewed multiple times, donated artifacts that he had, wrote letters, anything I needed.

A lot of this book's design was taken directly from Mr. Jacobson's written memoirs, supplemented with our interviews. While I've read every account from every member of the *Flier* I can get my hands on, when two accounts differed, I often fell back to Mr. Jacobson's memories. Other research helped flesh out the environment Al and his crewmates passed through, from the Filipino guerillas to the Coastwatchers, to contemporary accounts of intelligence (which often differ from what is accepted now as established fact, as in the case of the *Robalo*), to general descriptions of submarine life.

All I can say is that to this day, I'm still in awe of him, what he survived in 1944, and what he contributed to his family, business, and community when he returned.

WWII veterans, many who have since passed into "Eternal Patrol," protected this country while they should have been in school, in college, starting families, or beginning careers. They are the Greatest Generation because they did what it took to protect their country regardless of personal inconvenience or loss. Some sacrificed their youth, some their health, some their sanity, while several thousand sacrificed their lives as well. These submariners have not forgotten their crewmates, nor has any veteran I've ever met forgotten those they knew who didn't come home. Even more amazing, many of these men went on to re-establish a kind of "normal" life when they returned home.

There are only seven WWII era submarines left in the United States, all of them museums. These seven boats stand as a memory of the fifty-two submarines which were lost, the nearly 200 more that served, and the men who served on them.

When this book was researched and the bulk of it written, Al was the only man alive from the *Flier's* doomed second patrol, all others having passed on between 1997 and 2005. Al died October 16, 2008, before this book was published. His two great desires were to see this story told to the public, and to find the *Flier's* resting place. I have tried to present this story to the best of my ability, and his family fulfilled the other dream. My only regret is that Al never saw either, and his family has said that they wish he had been there on that boat when *Flier* revealed herself for the first time in 66 years.

I have lived with this tale for nearly five years now, and I know I'll miss it. Yet, it is only one of thousands of stories about a time where "courage was commonplace, and self-sacrifice the norm."

ADDENDUM: It didn't leave me. During the National Memorial Service for *Flier*, I met so many family members of *Flier* as well as James Alls and Heather Sutherland, and learned so much more that I felt the story that was launched that weekend was now lacking so much detail.

So I went back, and included many stories, including the details of Daggy's surgery at Midway, Al's bet with Don See on the outcome of the 1944 OSU v. U of M game, Heather Sutherland's account of what her family went through at Brooke's Point, and more. I hope the details were worth the second edition.

Someday, maybe, this story will leave me, but maybe it never will.

I think I'd be okay with that.

Flier's commissioning crew, photographed at Longo's Inn, Groton, Connecticut, during the Commissioning Party, 1 October 1943. Official US Navy Photo.

SUBMARINES AND WWII PACIFIC WARFARE

From the beginning of the U.S. Naval Submarine Force in 1900 to the immense nuclear vessels that prowl our oceans today, the submarine holds a unique place in the Navy, and indeed, in the human imagination.

Man has long wanted to dive beneath the waves, and submarine plans can be found as far back as the Renaissance. The first "submarine" was Cornelius Drebbel's design that demonstrated in the Thames River in 1620, but it wasn't until the mid-19th century that technology had developed sufficiently enough for people to have a "true" submarine. The *CSS Hunley* became the first submarine to sink a ship in battle in 1864, during the American Civil War.

It wasn't until John P. Holland invented the "Holland" boats that a submarine, as a naval vessel, became cemented in the minds of people all over the world. Holland figured out that each submarine needed two engines: a diesel/gas engine for running on the surface, and an electric engine for running underwater. The diesel engine charged the batteries for the electric one, and the boat's capabilities were only limited to the amount of fuel carried on board. Holland sold his boats to anyone who was willing to purchase or commission one, and is the father of the American, English, Russian, Japanese, and Dutch Submarine Forces.

In America, submarines, while considered useful, were a bit of a curious misfit until WWII. They were assigned to guard harbors and patrol shorelines watching for enemy vessels. The attacks of the German Wolf Packs during WWI proved that submarines, if designed right, had more versatility. These new post-WWI American boats, patterned after the captured German U-Boats, were called "Fleet Boats" and were designed to travel with convoys to provide protection. However, with the destruction of the American Fleet at Pearl Harbor on December 7, 1941, submarines, none of which had been attacked, were left as the largest line of defense between the Imperial Japanese Navy and the western coast of America.

This became the golden hour of the submarine. There were only twenty-one submarines in the Pacific on December 7, 1941, one of which would be destroyed during the attack on Manila Bay December 8, 1941. By the end of the war, over three hundred twenty-seven submarines had served and fifty-two paid the ultimate price, along with their crews. These boats and their crews compromised only 1.6% of the total Navy, yet they caused over 60% of Pacific wartime enemy losses: over six million tons of ships, submarines, planes and one train[46] were destroyed by these boats and their crews. The losses in the submarine service were equally devastating. One in five men who signed up for the service never came home.

Foot for foot, the submarine is the most complex weapon in the naval arsenal, then and now. As a *Gato-class* submarine, *Flier* sported ten torpedo tubes (six in the bow, four in the stern) and twenty-four torpedoes. These could be fired when the submarine was surfaced or submerged. In addition, on her decks, *Flier* carried three guns intended for last-defense warfare, because she would have to be surfaced and exposed to use them. These guns were a large 3-inch .50 caliber deck gun (later replaced by an even larger 4-in .50 caliber), and a 20 mm and 40 mm anti-aircraft guns.

The deck on which the smaller two guns were located was called the Bridge, and that was where the officers would stand watch while the submarine was surfaced. Above the Bridge on *Flier*, there was yet another tiny deck with just enough space for the four lookouts to stand, called the "Lookout Platform."

She controlled her depth using two pairs of diving planes, one near the bow, and one near the stern.

She also had two propellers, more commonly called "Props" or "Screws." These could be used together or use opposing forces to maneuver the submarine swiftly. For a hard turn, for example, one prop would pull full speed forward, while its twin would pull backward. On the surface, these five-foot brass props could propel the submarine at speeds up to 20 knots, while underwater, the limit was around eight knots.

Inside, the submarine was relatively simple. Photographs of construction show the interior of a WWII submarine was essentially a long tube, divided into eight sections, each room having an upper and lower level. Over the third section, the Control Room, there was a smaller tube sitting on top, which contained the Conning Tower. The eight rooms were,

---

[46] The crew from *USS BARB* "sank the train" on July 23, 1945.

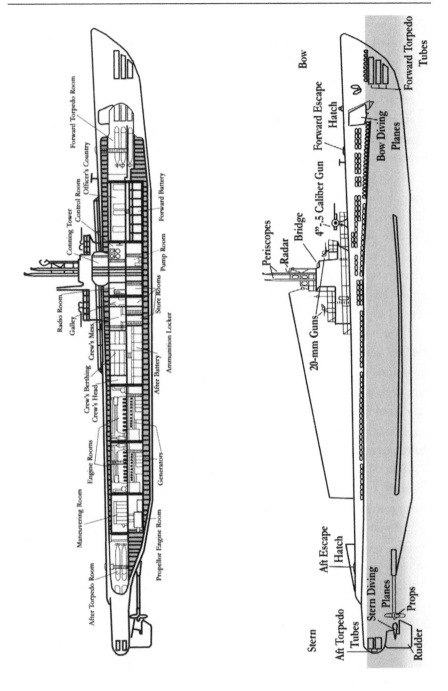

in order: Forward Torpedo Room, Forward Battery (also known as Officers' Country), Control Room, After Battery which contained the Galley, Crew's Mess, Crew's Berthing, and Crew's Head (Bathroom), and was followed by the Forward Engine Room, After Engine Room, Maneuvering Room, and finally, the After Torpedo Room. The Conning Tower, as before mentioned, was located above the Control Room, and accessed by a steel ladder.

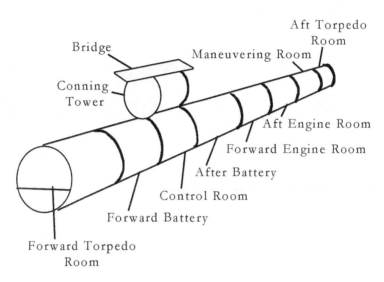

Simplified Interior Submarine Plan

FORWARD TORPEDO ROOM

This room was the largest and most heavily-armored room in the submarine. It contained six torpedo tubes and sixteen torpedoes. It also housed sixteen men, most of whom were Torpedomen.

Each man was given a bunk and a small (about one foot cubed) locker in which to keep his personal items. Due to the space constraints on a submarine, each man was limited to one change of clothes and one set of shoes, along with anything else he could pack in his locker. To save space, most men stowed their clothes under their mattress. There was no real second level in this room, just enough storage space for two spare torpedoes.

The forward torpedo room also contained the main escape hatch. This

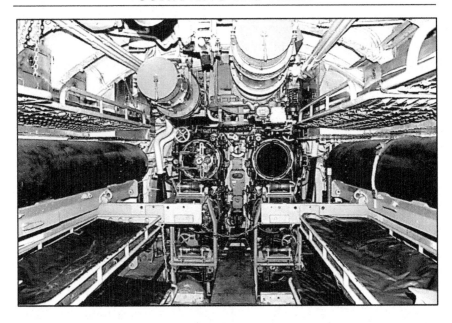

hatch was designed to be used by the men to escape if the submarine sank in around two hundred feet of water. For deeper rescues, (two hundred to five hundred feet deep,) this hatch could link with a Submarine Rescue Chamber, also called a McCann chamber, or Diving Bell. If the submarine sank in over five hundred feet of water, the inner hull would likely rupture due to the water pressure at those depths.

FORWARD BATTERY A.K.A. OFFICER'S COUNTRY

The next room was the Forward Battery, and to access it, one would have to step through a tiny water-tight door. The first of two battery arrays sat under the floor, giving the room its name. These wet cell batteries provided the submarine with anywhere from four to forty-eight hours of energy, depending on how much power the submarine was using. They had to be cleaned every day with pure distilled water. Any amount of salt in the mix had the potential to cause a massive chlorine gas explosion, which could destroy a sub.

The main level was Officers' Country. In addition to housing the officers' bunks, there as a pantry where food was kept warm for the officers, the Wardroom where the officers ate, relaxed, and also discussed business, and lastly, the Yeoman's office. The Yeoman kept all the records

On the left, the wardroom of USS Silversides, on the right, an XO's stateroom. Flier's Wardroom and cabins would have looked similar. Courtesy of Great Lakes Naval Memorial and Museum and Dr. Steven Demos.

of the submarine for the voyage. Five cabins housed a total of eight officers and four of the most senior enlisted men.

CONTROL ROOM

The Control Room was, with the Conning Tower, the heart of the submarine. The Control Room contained the air systems for blowing and flooding the ballast tanks, the Helm, the electrical panels for the boat, and the planes wheels, which controlled the diving planes.

In the center of the room sat a gyroscope compass which always pointed true north and a map table. At the far stern-end of this room was the Radio Shack where two men would monitor incoming and, occasionally, outgoing messages. Beneath this room was the Pump Room, which pumped water into the ballast tanks, but also could pump out the occupied areas of the submarine if necessary.

CONNING TOWER

The Conning Tower was where the real action took place. The periscope viewing stations were up there, as well as the Radar Stations, and the Torpedo Data Computer, which helped compute the torpedoes' trajectories based on the submarine's course and speed as well as the target's distance, course, and speed. The first of two firing buttons were also located here (the second buttons were located in their respective torpedo rooms). There was a ladder going from the Conning Tower to the Bridge overhead, and while on patrol, this was the only easily-accessible

Conning Tower of USS Silversides, looking aft. The silver column is the periscope, fully retracted. Courtesy of The Great Lakes Naval Memorial and Museum and Dr. Steven Demos.

exit. The others either were bolted shut or were difficult to access without attaching their ladders.

Gato- and *Balao-*class submarines contained two periscopes. The forward and larger periscope was the "Target Acquisition Periscope." It had a larger field of view, including an angled lens to view the sky for air patrols, and was able to magnify for greater detail. It was, however, so large in circumference that it made a large wake in the water. So the second periscope, the "Attack" Periscope was added. It had no ability other than simple viewing, but it was slender and nearly impossible to see in the waves.

Like her sisters, *Flier* had two types of radar, both of which were used primarily to scout for airplanes. Submarines did not fight airplanes unless they were unable to dive. An airplane was nearly impossible to shoot down, while a submarine was an easy target for any plane loaded with bombs.

AFTER BATTERY

This room was one of the more complicated in terms of the amount of things packed in there. On the main level, a four-foot wide, seven-foot deep steel-clad room was the Galley, where Breakfast, Snack, Lunch, Snack, Dinner, and Snack, along with gallons of coffee, were made daily for seventy-two to eighty-five crew members. Usually five men were assigned to the cooking duties, and unlike most surface ships, enlisted and officers ate the same food. Submarines got the best food in the Navy, and actually better than most of the American Armed Forces. While most WWII vets groan at the mere thought of canned or freeze-dried food, submariners had

On the left, the Crew's quarters, bunks three high for a total of thirty-four in the room. On the right, the Crew's Mess of USS Silversides. Courtesy of Great Lakes Naval Memorial and Museum and Dr. Steven Demos.

fresh meat, cheeses, and anything else they could desire. Recipes from a published WWII Submarine recipe book include items like Teriyaki Steak, Shrimp Creole, BBQ Ribs, and French Silk Cheesecake. Not surprisingly, some men signed up just for the food.

Next to the Galley was the Crew's Mess, where four four-foot long tables were expected to seat twenty-six men at a time. It took three whole seatings for each of the three major meals (the snacks were simply left out for those who wanted or needed it). This room, between meals, was the main area the men could go to relax, write home, play cards, or do anything else. In an effort to improve morale, the Navy also gave them the makings of their own movie theater, a tradition that has since continued. James Alls of the *Flier* said sometimes, when two submarines passed each other in the ocean, they would rig a line back and forth to exchange reels for more variety. He specifically mentioned seeing "Saratoga" more times than he cared to remember.

While in dock, the main access to the sub was also in this room.

Beyond this was the Crew's Berthing, featuring thirty-six to forty-two racks piled three high. This was also the area where the Pharmacist's Mate worked. Submarines were so dangerous and medical personnel so valuable that doctors and nurses were not permitted to serve in the submarine force. The Pharmacist's Mate was expected to keep the crew comfortable and alive until the submarine could rendezvous with a friendly ship somewhere if greater help was required. Despite these restrictions, records exist of at least three successful appendectomies and other minor surgeries.

Finally, there was the small and cramped Crew's Head. Two toilets, two showers, two sinks, and a washer and dryer, served sixty-eight enlisted personnel.

Beneath the Galley and Crew's Mess there were three storerooms for food, and one for the surface gun's ammunitions. Under the Berthing and Head was the second battery array.

Engine Room of USS Silversides, featuring Fairbanks-Morse Engines. USS Flier had Winton V-16 Engines, similar to those depicted in the inset. Photo courtesy of the Great Lakes Naval Memorial and Museum and Dr. Steven Demos.

ENGINE ROOMS

There were two Engine Rooms, identical mirror images of each other. *Flier* and other Groton-built boats were usually equipped with four General Motors V-16 engines. Each engine was 1600 horsepower; two in the Forward Engine Room and two in the After Engine Room. They were split into two rooms separated by the water-tight door instead of being housed in one room, just in case one room flooded or became inoperable. Each engine was connected to an electrical generator. There was one hatch to the deck in the After Torpedo Room, but this also was bolted shut before leaving on patrol. A submarine is 100% electric, from the propulsion to the light bulbs. Prior to nuclear submarines, the engine's sole duty was to run the generators which would charge the batteries in the Forward and After Battery compartments. The engine's air consumption alone meant that a submarine could only run her engines on the surface, and they would be shut down while underwater, which meant her first limitation as a submarine was not breathable air, but how long her batteries could continue to provide energy.

With the introduction of nuclear submarines, (which operate on the same principle: the nuclear plant runs a generator which creates electricity which powers the boat) diesel submarines were slowly phased out of the US Navy. The last diesel electric boat, *USS Blueback*, was decommissioned in 1990 and is now a museum ship in Portland, Oregon. Still, modern diesel electric submarines form the backbone of a number of navies, and in many ways, once submerged, they are quieter than their nuclear counterparts

MANEUVERING ROOM

This room was the most critical room in terms of the submarine functioning. All of the electrical systems originated from this room, and because all the systems fed off the batteries, anything that damaged this room had the potential to paralyze the submarine. The center of the room was occupied by a large cage which contained all the live wires and switches. This left less than two feet of width in the passage along the port side of this cage for the men to work. Beneath this room were the main motors that ran the props.

AFT TORPEDO ROOM

This room was nearly identical to the forward with a few exceptions. Four, rather than six torpedo tubes were housed here, as were only eight, rather than sixteen torpedoes. A Signal Ejector Tube, used for firing flares and later, bubbling devices to drown out enemy sonar, was here as well. Twelve to thirteen men, bunked here, and there was a tiny office for the engineers.

There was another escape hatch in this room, but it was not designed to be used with an exterior rescue device like the McCann Chamber. The only way the men could get out would be to swim out using Momsen Lungs or Steinke Hoods to help them get to the surface.

BIBLIOGRAPHY

Allied Warships. *USS Flier (SS-250) Submarine of the Gato Class.* n.d.
    http://uboat.net/allies/warships/ship/2996.html (accessed August 31,
    2006).

Alls, James. *Behind the Badge.* n.d.
    www.behindthebadge.net/bloodstripes/memory/mem_s.html (accessed
    August 31, 2006).

Alls, James, interview by Rebekah Hughes. *Brag Rags, Disney and the Flier, Sinking the
    Hakusan Maru* (March 12, 2011).

Alls, James, interview by Rebekah Hughes. *Daggy's Surgery* (August 13, 2010).

Alls, James, interview by Rebekah Hughes. *Radio shows and the sports pools* (March 9,
    2011).

Alls, James, interview by Rebekah Hughes. *Red Snyder's borrowed uniform* (March 26,
    2011).

Alls, James, and Jackie Alls, interview by Rebekah Hughes and Justin Hughes. *USS
    Flier and her Crew* (November 13, 2010).

Amunrund, Peter. ""Men Against the Sea: The Loss of the USS FLIER SS-250."
    US Submarine Veterans of WWII. n.d.
    ussubvetsofworldwarii.org/FLIER.html (accessed June 14, 2006).

Arellano, Renato, and Josie Arellano. "Christmas Letter 2000-2001." December
    2000: 1.

Associated Press Writer. "Japs Losing Two Palau Isles, Yanks Raid S. Philippines."
    News Clipping from Scrapbook of Lt. James Liddell, 1944.

Austin, Marshall H. *Report of Fourth War Patrol of USS REDFIN SS-272.* Naval War
    Patrol Report, United State Navy, 1944.

Austin, Marshall H. *Report of Third War Patrol of USS REDFIN SS-272.* Naval War
    Patrol Report, United States Navy, 1944.

Austin, Marshall H. *Serial 0011, 4 September 1944: Special Mission 23-31.* US Navy,
    1944.

Bartholomew, Bart. "The Fremantle Submarine Base." *Homepage of Paul W. Wittmer.*
    n.d. http://www.subvetpaul.com/TheFremantle.htm (accessed June 14,
    2006).

Baumgart, Earl, and Edwin Keifer. ""The Motor Mac's Tale"." *Submarine Journal,*
    Spring 1998: 105-111.

Beach, Edward. *Submarine.* New York: Pocket Star Books, 1946.

Bos, Abigail. "Grand Haven Man Comes Back from Lost Sub." *Grand Rapids
    Herald,* News Clipping from Scrapbook of Alvin Jacobson, Jr. n.d.

Buffalo Courior Express. "Eight Survive Explosion; Sinking of US Submarine."
    December 8, 1944.

Burns, Lieutenant Colonol R.C., USMC. "Palawan Rescsue." *U.S. Naval Institute Proceedings*, June 1950.

Calvert, James F. *Silent Running: My Years on a WWII Attack Submarine*. Wiley; New Ed edition , 1997.

Campbell, Douglas. *Eight Survived: The Harrowing Story of the USS Flier and the Only Downed World War II Submariners to Survive and Evade Capture*. Guilford: Lyons Press, 2010.

Cedar Rapids Gazette. "Eight Survivors of Lost Sub Saved by Guerillas." December 1944.

"Chart of North Balabac Strait and Vicinity." no. 14,326. Deptartment of Navy Hydrographic Office, April 1959.

Chicago Daily Tribune. "US Submarines Sunk 2 Jap Destroyers and 27 Cargo Ships." September 19, 1944.

Coastline News. "Obituary of Carlos S. Palacido." December 8, 2000.

Cole, William. "U.S. Submarine, Sunk in 1944, Found." *Honolulu Advertiser*. February 2, 2010. http://www.honoluluadvertiser.com/article/20100202/NEWS08/2020319/U.S.+submarine++sunk+in+1944++found (accessed February 2, 2010).

Coleman, Larry. *1944 Ltr*. E-mail to Rebekah Hughes. February 27, 2007.

Coleman, Larry. *Coastwatchers*. E-mail to Rebekah Hughes. February 20, 2008.

Coleman, Larry. *Flier Survivor*. E-mail to Rebekah Hughes. February 25, 2007.

—. "Alastair's Prayer." *Looking Aft*, September 2001: 1-5.

Coleman, Larry. *Redfin Patrol Reports*. E-mail to Rebekah Hughes. November 19, 2008.

Coleman, Larry. *Serial 0011*. E-mail to Rebekah Hughes. February 27, 2007.

Coleman, Larry. *The Peso*. E-mail to Rebekah Hughes. February 26, 2007.

Commander Submarine Force. "Press Release of Confirmed Discovery of USS Flier SS-250." Pearl Harbor, Hawai'i: Commander Submarine Force, February 1, 2010.

Commander Submarine Force, U.S. Pacific Fleet. *USS FLIER (SS 250) August 13, 1944 78 Men Lost*. n.d. www.csp.navy.mil/ww2boats/flier.htm (accessed May 1 , 2006).

Coye, Cmdr. John. *Report of Tenth War Patrol of USS Silversides SS-236*. United States Navy, 1944.

Crowely, John D. "Second Letter to John J. Casey concerning Lt. John Edward Casey." New London, Connecticut: United States Navy, December 19, 1944.

Crowley, John D. "Letter to Mr. John F. Casey Concerning Fate of Lt. John Edward Casey." Washington D.C.: United States Navy, October 28, 1944.

—. "Letter to Mrs. Mary Frances Casey Concerning the Fate of Lt. John Edward Casey." 1944, Washington D.C.: United States Navy, October 28, 1944.

Crowley, John D. *Narrative: of the Second War Patrol of U.S.S. Flier (All Times HOW and Approximate).* United States Navy, 1944.

Crowley, John D. *Report of First War Patrol of U.S.S. Flier SS-250.* Naval War Patrol Report, United States Navy, 1944.

—. "Speech About USS Flier." From Records of Lt. James Liddell , n.d. 16.

Croyle, William. "Sub's Fate Haunts Veteran." *The Kentucky Enquirer*, November 7, 2010.

Cundall, Peter, Bob Hackett, and Sander Kingsepp. *IJN Minelayer Tsugaru: Tabular Record of Movement.* 2007. http://www.combinedfleet.com/tsugaru_t.htm (accessed 6 15, 2007).

Dana, Sylvia. "Remembrance of local legend Alvin Jacobson." *Grand Haven Tribune*, October 17, 2008.

Dealey, Sam. *Report of Fifth War Patrol of USS Harder SS-257.* Naval War Patrol Report, United States Navy, 1944.

Dealey, Sam. *USS HARDER Fifth War Patrol Log.* United States Navy, 1944.

Denfeld, L.E. "Letter to Mr. and Mrs. A.E. Jacobson concerning Alvin E. Jacobson, Jr." Washington D.C.: United States Navy Department Bureau of Personnel, September 14, 1944.

Department of the Navy--Naval Historical Center. *USS Flier (SS-250), 1943, 1944.* n.d. www.history.navy.mil/photos/sh-usn/usnsh-f/ss250.htm (accessed May 1, 2006).

Detroit Free Press. "8 of 17 in Sub Survive Sinking." December 3, 1944.

Dierking, Gary. *Outrigger Sailing Canoes.* n.d. http://outriggersailingcanoes.blogspot.com/ (accessed May 20, 2011).

"Escaped Gob Outwits Japs for Two Years." *News Clipping from Scrapbook of Lt. James Liddell.* December 1944.

A.E. Jacobson Jr.: 75th Birthday Celebration. Directed by Jacobson Family. 1997.

Fisher, Ray. "Letter to the Editor of Muskegon Chronicle." *Muskegon Chronicle*, December 7, 1944.

Dive Detectives: Submarine Graveyard. Documentary Film. Directed by Jeff Vanderwal. Produced by Eliott Halpern. Performed by Michael Fletcher and Warren Fletcher. 2010.

Forrestal, James. "Letter to Mrs. Mary Frances Casey changing his status to KIA." Washington D.C.: United States Navy, February 5, 1946.

Gilpatrick, Kristin. *The Hero Next Door Returns: More Stories from Wisconsin's WWII Veterans.* Middleton: Badger Books LLC, 2001.

Grand Haven Tribune. "A. Jacobson Jr. Survives Loss of Submarine." September 20, 1944.

Grand Haven Tribune. "A.E. Jacobson Jr. to be Commissioned Ensign." October 21, 1943.

Grand Haven Tribune. "Ensign Escapes Death in Sinking Sub." 1944: News Clipping from Scrapbook of Alvin Jacobson Jr.

Grand Haven Tribune. "Ensign Jacobson Swam 18 Hours." December 2, 1944.

Grand Haven Tribune. "Happy Reunion in Jacobson Family." October 26, 1944.

Grand Haven Tribune. "Sub Still Best Offensive Weapon, Says Jacobson." 1979: News Clipping from Scrapbook of Alvin Jacobson Jr.

Grand Haven Tribunes. "Ensign Jacobson Arrives Home." November 6, 1944.

Grand Rapids Press. "Grand Haven Man Escapes as Sub Sinks." December 2, 1944.

Guttery, Randy. 1996. http://www.tendertale.com/ (accessed September 11, 2006).

Guttery, Randy, interview by Rebekah J. Hughes. *Questions About Tender USS ORION* (September 8, 2006).

Guttery, Randy, interview by Rebekah J. Hughes. *Thansk you for your reply--need a tiny bit of clarification* (September 11, 2006).

Haywood, J. "Businessman Alvin Jacobson Jr. dies at age 86." *Grand Haven Tribune,* October 17, 2008.

Henley, Walter EM2 (ss). "The Letdown: The Near Sinking of the USS IREX." *Irex Sea Storied.* n.d. http://www.hartford-hwp.com/Irex/docs/doc09.html (accessed August 31, 2006).

Hinman, Charles. *On Eternal Patrol: USS Flier.* n.d. http://www.oneternalpatrol.com/uss-flier-250.htm (accessed May 17, 2006).

—. *On Eternal Patrol: USS Robalo.* n.d. http://www.oneternalpatrol.com/uss-robalo-273.htm (accessed May 17, 2006).

—. *USS Flier.* Janurary 27, 2010. http://www.ussflier.com (accessed January 30, 2010).

HMAS Mildura Association. "HMAS MILDURA--The Other Milduras 1941-1965." *HMAS Mildura J207.* July 8, 2006. http://home.vicnet.net.au/~mildura/the_ship2.htm (accessed August 1, 2006).

Holmes, Harry. *The Last Patrol.* Annapolis: US Naval Institute Press, 2001.

Howell, Arthur Gibson. "Letter to Mrs. Mary Frances Casey about Lt. John Edward Casey." 1944, Connecticut: Personal Letter, December 10, 1944.

Hoyt. *The Destroyer Killer.* New York: Pocket Books, 1989.

i. n.d.

Jackson, Kent. "Discovery of Late Brother's Sunken WWII Sub Soothes City Woman." *Standardspeaker.com.* February 12, 2010. http://standardspeaker.com/news/discovery-of-late-brother-s-sunken-wwii-sub-soothes-city-woman-1.613586 (accessed February 16, 2010).

Jacobson, Alvin E., interview by Rebekah Hughes. (November 24, 2007).

Jacobson, Alvin E. Jr. *Survivor's Story*. Grand Haven: Self, 1997; 2002.

Jacobson, Alvin E. Jr., and Edna Jacobson. "Report of Flier Incident August 1944." Unpublished, October 1944.

Jacobson, Alvin E. Jr.,. "Cirriculum Vitae of Alvin E. Jacobson Jr." Self, n.d.

—. "Letter from Al Jacobson to Muriel Jacobson." July 2, 1944.

—. "Survivor's Story." *Submarine Journal*, Spring 1998: 1-101.

Jacobson, Alvin E., interview by Rebekah J. Hughes. *Mr.* (August 28, 2006).

Jacobson, Alvin Emmanuel. *A Survivor's Story: Submarine USS Flier lost August 13, 1944*. Self, 1944.

—. "Survivor's Story." *Submarine Journal*, Spring 1998: 1-101.

Jacobson, Mr. Alvin Emmanuel, interview by Rebekah J. Hughes. (August 28, 2006).

Jacobson, Nelson, interview by Rebekah Hughes and Justin Hughes. (March 12, 2010).

Jacobson, Nelson, interview by Rebekah Hughes. (May 21, 2010).

Jacobson, Nelson, interview by Rebekah Hughes and Justin Hughes. (March 12, 2010).

Johnson, David. "Wreckage of WWII Sub Found." *Odessa American Online*. April 2, 2010. http://www.oaoa.com/news/knees-45317-german-world.html (accessed April 3, 2010).

Jones, Dave. *Capt. David Hayward McClintock*. 11 1, 2007. http://www.findagrave.com/cgi-bin/fg.cgi?page=gr&GSln=McClintock&GScid=1341&GRid=22596682 & (accessed 10 26, 2009).

Jr., Clay Blair. *Silent Victory*. Emreyville: J.B. Lippencott Company, 1975.

Judd, Terry. "Family of USS Flier Explosion Thrilled about Submarine's Discovery." *Muskegon Chronicle*. Muskegon, February 9, 2010.

Keifer, Edwin. ""Tale of the Chief Radio Technician"." *Submarine Journal*, Spring 1998: 114-118.

—. ""The Captain's Tale"." *Submarine Journal*, Spring 1998: 102-104.

Keilen, Brian. "Sunken Sub ID'd as One Al Jacobson Served On." *Grand Haven Tribune*. February 3, 2010. http://www.grandhaventribune.com/paid/301379707894166.bsp (accessed February 3, 2010).

Kit J. Pourciau of the USS Flier. November 3, 2009. http://www.footnote.com/spotlight/13447/kit_j_pourciau_of_uss_flier_ ss250/\ (accessed November 15, 2009).

Krill, Naeter. "Letter to Mr. Hayes Kisamaore from Mrs. Naeter Krill regarding Oliver Krill, USS Flier crewmember." January 28, 1945.

Lavelle, James M. *USS Gunnel 5th War Patrol.* n.d. http://www.jmlavelle.com/gunnel/patrol5.htm (accessed September 15, 2006).

Lavelle, James. *USS Gunnel 6th Patrol.* n.d. http://www.jmlavelle.com/gunnel/patrol6.htm (accessed April 24, 2007).

Leffler, Jessica. *WWII Sub Found;Grand Haven Family Elated.* News Broadcast. WOOD TV-8. Grand Rapids, Michigan, Febrary 2, 2010.

Leone, Diana. "Northwest Islands Trip Yields Preservation Data." *Honolulu Star Bulletin,* June 8, 2005.

Liddell, Kirk, interview by Rebekah Hughes and Justin Hughes. (May 15, 2010).

Loughman, Tim. *USS Macaw.* n.d. http://www.ussmacaw.org/ (accessed April 9, 2011).

Loughman, Timothy, interview by Rebekah Hughes. *USS Macaw's grounding at Midway* (May 6, 2011).

Lupo, L. "Alvin Jacobson, JSJ Corp. founder, died at 86." *Muskegon Chronicle,* October 17, 2008.

Mansfiled, John G. Jr. *Cruisers for Breakfast: The War Patrols of the USS Darter and the USS Dace.* Media Center Publishing, 1997.

March of Time Radio Spot. *"Chief Howell Spot".* 1944. Radio Program.

March, Jack. "3rd War Patrol." *Official Website of the USS REDFIN.* n.d. http://www.ussredfin.com/ss-272/warpatrol3/warpatrol3.htm (accessed September 15, 2006).

—. *USS FLIER (SS-250).* n.d. www.ussredfin.com/ss-272/ussflier/uss_flier.htm (accessed August 31, 2006).

March, Jack. *USS REDFIN.* E-mail to Rebekah Hughes. September 29, 2008.

—. "USS REDFIN's 2nd Patorl." *Official Website of USS REDFIN (SS 273).* n.d. http://www.ussredfin.com/ss-272/warpatrol2/warpatrol2.htm (accessed September 15, 2006).

—. "USS REDFIN's 4th Patrol." *Official USS REDFIN website.* n.d. http://www.ussredfin.com/ss-272/warpatrol4/warpatro43.ht (accessed September 15, 2006).

McGee, Eugene D. "To Sink and Swim: The USS FLIER." *Submarine Journal,* October 1996: 94-98.

McMahon, Charles. "Closure at Long Last: Kittery Woman Learns Fate of Brother's Sub, Sunk 65 Years Ago in World War II." *Foster's Daily Democrat.* February 3, 2010. http://www.fosters.com/apps/pbcs.dll/article?AID=/20100203/GJNEWS_01/702039947 (accessed February 3, 2010).

Mendenhall, Corwin. *Submarine Diary: The Silent Stalking of Japan.* Annapolis: US Naval Institute Press, 1995.

Military Times Hall of Valor. 2009. http://militarytimes.com/citations-medals-awards/recipient.php?recipientid=20668 (accessed October 26, 2009).

Miller, Bruce, interview by Rebekah Hughes. *Wesley Bruce Miller and the USS Flier* (September 6, 2010).

Miller, Vernon J. "Letter to Capt. John D. Crowley, USN (Ret.) from Vernon J. Miller." Arbutus, Maryland, September 3, 1985. 1.

Milton, Keith M. *Subs Against the Rising Sun: U.S. Submarines in the Pacific.* Las Cruces: Yucca Tree Press, 2000.

Morison, Smuel Eliot. *History of United States Sumbarine Operations in WWII.* Little, Brown & Co., 1949.

MTCM(SS)(Ret.), Royal Weaver. "USS FLIER (SS-250)." *Geocities Pentagon Base.* n.d. www.geocities.com/Pentagon/Base/7660/lost_boats/pages/FLIER.htm ?200614 (accessed June 14, 2006).

Muskegon Chronicle. "Ensign Jacobson and Band Had Harrowing Experience." December 4, 1944.

New London Day. "Awards Ceremony at Sub Base Discloses Story of Heroism in Loss of Submarine Flier." January 4, 1946.

New London Day. "Crew Member of Submarine Flier Now Listed as Dead; Story of Sinking Told." April 16, 1946.

New York Times. "Submarines Sink 29 More Vessels." September 20, 1944.

News Clipping from Milwaukee Paper in Scrapbook of Alvin Jacobson Jr. "Survivor Here from Sunken Submarine Suffered Too Much, Too Little Water." December 1944.

News Clipping from Scrapbook of Lt. James Liddell. "Sub Blown Up, 8 Escape Japs." December 2, 1944.

Online Obituary for David Capt. David H. McClintock. n.d. http://www.memorialobituaries.com/memorials/memorials.cgi?action=Obit&memid=49861&clientid=canale (accessed 10 21, 2009).

Palacido, Sgt. Carlos S. *Mission Report of Sgt. Carlos S. Palacido.* US Army Summary Report, 978th Signal Service Company, United States Army, United States Army, 1945, 21.

Parker, Richard. *Siargao Island-Boats and Boat Building.* April 2005. http://www.coconutstudio.com/Boats.htm (accessed May 20, 2011).

Patton, Meagan. "Sunken Sub that Claimed Ottowan's Life now Headed for TV." *The Ottawa Herald.* Ottawa, Febrary 23, 2010.

Pearson, Jake. "Familes Learn War Heroes Fate: WWII Sailors Killed On Sub Recently Discovered in South China Sea." *New York Daily News.* New York, New York, June 22, 2010.

Poel, Clarence. "Local Veteran Retraced Survival Route ." *Grand Haven Tribune,* News Clipping from Scrapbook of Alvin Jacobson Jr. 1998.

Record of Proceedings of an Investigation... [into the] Circumstances Connected with the Loss of the USS Robalo and USS Flier. (United States Naval Court, September 14, 1944).

"Recorder, Febrary 6, 1946 F1/c Victor J. Murawski." *The Judge Report.* February 6, 1946. http://rgoing.livejournal.com/383031.html (accessed February 3, 2010).

Riddle, Phil. "Sailor with Local Ties Recovered in WWII Submarine." *The Weatherford Democrat.* Weatherford, March 28, 2010.

Schwertfeger, Charles "Red". ""God's Patrol" ." September 2001.

Schwertfeger, Charles, interview by Rebekah Hughes and Justin Hughes. (October 11, 2008).

Sharp, Cmdr. George A. *U.S.S. Florikan (ASR-9) Report: Towing U.S.S. Flier.* United States Navy, 1944.

Starmap for Balabac Straits, August 13, 1944 at 10:15 p.m. n.d. http://starmap.causeway.co.uk/starmap.sky?place=Balabac&lat=8+5+North&long=117+1+West&date=1944%2F8%2F13&time=10%3A15+pm&dst=0&step=0&unit=Dys&img=SVG&action=Calculate+...&show=S&show=P&show=C&show=N&show=B (accessed November 10, 2006).

Stum, David. "Sub Sank, Liddell Swam for Help." *Intelligencier Journal,* June 11, 1987.

Sturma, Michael. *Death at a Distance: The Loss of the Legendary USS Harder.* Annapolis, Maryland: Naval Institute Press, 2006.

—. *Surface and Destroy: The Submarine Gun Battle in the Pacific.* Lexington: University Press of Kentucky, 2011.

—. *The USS Flier: Death and Survival on a World War II Submairne.* Lexington: University of Kentucky Pess, 2008.

Tactical and Technical Trends. "Atrabine for Malaria form Tactical and Technical Trends." *Lone Sentry.* June 3, 1943. http://www.lonesentry.com/articles/ttt09/atabrine.html (accessed April 30, 2010).

"Tells How Joliet Girl's Husband Swam 18 Hours in Sea After Loss of Sub." *News Clipping from Scrapbook of Lt. James Liddell.* December 1944.

The Evening Bulletin. "Capt. Rauch Now Listed As Dead." February 22, 1946: 1.

The Herald Examiner. "Philippine Patriots Save 8 Yanks After Sub Blas." December 2, 1944: Found in Scrapbook of Alvin E. Jacobson, Jr.

Tremaine, Don. ""Tale of the Firecontrolman 3"." *Submarine Journal,* Spring 1998: 112-113.

Trumbull, Robert. *Silversides: Hunter Killer Attack Sub of WWII.* New York, New York: Henry Holt and Company; Reprinted P.W. Knutson & Co., 1945.

Tuohy, William. *The Bravest Man: Richard O'Kane and the Amazing Submarine Adventures of the USS Tang.* New York: Presidio Press, 2006.

United States Army. *Report of the History of the 978th Signal Service Company*. Army Summary Reports, United States Army, 1945, 18.

United States Navy. *Deck Log of USS Flier SS-250 October 1943-June 1944*. United States Navy, 1944.

—. "Departure List: Results of U.S. Submarine War Patrols listed Chronologically by date Underway for Patrol Based on Task Force Commanders Assessments ." United States Navy, Oct 22, 1945.

United States Navy Historical Center. "Pearl Harbor Submarine Base: 1918-1945." *Naval Historical Center*. May 15, 2001. http://www.history.navy.mil/faqs/faq66-5a.htm (accessed September 15, 2006).

—. *Ship Lookup: USS FLIER*. n.d. www.nwc.navy.mil/usnhdb/ShipLookup.asp?ShipID=USSS00250 (accessed August 31, 2006).

United States Navy. *N.D. Communique No. 540 September 6, 1944*. September 6, 1944. www.ibiblio.org/pha/comms/1944-09 (accessed September 6, 2006).

—. *N.D. Communique No. 545, September 19, 1944*. September 19, 1944. www.ibiblio.org/pha/comms/1944-09 (accessed September 6, 2006).

—. *N.D. Communique No. 565, January 2, 1945*. January 2, 1945. www.ibilio.org/pha/comms/1945-01 (accessed September 6, 2006).

—. *Online Navy Art Collection*. n.d. http://www.history.navy.mil/branches/org6-2.htm (accessed July 1, 2011).

—. "Operation Order No. 100-44." Perth, West. Australia: United States Navy, July 31, 1944.

—. "Press Release announcing awarding of Silver Star to Lt. John Edward Casey." Norfolk, VA: United States Navy, April 9, 1945.

—. *Submarine Lost in Pacific During Training Exercises*. July 11, 1944. www.ibiblio.org/pha/comms/1944-07 (accessed September 6, 2006).

—. "USS ROBALO (SS 273) July 26, 1944--81 Men Lost." *Commander Submarine Force, U.S. Pacific Fleet*. n.d. www.csp.navy.mil/ww2boats/robalo.htm (accessed June 14, 2006).

USS Flier SS-250. "Sailing List of USS Flier SS-250." Fremantle, Western Australia, August 2, 1944. 5.

Walters, Bill. "USS Flier Dedication." *The Cabot Chronicle*, May 31, 2008.

What's On Vancouver. *Dive Detectives*. Vancouver, March 26, 2010.

Wilbanks, Bob and McDole, Glenn. *Last Man Out: Glenn McDole USMC, survivor of the Palawan Massacre*. Jefferson: McFarland & Company Inc., 2004.

Wilbanks, Bob. *Last Man Out: Glenn McDole USMC, survivor of the Palawan Massacre*. Jefferson: McFarland & Company Inc., 2004.

—. *Last Man Out: Glenn McDole, USMC, survivor of the Palawan massacre in WWII.* Jefferson : McFarland & Coompany Inc,. Publishers, 2004.

Wittmer, Paul. ""Flier (SS-250)"." *Sub Vet Paul.* n.d. www.subvetpaul.com/LostBoats/Flier.htm (accessed June 14, 2006).

Wolfe, Bill. "Do you remember this USS REDFIN?" *USS Redfin SS/ASR/AGSS-272 Links.* n.d. http://www.geocities.com/Pentagon/Base/7660/RemThisRedfin.html (accessed December 14, 2006).

Wolfe, Bill, and John D. Crowley. ""Loss of the USS FLIER"." *Plolaris,* June 1981.

YAP Films. *Toronto-based Television Production Company YAP Films Discovers Missing WWII Submarine.* Toronto, March 30, 2010.

Yount, Dan. "Cincinnatti Family: Discovery of WWII Submarine Wreckage Where Cousin Died Brings Closure." *The Cincinnatti Herald.* Cincinnatti, April 24, 2010.

Chief Petty Officers of Flier taken during Commissioning Party, 1 October 1943. Courtesy Submarine Force Museum, Groton, Connecticut.

Top, left and right: Flier's sponsor, Mrs. Pierce, christens Flier then launch, 11 July 1943. Submarine Force Museum, Groton, CT. Middle: Commissioning Party of USS Flier, courtesy of family of Cmdr. John D. Crowley. Bottom left: Radio Comm team at Hawaii Barbecue, courtesy of family of Walter "Bud" Klock. Bottom Right: Cmdr. Crowley and Lt. Liddell, courtesy of family of Lt. Liddell.

NEVER FORGOTTEN

CPSIA information can be obtained at www.ICGtesting.com
Printed in the USA
BVOW06s0042140116

432630BV00010B/109/P